SOCIAL EXCLUSION AND THE REMAKING OF SOCIAL NETWORKS

Social Exclusion and the Remaking of Social Networks

ROBERT STRATHDEE
Victoria University of Wellington, New Zealand

ASHGATE

Published by
Ashgate Publishing Limited
Gower House
Croft Road
Aldershot
Hants GU11 3HR
England

Ashgate Publishing Company
Suite 420
101 Cherry Street
Burlington, VT 05401-4405
USA

Ashgate website: http://www.ashgate.com

British Library Cataloguing in Publication Data
Strathdee, Robert
    Social exclusion and the remaking of social networks. -
    (Voices in development management)
    1. Youth - Employment 2. Youth - Employment - Government
    policy 3. Youth - Social networks
    I. Title
    331.3'4137

Library of Congress Cataloging-in-Publication Data
Strathdee, Robert.
    Social exclusion and the remaking of social networks / Robert Strathdee.
        p. cm. -- (Voices in development management)
    Includes bibliographical references and index.
    ISBN 0-7546-3815-4
    1. Youth with social disabilities--Government policy. 2. Unemployed youth. 3.
Youth--Social networks. 4. Vocational education. 5. Labor market. 6. Social capital
(Sociology) I. Title. II. Series: University of North London voices in development
management.

    HV1421.S77 2004
    362.7'083--dc22

                                                                          2004062397
ISBN 0 7546 3815 4

Printed and bound by Athenaeum Press, Ltd.,
Gateshead, Tyne & Wear.

Contents

List of Figures

List of Abbreviations

CBET	Competency-based education and training
E2E	Entry to Employment
ITO	Industry Training Organisation
MAS	Modern Apprenticeship Scheme
NCEA	New Zealand Certificate in Educational Achievement
NEET	Not in Employment, Education or Training
NPM	New Public Management
NQF	National Qualifications Framework
NZQA	New Zealand Qualifications Authority
PA	Personal Advisor
PTE	Private Training Establishment
TEC	Tertiary Education Commission
TO	Training Opportunities
VET	Vocational Education and Training
WINZ	Work and Income New Zealand
YT	Youth Training

Acknowledgements

The central argument within this book concerns the declining value of familial and kin-based social networks that lead to employment. In the past, young people could make effective transitions into employment through the utilisation of resources made available through personal social networks. However, for a variety of reasons, which are detailed within this book, the value of these resources has declined. The erosion in the value of social networks is problematic because it reduces the significance of 'cultural codes' and other kin-based resources that facilitate transitions into work. This book addresses the strategies implemented by the state that act to replace these resources and better regulate transition into work.

Although I have been developing this argument for a number of years, the original idea, forming the basis of this book, comes from Professor Hugh Lauder (University of Bath). It was Hugh who first pointed out to me the relationship between social networks, employment and the vocational education and training system. I developed Hugh's idea more fully in my PhD thesis on vocational education and training in New Zealand, which I completed in 1999 and in subsequent journal articles. During this period, David Hughes (formerly of the University of Canterbury) also helped me frame my ideas and assisted me in presenting them in a useful form. However, it was an interview with a senior government official who commented that his department was 'purchasing' access to social networks that first alerted me to the commodification of networks (Strathdee and Hughes, 2000). This book builds upon that idea and my earlier work by broadly addressing the strategies used by the state to remake networks within New Zealand and England.

There are many other people to whom I am indebted. In particular, I would like to thank Val Rose, the commissioning editor of the Voices in Development Management series at Ashgate, for support of the book and Ashgate's offer to publish it as part of the 'Voices in Development Management Series'. Along the way, I also received help and advice from a number of people including Margaret Grieco, John Freeman-Moir, Alan Scott, Phil Brown, Judie McNeill, Steve Jordan, and Tony Taylor. The empirical chapters of the book are based upon interviews that were conducted with tutors working in a range of programmes in New Zealand, with personal advisors working within the Connexions Service and with tutors working in the Entry to Employment Programme in England. Without their help this book would not have been possible. A special thanks is due to my partner, Charlotte Clements, who spent many hours editing and critiquing this book and to Claire Pickering who transcribed the interviews and helped edit the final manuscript. Of course, the views expressed in this book are my own and do not necessarily reflect those of the Tertiary Education Commission, the Connexions Service or Entry to Employment providers.

Chapter 1

Introduction

This book explores changes in the delivery of social welfare related services and vocational education and training (VET) to young people. The major argument is that recent changes in society, such as an increase in the proportion of young people growing up in work-poor households, have eroded the value to the state of familial and community-based social networks. As a result the state has adopted some of the functions formerly undertaken by these networks in order to facilitate transition into work. Until recently, the presence of familial and community-based social networks, which were deeply rooted in the social infrastructure, enhanced the effectiveness of the state by minimising the cost of integrating young people into the labour market. Although the precise configuration of these networks varies between eras, there exists a long history of social networks facilitating transitions into work through, for example, existing employees, 'speaking to the guv'nor' on behalf of job seekers' (Young and Willmott, 1957, p. 76). Historically, familial networks have also played an important role in transmitting skills between generations (Grieco, 1996). For example a study of East London families described how fathers who worked on the docks 'kicked their sons' arses until they did lay the ropes right' (Young and Willmott, 1957, p. 76). As exemplified, networks helped build labour market attachment ensuring that young workers obtained the required skills and helped them form appropriate identities as workers.

The presence of these networks aided the goals of the state by shaping the conditions under which labour power was bought and sold. For example, they helped shape the labour market by assigning work roles, connecting job seekers with employers, and transmitting pro-work attitudes and values. The role of social networks in regulating labour was buttressed within the schooling system by selective assessment practices that were designed to limit achievement and reduce the proportion of young people progressing to higher levels of schooling. These practices proved to be highly effective when there was strong demand in the labour market for poorly qualified school leavers. However, since the mid-1970s, changes in the workplace – particularly those brought about by the introduction of new technologies – have altered the range of skills young workers are required to have. Concurrently, the credential level needed to secure some forms of employment has increased.

Such changes have led to increases in youth unemployment in New Zealand (Blaiklock et al., 2002), the United Kingdom (Brown and Lauder, 2001) and elsewhere. Young people with no or limited school qualifications and those working in unskilled and semi-skilled segments of the labour market have been particularly vulnerable to the adverse effects of these changes (Murnane and Levy, 1993). These young people have experienced a comparatively high rate of unemployment and declining wage levels.

For the state the rise in youth unemployment and the declining value of labour power in semi- and unskilled segments of the labour market are problematic, as young people cannot leave school and obtain employment as readily. Furthermore, the economic incentives for doing so are low. A resulting consequence is the emergence of a pool of young people who achieve poorly in the schooling system and, despite the state's attempt to create pro-learning identities, remain sceptical of the value of the qualifications they are studying towards and remain poorly motivated to achieve. Nevertheless, they remain in education as 'discouraged workers' because of the uncertainty inherent in entering the labour market (Biggart and Furlong, 1996) and because they are encouraged to do so by the state. In an earlier era, young people could reject the culture of schooling and obtain relatively well-paid employment in semi- and unskilled segments of the labour market or they could obtain craft apprenticeships as soon as they reached the minimum school leaving age (Willis, 1977). However, discouraged workers tend to remain in education and drift through schooling without clear goals. The emergence of the discouraged worker effect and other problems for the state, such as the proportion of young people not in employment, education or training (NEET), suggests a decline in the ability of social networks to regulate labour in ways supportive of the state's goals.

The problems of poor student motivation, poor levels of achievement and comparatively high proportions of young people NEET, which can be linked to the decline in the value of semi and unskilled labour, has prompted policy makers in New Zealand, the United Kingdom and elsewhere to develop a range of interventions designed to resynchronise societal regulatory systems with labour market changes. For example, the so-called 'Third Way governments', such as New Labour in the United Kingdom and the Labour-led Coalition[1] in New Zealand, have continued extensive reform programmes within education introduced by previous administrations. These are designed to promote achievement, motivate young people to learn, reduce truancy, provide better systems of career guidance, and to generally reduce social exclusion through reconnecting young people to the labour market. For example, in New Zealand

and the United Kingdom, the development of competency-based assessment, qualifications frameworks, and careers advisory and mentoring services, such as New Labour's Connexions, are designed to help create new, increasingly relevant and motivating 'ladders of opportunity'.

Concurrently, increases in the rate of unemployment and inactivity amongst adults have resulted in growth in the proportion of work-poor households and work-poor communities. This is seen by New Labour and the Labour-led Coalition to have led to the creation of dependency cultures that are being transmitted across generations. By modelling their behaviour on that of their parents, the children of unemployed are at risk of developing a form of learned helplessness in relation to the labour market. Thus, they are more likely to fail to attach to the labour market and to become unemployed themselves when they leave school.

Youth unemployment and inactivity is seen as a cost to the state and a source of economic inefficiency. A reason for this concerns the high cost of maintaining and expanding training and welfare systems, which represents a cost to capital in that the level of surplus value that can be extracted from the labour process is reduced. This is because the state is forced to appropriate revenue from the economic system through taxation. This ultimately emerges as a cost to capital through the requirement that higher wages be paid to workers. Higher costs also result from reduced competition between workers for employment and through workers' demands for higher wages as a result of training. To reduce unemployment and inactivity amongst youth, and thus increase the efficiency of the economic system, Third Way governments are building up on strategies introduced by conservative predecessors by further developing so called 'active' welfare systems. Essentially, policies of this nature, such as New Labour's New Deal for Young People, are designed to regulate youth by decreasing the incentive to remain on welfare without increasing the cost of labour to employers. By reducing wage pressure the New Deal has increased total employment (White and Riley, 2002). However, it is not clear that New Labour's strategies are effective in other ways. For example, recent evidence suggests that approximately one in 10 young people in the United Kingdom are NEET. In New Zealand the figure is perhaps higher with an estimated 10 to 17 per cent of young people aged 15 to 19 years not undertaking formal education, employment or training. This figure is much higher in economically disadvantaged groups such as Maori (Department of Labour, 2003).

Other accounts, detailing a decline in the employment prospects of young people, have described in great detail how economic change has eroded employment conditions in the youth labour market. This book builds upon these accounts by examining related changes in the social infrastructure and explaining why, in the contemporary era, the state has come to adopt interventionist strategies. Changes, including deindustrialisation, increases in adult unemployment, increases in the proportion of young people growing up in work-poor families, and credential inflation, have resulted in important changes in the social infrastructure that have reduced the ability of people to access employment through their social networks. For example, young people from work-poor backgrounds are unlikely to know someone who can 'speak to the guv'nor' at their own places of work. The erosion in the value of social network capital aids an understanding of the wider effects of structural change, which in turn, challenges the individual deficit accounts as presented in right wing accounts of youth unemployment and other social problems. In this context, it is important to recognise that although employment networks have arguably declined, broader networks remain a vital source of support for young people (Newman, K., 1999). Indeed, the debate is not about whether or not young people participate in social networks. Rather, it is about the kind of networks young people participate in and the impact these networks have on transitions into employment.

The Third Way and the Regulation of the Youth Labour Market

In this book three major strategies are identified as being utilised by Third Way governments to regulate the youth labour market in response to the eroding value of social networks. The first strategy involves creating better VET systems, including the development of new qualifications and ways of delivering knowledge, which aim to reconnect people with the labour market by motivating them to achieve qualifications that will enable them to secure and hold a job in the emerging high-wage/high-skill labour market. Accordingly, high levels of investment in education and training and the deployment of new forms of educational technology designed to motivate achievement are required. In other words, the aim of VET is to re-engineer intelligence and its measurement in ways conducive to the labour markets of deindustrialised economies. The second strategy involves motivating young people to take up work by manufacturing risk through reforming welfare systems (Giddens, 1998). This reform is thought to reduce the development of welfare pathologies by breaking the so-called 'cycle of dependency', increase the incentive to learn, and strengthen the role of families in transmitting pro-work attitudes and values. The third strategy involves developing the Connexions Service in England, which is a new career advisory service for youth. Here the aim is to replace functions formerly completed by social networks in the recruitment process by providing quality advice about training and employment opportunities. Closely related to the Connexions Strategy is the development of a new programme known as Entry to Employment (E2E). Connexions advisors place young people who they deem in need of more intensive assistance in E2E to assist them to obtain work-based training.

The Third Way and Social Capital

The development of strategies that attempt to reconnect young people with the labour market form part of a broader attempt by Third Way administrations in New Zealand and the United Kingdom to create social capital. According to the Third Way, neoliberal reforms have injured social capital by destroying trust and social cohesion within the community. Third Way administrations claim they want to create social capital and believe the judicious use of market and non-market strategies is likely to achieve this. Third Way governments are negotiating a path between these strategies and are focusing on 'what works' in terms of their stated policy goal of increasing the proportion of young people in paid employment or training. Of relevance here is the introduction of new modes of delivering social welfare related services to young people. Within New Zealand, the adoption of neoliberal funding methods, where the state purchases outcomes from public and private sector providers of VET and related welfare services, is particularly important. Consistent with the Labour-led Coalition's emphasis on increasing the number of young people in employment, employment outcomes have become a key criterion upon which funding is allocated to providers. This aids the establishment of competition within the New Zealand training market. This approach has proved to be a highly effective and efficient method of attaching people to the labour market, at least temporarily. However, its contribution to social capital remains unclear. For example, the relationship between the Third Way's focus on getting single parents back in to work and their desire to create social capital in the form of trust and community engagement remains unclear.

It is widely assumed that young people compete for employment in the open labour market on the basis of the qualifications they have achieved in education. However, evidence suggests there exists a complex relationship between qualifications, social networks and employment. Arguably neoliberal funding models and the focus upon employment outcomes have thrown the relationship between qualifications and employment into focus and underpin the state's role in building social capital by remaking networks. In New Zealand, outcomes-based funding is used in the flagship training programmes for youth – youth training, the modern apprenticeship scheme and gateway.[2] The impact of these programmes on young people and on social capital is the subject of Chapter 7. This chapter aims to show that outcomes-based funding has encouraged providers of VET to make social networks and has resulted in the introduction of new forms of regulation for the work of youth professionals. Youth professionals are increasingly finding they are compelled by the new method of funding to deliver the training and employment outcomes purchased by the state. Mizen (1999) argues that welfare reform in the United Kingdom has created dilemmas for youth professionals, who are torn between managing the constraints imposed by the state and its focus on employability and delivering a youth-centred service. Thus, neoliberal funding methods have emerged as means of forcing cultural change in targeted groups of young people and in the institutions working with them. The implications of this are particularly significant for community organisations, many of which rely upon the state to finance at least some of their activities. Within New Zealand, Australia and the United Kingdom, there is debate that the kinds of practices governments sponsor are inconsistent with the underlying values of these organisations. Of particular concern is the focus on quantitative rather than qualitative outcomes regarding the work of these organisations. For example, community organisations may demonstrate that they have helped disadvantaged people improve their lives, yet these outcomes go unrecognised and ultimately, unrewarded because these qualitative improvements are not valued in work-focused welfare systems. Indeed, such funding methods may actually stifle innovation and create new forms of Taylorism among human service practitioners.

Similar concerns have been expressed regarding the Connexions service, which is the subject of Chapter 7. For example, Smith (2002) argues that youth work, which has traditionally been concerned with developing relationships between youth workers and young people, is being transformed into a form of schooling driven by the attainment targets. Accordingly, practitioners are forced to focus on meeting quantitative targets irrespective of the quality of the service they deliver. Stephen Twigg, the British Member of Parliament for the Labour Party and Parliamentary Under Secretary of State Schools, pointed out that reducing the proportion of young people not in education, employment or training will be the key measure of the effectiveness of Connexions. Thus, by 2006, the Connexions service will need to prove it is making a quantitative difference in the lives of young people (Twigg, 2002).

State Intervention and Legitimation

Within the book, the role assumed by the state in the recruitment, training, and placement of workers or the remaking of social networks is seen as an attempt to address concerns about the legitimacy of state education systems and welfare systems. Increasing the efficiency of transitions into work will address concerns expressed by critics regarding the efficacy of the state. While the concept of legitimation appears to have been marginalised since the mid-1980s in the debate around the role of schooling and welfare systems, it nevertheless remains that the state is continually restructuring and reorganising schooling and welfare systems in response to problems posed by capitalist production (Piven and Cloward, 1972). Whilst these problems, including the discouraged worker effect, the entrenched proportion of young people NEET, youth unemployment, and welfare dependency, within themselves may not fundamentally challenge the legitimacy of the state, they have led to questions concerning the effectiveness of the state and its solutions to current economic and social problems (Young, 1990).

The possibility that the state is assuming a greater role in facilitating transitions into work in order to enhance the legitimacy of the system provides a way to link the claims made above with those made by critical theorists, such as Habermas (1976). This link is useful as it situates the regulation of youth within a theoretical tradition that can be utilised to connect the erosion in the value of social networks to the emergence of legitimation deficits within capitalist economies. In addition, it also provides a way to demonstrate how and why the state is increasingly monopolising the structure, content and form of education. Broadly speaking, this monopolisation has ensured that educational policies support the maintenance of the social relations of production. An essential part of this process is the state's expansion and penetration into the lives and activities of individuals. While social and educational policies are often implemented by supposedly neutral organisations, the effect has been to create an increasing number of technocrats who have restructured the lives of workers and their families in an attempt to ensure the reproduction of profitable forms of labour power (Donzelot, 1977; Jones and Novak, 1980).

The argument presented in this book is premised on the notion that an important role of the state is to ensure the reproduction of capitalist society. In fulfilling this task the state should not be viewed as an instrument of the ruling class as this leads to a functionalist view of the state. Instead, the role of the state evolves amidst competing classes and interest groups that attempt to define its role. As Piven and Cloward (1972) noted over 30 years ago, the state plays a central role in the maintenance of capitalism because it is an unplanned and anarchic system that cannot spontaneously produce and reproduce itself. For example, in terms of labour power, the state develops and maintains an educational system that enhances the viability of the economic system by training, sorting, selecting and certifying able and willing workers (Bowles and Gintis, 1976). Concurrently, the state reproduces and legitimates inequalities through its certification and credentialing systems, which are a result of the natural functioning of the current economic system.

Readers might object to this premise and point out that the state itself should be subjected to a more nuanced analysis and that treating it in a unitary and abstract fashion is a weakness. After all the state takes many different forms in different nations and adopts different responses to social and economic problems. Subjecting the state to a more nuanced analysis has obvious value. However, this book is not the place to rehearse unresolved debates, for example, those within Marxism. Rather, the book proceeds on the basis that it is sufficient to claim that the state has an interest in facilitating transitions into employment and training and that a desire to reproduce the social relations of production is a key motivating force.

The emergence of the discouraged worker effect, youth unemployment and the entrenched proportion of young people NEET suggests the emergence of what critical theorists such as Habermas (1976) and those who draw on his work (Codd, 1995; Hargreaves, 1989), refer to as a 'crisis of motivation'. A source of this crisis is the erosion of the cultural supports or norms of behaviour that formerly provided individuals with guidance. For instance, traditional methods of skilling typically involved an 'apprenticeship' model in which older workers provided younger and less experienced workers with the training they required in order to function effectively in the workplace and in the home. This included training in the technical skills and social skills young workers required to be effective in the workplace. For example, older workers took responsibility for inculcating younger workers into the social relations of the workplace and policing challenges to appropriate behaviours (Grieco, 1996; Young and Willmott, 1957). Family and community networks built labour market attachment and ensured that young workers obtained the skills required to be effective in the labour market. For young females the process was similar, though linked to their future roles in the home. In the past, these cultural supports or norms of behaviour have supported capitalist production by enhancing the productivity of labour power (Willis, 1977).

Like Marx, critical theorists maintain that economic development and state intervention have eroded the ability of these cultural supports to give meaning and motivation to life, at least in ways conducive to the needs of the economic system. As the current focus on improving individual incentives to take up work demonstrates, maintaining the social relations of production necessitates State intervention in community and family life (Hargreaves, 1989). To aid legitimation processes, the state relies on experts and their technocratic strategies. These are designed to create sets of institutional arrangements that attempt to satisfy individual needs and aspirations (Ewert, 1991). However, the inability of these interventions to resolve contradictions within the economic system inevitably leads to questions regarding the effectiveness of the new arrangements. This comprises a second source of the motivation crisis. For example, the development of new forms of schooling and new ways of assessing learning are designed, in part, to provide a new set of institutional arrangements to satisfy individual needs and aspirations. However, as the discouraged worker effect suggests, increases in youth unemployment led some students to ask why they should work hard to obtain qualifications perceived as worthless.[3] Evidence that educational reforms have failed to motivate all young people to attend class, let alone to work hard when they are there, is not difficult to find. For example, in 2002 it was estimated that about 50,000 students per day were absent from school in the United Kingdom. The fact that this truancy appears to be sanctioned by parents suggests that they also do not have faith in the schooling system (Smithers, 2002).

In response to such problems, the state is attempting to develop forms of educational technology by creating new methods of schooling and assessment techniques that are believed to be more motivating for students. From a Habermasian perspective, interventions such as competency-based training and the 'Graduation Certificate' in Britain are designed to replace cultural supports that previously gave individuals meaning and motivation. However, students and parents who do not respond to the new measures will encounter more authoritarian measures. For example, parents who do not ensure that their children attend school may face fines of up to £2,500 or terms in jail (ibid., 2002).

The views of the critical theorists resonate with views of sociologists such as the late James Coleman who saw the loss of those informal and community structures, which created sanctions and norms of behaviour consistent with the aims of society as a loss of social capital. He traces the decline of 'primordial' institutions based on the family that he describes as the central element of social organisation and the means through which social control was exercised. The sources of this control were located in social norms, status, reputation and moral force. In primordial societies such forms of control were 'born of informal processes that depend[ed] on a dense and relatively closed social structure that has continuity over time. Closure and continuity provide[d] a form of social capital' (Coleman, 1993, p. 9). However, technological change has expanded social circles and erased the geographical constraints on social relations and has reduced the ability of social networks to control behaviour through social closure. For example, prior to the Industrial Revolution, patterns of economic dependence between generations within families created intergenerational solidarity. When parents became economically inactive, norms in the extended family and in the community meant children were obliged to support their parents. For Coleman (1993), the emergence of pension funds and government old-age assistance has contributed to a weakening of this obligation and a loss of incentive on the part of parents to raise their children to be productive. In contemporary society, the state has a strong interest in ensuring that young people become useful and productive members of society. In this context, one task of sociology is to guide the process of social engineering that replaces the now eroded primordial ties with rationally devised incentives and rewards. This prevents the emergence of a social vacuum that is likely to have deleterious impact on all, particularly children.[4] In other words, solving contemporary social problems rests in developing new social technologies.

State Intervention and the Remaking of Social Networks

The development of new forms of VET, new careers advice services, and active labour market policies are examples of new social technologies and represent important developments in the state's response to the erosion in the value of social networks. Arguably, what is unique to the contemporary period is the way networks are being remade by the state through changes in the delivery and aims of VET and social welfare. Particularly, it is argued that outcomes-based funding has created strong incentives for those who work with youth to deliver the outcomes purchased by the state. Where employment outcomes are an important performance measure, as in the New Zealand version of the Modern Apprenticeship Scheme (MAS), youth workers are provided with strong incentives to place young people into employment. Producing such outcomes is dependent on the ability of tutors in such schemes to make effective networks with training providers and employers. Evidently, one reason for the effectiveness of this approach rests in the function completed by the tutors who match the recruitment of young people with placement into employment. Through an understanding of the skill requirements and cultural practices found in places of work, the tutors are able to maximise the likelihood of a successful placement. This matching function cannot be efficiently completed in bureaucratic systems, such as the VET system.

Earlier accounts of the role of the state in the regulation of labour have correctly argued that capitalism is a fluid system in which entrepreneurs seek out new markets and ways of maximising profit margins (Piven and Cloward, 1972). These developments create demand for new forms of labour and workers in alternative locations. In the process, traditional forms of skilling and allocating workers have been rendered inefficient. Neither can these functions be efficiently performed within the bureaucracies of central governments. The competitive pressures of capitalism require these functions to be performed in the market place. As Piven and Cloward (1972, pp. 4–5) point out that '[i]n the place of tradition or government authority, capitalist societies control people and work tasks precisely as they control goods and capital – through a market system'.

While overall Piven and Cloward's (1972) case is compelling, their claim that capitalism requires new kinds of workers and that 'traditional' methods of allocating labour power are inefficient requires closer examination. In this respect, their analysis resonates with the functionalist sociology of Parsons (1951). Accordingly, a diminished significance of social networks in the recruitment process is predicted as the proportion of employment requiring high levels of skill and technological expertise increases.

The prediction that capitalist methods of production have reduced the importance of traditional methods of allocating labour power is an overstatement. There are two main reasons for this. Firstly, although the proportion of young people who obtain basic school qualifications has grown dramatically in recent years, skill demands have not increased to the same extent, despite technological change and economic modernisation in many segments of the labour market. Strong demand for workers who have only basic skills remains (Livingstone, 1999; Wolf, 2002). Secondly, recruitment through 'traditional' methods, such as social networks, remains a feature of modern labour markets despite economic change (Rosenbaum, 2002). Indeed, it is likely that in some respects informal methods of recruitment have increased in importance as the proportion of young people who hold qualifications increases, thus reducing their signalling capacity to employers. In subsequent chapters, it is argued that market methods are being used by Third Way governments to regulate the transitions into work of disadvantaged people who lack access to valuable social networks, in terms of job information, training information, and actual vacancies. In such settings networks are a form of social capital and they have assumed a commodified form.[5]

This book argues that the commodification of social networks is a result of two inter-related developments. The first is the inability of VET to replace functions formerly served by social networks. Secondly, the development of new methods of governance, particularly the increasing use of outcomes-based funding in the provision of VET and in the provision of welfare services to disadvantaged youth.

It is important to note that the erosion in the value of social networks and their subsequent remaking is not unique to the contemporary period. During episodes of economic disruption, such as that which occurs through the demise of particular industries, whole communities have found that employment networks suddenly lack value. Over time, displaced workers have been attracted by the growth of new industries in other regions. Social networks have been a key resource facilitating the movement across large geographical distances (Tilly, 1998).[6] During such periods, the state has intervened to remake networks. For example, during the workhouse era in nineteenth-century Britain, the development of relief under the Poor Law went hand-in-hand with urbanisation and the development of wage labour markets. In this context, relief served as a support for labour markets disrupted by economic depression and as a means of disciplining 'disturbed' rural immigrants (Piven and Cloward, 1972). In a similar vein, the process of determining eligibility for relief was also a process of labour market formation. The moral and administrative categories concerning marital status, length of residency, place of origin, and the like 'both defined access to extramarket subsistence and determined patterns of participation in wage labor' (Peck, 2001, p. 62). Later, the labour exchanges which were established in the United States and in the United Kingdom performed similar functions (King, 1994).

Unlike earlier periods, the current commodification of social networks is symptomatic of a broader shift in the locus of employment-related social networks, away from familial, community, and workers' networks towards professional networks that are located in the relationships between employment brokers/VET providers and employers. It also represents the transference of relationships formerly untainted by commerce, into commercial relationships (Jacob, 2003).[7]

To make this case, the following chapter argues that the relationship between educational credentials, social class and social networks has become more complex. Chapter 3 shows that growth in the proportion of work-poor families, the decline in the quality of work available, and credentialism have reduced the extent to which employment rich networks are embedded in the social infrastructure. Chapter 4 canvasses the state's response to problems created by the decline in the value of social networks. The purpose is to briefly establish the relationship between Third Way approaches to political management and social capital and to introduce the contrasting solutions to the disruption described above. Chapter 5 provides a critical evaluation of the ability of the VET system to re-engineer intelligence in ways conducive to the labour markets of deindustrialised economies. Chapter six focuses on New Zealand, where qualitative data gathered in interviews with trainers participating in a variety of VET and workfare programmes in New Zealand are used to explore the relationship between VET, market methods, and social networks. The argument presented in Chapter 6 provides a basis for Chapter 7, where an assessment of the Connexions Service and the E2E Programme is offered. In addition to drawing on policy debates as these relate to the likely impact of Connexions, data gathered in a small number of interviews conducted with personal advisors and E2E tutors will be used to explore the impact of the Connexions Service on transitions to work and training. Chapter 8 concludes by discussing the relevance of critical theory in light of the findings and by considering the limits and possibilities of social capital.

Notes

1   The Labour Party formed a coalition with the centre-left Alliance Party to form a government in 1999 and with the centrist Progressive Coalition in 2002. Labour also relies upon the support of the conservative United Future party in order to govern.
2   The Youth Training programme is designed to assist young people with low levels of formal qualifications to obtain work. Training providers receive a fee for providing training and placing young people into employment. The Modern Apprenticeship Scheme involves using brokers who are contracted on a fee per placement and ongoing management of trainees to arrange apprenticeships on behalf of young job seekers. Gateway is designed to provide senior school students with work experience.
3   Although Habermas' thesis awaits firm empirical proof from the perspective of educational policy, it is the public perception of the crisis and readings of the educational and employment trends that is of primary significance. This provides much of the impetus underpinning educational reform (Hargreaves, 1989).
4   It is important to stress that Coleman's (1993) account is highly stylised. More nuanced accounts have stressed that the analysis of the impact of kinship remains generally unfinished (Neven, 2002).
5   Debate exists concerning the appropriateness of describing social relationships as 'capital' (Robison et al., 2002). For example, some argue that it is inappropriate to describe social relationships in this way as – unlike financial, human, and physical capital – social capital is not 'located' within actors but located 'between' actors. That is, no one person can own

a network (Adler and Kwon, 2000). Conversely, Coleman (1988) stresses that, like other forms of capital, social capital can be appropriated. For example, it can be used by an individual to secure employment ahead of other individuals. In addition, it can be converted into other forms of capital (Lin, 1999). Although debate will continue regarding the merit of calling certain social relationships capital, this difference is not great in the context of the similarities social capital shares with other forms of capital (Robison et al., 2002). This book proceeds on the basis that it is appropriate to define networks in this way.

6   Historical studies confirm the construction of networks by merchants who were keen to expand their trade across large geographical areas (Bull, 2002). An initial step into business was the admittance of an individual as an apprentice, followed by the establishment of an independent business. Family supported young people throughout, from arranging an apprenticeship through networks to providing recommendations needed to become established as an independent merchant. The recommendations were seen as guarantees that the appropriate social capital and cultural capital were present. Thus, they indicated that young merchants came from the 'right' social class. Marriage was a key strategy for expanding as opportunities because it expanded the network structure.

7   It is important to recognised that the commodification of social networks is a small part of broader social changes occurring in society. In this respect, other aspects of society, such as knowledge, are being reduced to a format through which an exchange value can be determined and are being exposed to market forces in order to better regulate social practices (Jacob, 2003).

Chapter 2

Educational Credentials, Social Class and Social Networks

The opening of America, Australia, and New Zealand to European immigrants in the nineteenth century was perceived by many as sowing the seeds of new, egalitarian societies. It was believed that ordinary individuals in these nations would be given an opportunity to break free of the rigid class structures found in home nations. *The Australian Bulletin* expressed this sentiment:

> By the term Australian we mean not just those who were merely born in Australia. All white men who come to these shores – with a clean record – and who leave behind them the memory of the class-distinctions and religious differences in the Old World; all men who place the happiness, the prosperity, the advancement of their adopted land before imperialism are Australians. (*The Australian Bulletin*, 1887, p. 4)

This optimism was also apparent in Britain, where the reconstruction of society following the destruction caused by World War II provided an opportunity to build an egalitarian society. The state had a central role in creating such a society and it was believed that it could ameliorate, though not eliminate, inequalities. The idea was to create a more socially cohesive and equal society, and to insure against the economic and social risks and uncertainties apparent in earlier phases of capitalist development.

The view that the government could have a defining impact on the relationships between individuals and help reduce inequality provided the impetus for the creation of the welfare state. In T.S. Marshall's view the welfare state would lead to a:

> ... general enrichment of the concrete substance of life, a general reduction of risk and insecurity [and] an equalisation between the more and less fortunate at all levels – between the healthy and the sick, the employed and the unemployed, the old and the active, the bachelor and the father of a large family. (Cited in Ellison, 1997, p. 698)

The sense of optimism associated with immigration and reconstruction of a socially just society provided the initial basis for an egalitarian society. However, it was the economic argument that western societies could no longer afford to waste the pool of ability found in working class and ethnic minority groups that proved decisive in shaping the competition for advancement through education that was eventually organised in these nations. In an era of rapid technological change, the notion that all people could achieve according to their level of ability and motivation was implausible without education. This view was also politically appealing as it meant the state did not need to intervene directly to create equality through, for example, breaking down property rights.

This chapter briefly considers some of the economic and social forces that underpinned the development of mass education and contributed to the emergence of individualisation theories. According to these theories, the development of mass schooling freed young people from their social origins and led to an erosion in the significance of social class. Status is achieved rather than ascribed and young people become the authors of their individual destinies. Based on this view, the role of social networks in the recruitment process has declined through the creation of open labour markets which are the result of economic development, the expansion of education systems, the development of institutional-based trust in the form of educational credentials and the development of bureaucratic selection mechanisms in the labour market.

This position is challenged here in that the demise of the significance of social networks in the process of obtaining employment and the credentials needed to obtain employment has not taken place. Rather, in some segments of the labour market credentials do not function in the manner predicted and in other segments the relationship between credentials, networks and employment has become more complex. Work-bound school-leavers attempting to make the transition into work but lacking access to valuable networks can be seen to experience disadvantage compared to those with access to such networks. By the same token, young people who have access to valuable knowledge concerning which qualifications are in demand and the best institutions in which to obtain these are advantaged relative to those who do not.

Educational Reform and the Erosion of Networks

Until the emergence of mass education systems in the early twentieth century, access to academic education was primarily limited to the male elite. For the working class, where if attendance at school occurred at all it was limited to preparation for employment. However, demand from egalitarian social reformers and the parents of able, working class youth to be afforded the same opportunities as their upper class peers pressured governments to deliver the egalitarian vision upon which the new societies were founded. For example, in New Zealand at the turn of the twentieth century, pressure to satisfy demand from the public with academic ambitions for their children for more secondary school places led to the introduction of the Free Secondary Places Legislation. This provided those formerly excluded by cost with access to secondary schooling and thus with access to the credentials that held the promise of social mobility. As a result, secondary school rolls began to increase. This created strife for the government, which argued that an academic curriculum geared to preparing students for university was only necessary if every student intended to go down this path. This was clearly not the case as only one in 20 students advanced to university (Lee and Lee, 1992). Consequently, schools were seen to be producing graduates with credentials that did not reflect individual future destinations. In addition, in a view that resonates with contemporary educational debates, it was feared the professions were likely to become overcrowded unless something was done to create a bias towards industry and manufacturing. However, attempts in the early twentieth century to reduce the number of working class people in academic education by introducing new forms of technical and vocational education largely failed. A common fear was that, should youth be directed into technical curricula, vocational opportunities would be restricted. For example, McKenzie et al. (1990, p. 4) reported that working-class people 'wanted little to do with "technical schooling" that they suspected to be chiefly designed to keep their children in the factory'.

Pressure from ambitious working class parents and from egalitarian social reformers led to minor changes in assessment and curriculum in New Zealand but the basic thrust to limit participation and achievement in academic education to the elite was retained. However, during the post-war economic boom of the 1950s and 1960s, producing the number of educated workers needed to fill the growing number of middle class positions from within the ranks of the middle classes proved difficult. It was at this point that extending educational opportunities to all people irrespective of their social backgrounds was seriously considered by the state. Thus, the creation of a new society and progressive education systems in paving the way for egalitarianism was originally a political strategy, though it ultimately transmogrified into an economic strategy. Indeed, it was the revolutionary nature of the capitalist system itself, which demanded access to a wider range of talent, that proved decisive. This idea was given academic credibility in the functionalist sociology of the mid-1900s, which maintained that in the shift from traditional to industrial society, selection on the basis of personal merit replaced selection on the basis of social background (Parsons, 1951). Accordingly, individuals were to be allocated to various positions in the labour market on the basis of what they could show they could do rather than on a basis of their family's position in the social structure and the value of their social networks. The role of schooling was to identify those with talent and reward this with educational credentials that would provide access to the most highly prized occupations. The erosion of the influence of kin and community in linking origins with destinations was seen as functionally necessary given the competitive pressures of capitalist production. Durkheim believed that if individuals could see that any resulting inequality was meritorious or the result of rational processes, they would accept it as fair. Thus, education could contribute greatly to social cohesion and stability (Parkin, 1992).

The strategy initially settled upon to identify individual merit involved devising fair, scientific assessment and selection procedures in schools (Scott and Freeman-Moir, 1990). To affect this, examinations were developed to assess the academic potential of students and to assign them to various roles in society. It was believed that the efficient allocation of labour power depended on devising ways to select the most suitable candidate for a given job. Accordingly, it was argued that 'scientific' selection methods allowed individuals to compete for highly prized educational credentials on the basis of personal merit rather than on the basis of social, cultural, or economic backgrounds. Examinations were perceived as providing the most accurate assessment of individual potential and thus the fairest way of allocating individual future roles in higher education or the labour market. The assumption was that intelligent people would opt for academic subjects leading to university study and professional or managerial jobs. By the same token, their less able peers would opt for practical subjects leading to associated semi- or unskilled jobs or unemployment (Brown and Lauder, 2001). However, this failed to deliver the expected rewards, and social and economic inequality continued (Scott and Freeman-Moir, 1990).

The next strategy used was to delay directing students into academic and vocational pathways until later in their schooling through providing a comprehensive secondary school education to all. The view was that this would better allow individuals to demonstrate their potential and to advance to destinations in the labour market, higher education, or vocational education depending upon their potential and irrespective of social background. In New Zealand, Labour Party politicians, who saw a differentiated schooling system as promoting and supporting social class divisions, supported calls for a common curriculum. A common core curriculum was needed to curtail the divisive effects of the development of technical and secondary schools and, irrespective of their ability, all learners had common needs. McKenzie et al. (1990, p. 22) describes the Labour Party's position on post-compulsory education from the time:

> First a commitment to added general education for all; second, a preference for this taking place in a common institution; third, opposition to any early course specialisation that might be reducible to narrow trade training; and fourth, acceptance that 'non-academic' subjects and activities had a worthy place as part of general education.

For varying reasons the development of a common core-curriculum was resisted. Some school principals felt it would disadvantage their academic pupils, whilst the Ministers of Education of the day saw the distinction between academic and technical education as justified because not all students were of equal intelligence (Lee and Lee, 1992). However, following the release of the Post-Primary Curriculum (Department of Education, 1943), the move towards a compulsory common core curriculum was given a decisive push. The Report recommended the development of a compulsory common core curriculum, claiming that such a curriculum was needed to educate all adolescents for their forthcoming roles as workers, neighbours, homemakers and citizens. The Report advocated that schools had an educative function to create individuals that were '… not only self-disciplined and free in spirit, gifted in work … but also responsible and generous in social life' (Department of Education, 1943, p. 5). However, this strategy also failed to deliver the promised social rewards and despite the massive expansion of higher education, individuals continued to move up and down the social scale at the same rate as always (Scott and Freeman-Moir, 1990).

In the contemporary period, Third Way administrations are attempting to introduce new forms of VET and methods of assessment to increase equality of opportunity and resynchronise what is produced in the schooling system with the demands of the labour market. The ability of the new measures to achieve the aims of Third Way administrations is the subject of Chapter 4. For the moment, the increase in the numbers of technological, professional and scientific workers and the economic necessity for equality of opportunity led to the claim that growth in technology had contributed to the creation of a classless society in which destinations had been separated from origins. An extension of this view is that occupational attainment becomes simply a matter of individual achievement and the labour market became freed from status restrictions and exclusions (Scott, 1996). This view gave rise to theories of individualisation and the related claim that the significance of social class backgrounds in influencing future destinations and the significance of social networks in the recruitment process had declined.

The Erosion of Social Class

The growing significance of educational credentials led some to declare that industrial and scientific progress contributed to the creation of a classless society. This belief is based upon a view that technological innovation, increased labour mobility, the need for greater numbers of professional, technological and scientific workers, and the competitive pressures created by capitalism eroded social divisions based on membership of a group. According to the technocratic/meritocratic thesis, as it has come to be known, industrialism opposes the tradition and status that is based on membership of particular groups, including family, race, or caste (Kerr et al., 1973). Instead, one's ability to secure a place in the emerging technologically advanced economy rests on the credentials obtained in the education system, which transmit to employers trustworthy information concerning one's skills. The increase in the importance of educational credentials signalled that traditional or informal methods of gaining skills were no longer able to achieve the level of skill required to secure a place in the technologically advanced economy. The aspects of society that formerly fulfilled these skill transmission and skill recognition functions, such as familial and community-based social networks, became of little value. Indeed, from an egalitarian and economic perspective, education programmes were designed to separate young people from networks that were likely to suppress their talents. In other words, credentials came to replace social networks in the process of allocating and regulating labour power. Variations on the basic theme that individuals have been freed from their social networks and bonds or that the transition into work has become individualised are apparent within contemporary sociological debates. Although these accounts are highly stylised and do not properly explain reality, they nevertheless provide a way to improve understanding of the contemporary debates regarding economic and social change and their relationship to social networks.

It is argued that modernisation and industrial development have freed individuals to write their own biographies and led to the individualisation of young people's situations (Chisholm and Du Bois-Reymond, 1993; Kelly and Kenway, 2001). Researchers argue that the erosion in the significance of kin also brought about broader changes in the process of individual identity formation. For example, some argue this erosion has freed individuals from their social backgrounds and allowed them the space to create their own identities (Beck, 1992). In the past, young people drew on resources such as social networks provided by their families and the communities in which they lived in order to make the transition into work. For example, in the Welsh collieries, older workers would take younger, male family members down the pit and train them to mine coal safely (Rees, 1997). The transmission of this skill and the reproduction of the social relations of production depended upon young men adopting identities as workers that were similar to those of their fathers in a baboushka doll-like fashion. The transition for women was different, although it still involved the reproduction of an identity supportive of the social relations of production.

However, in the contemporary era it is argued that modernisation, industrial development and labour mobility have brought about transformations in both families and work (Carnoy, 2000). This has freed individuals from adopting standardised roles and, though inequality continues, it is individualised rather than class-based. That is, '[t]he individual himself or herself ... becomes the agent of their own livelihood mediated by the market' (Beck, 1992, p. 130) and the creation of new networks becomes a key strategy for remaining embedded in the global economy (Carnoy, 2000). Thus, community and kin no longer shape individual identity to the extent they once did. The reproduction of the social relations of production and the attendant identities no longer occur within families and the communities in which they live. Rather, this occurs in other spheres and through other means – for example, in the VET system and via the mass media, particularly television – and it occurs through participating in new 'professional networks'.[1]

In a position that resonates with the neoconservative critique of the welfare state (Mead, 1986), a result of these transformations is that 'traditional' social structures, such as the extended family, social networks, and social class, no longer provide clear signposts for mapping one's life. Because it is thought to separate individuals, their families and the communities in which they live, schooling plays a key role in the process of reducing in significance 'traditional' social structures and in helping create new identities. As Beck, (1992, p. 93) expresses it:

> ... schooling means choosing and planning one's own educational life course. The educated person becomes the producer of his or her own labor situation, and

in this way, of his or her social biography. As schooling increases in duration, traditional orientations, ways of thinking, and lifestyles are recast and replaced by universalistic forms of learning and teaching as well as by universalistic forms of knowledge and language.

The reasons families and the communities in which they live no longer provide clear pathways for young people are varied and range from changes in working class cultures, changes in their communities, and the opening up of the non-work sphere in identity formation. In this respect, researchers have identified numerous other influences on identity formation (Bradley, 1996). For example, Fevre (2000) argues in support of Putnam (2000) by claiming television is strongly implicated in the creation of identities in the contemporary period and the decline of social capital. Television supplants social capital and creates commodified identities. Thus, television has taken on the role of 'substituting identities and networks itself ... in the new society a kind of ersatz social capital is created instead of the real, embedded social capital of identities and networks' (ibid., p. 108).

In this way, transitions into work are no longer effectively facilitated or regulated in the private sphere of families and the communities in which they live but are increasingly facilitated in the public sphere of schools and, for instance, through VET (Hollands, 1990). Concurrently, the weakening of institutional restraints on identity formation means that individuals face an increasing array of choices and are forced to take more responsibility for shaping their future.

> As soon as people enter the labour market, they experience mobility. They are removed from traditional patterns and arrangements ... they become relatively independent of inherited or newly formed ties (e.g. family, neighbourhood, friendship, partnership). *There is a hidden contradiction between the mobility demands of the labour market and social bonds*. (Beck, 1992, p. 94, original emphasis)

In addition, the weakening of institutional restraints, or disembedding, is thought to have contributed to greater risk and uncertainty for individuals, especially for those who are most disadvantaged in society, hence Beck's notion of the 'risk society'.

The Continuing Significance of Social Class

Whilst the prediction that mobility demands in the labour market and the expansion of education would free individuals from their social class backgrounds, evidence suggests that social origins remain important in determining future labour market destinations. For example, evidence suggests inequality is transmitted across generations (Levine, 1999). In other evidence, over 40 per cent of young men whose fathers were either unemployed or in the lowest income brackets in Britain in the early 1970s have themselves either been unemployed or are in the lowest income brackets (Johnson and Reed, 1996). In the United States Solon (1992) reached a similar conclusion.[2] In the United Kingdom social class inequalities measured in relative terms have either remained stable for the last three generations, despite the expansion of higher education (Halsey, 1993; Wolf, 2002), or have declined as Britain becomes less meritocratic (Galindo-Rueda and Vignoles, 2003). Recent evidence shows that Australians from lower socioeconomic backgrounds are half as likely to participate in higher education as those from medium and higher socioeconomic backgrounds (James, 2002). In this context, the argument that transition into work has been transformed by economic and technological change has proved unfounded and there exists a good deal of continuity between generations. Thus, although transitions into work may have become more attenuated with the expansion of education, mechanisms continue to ensure that the reproduction of social classes remains. Similarly, the notion that identities have become fragmented by economic and social change is likely to be an overstatement. Research indicates that the majority of young people hold views of themselves and the society in which they live that dovetail with those held by their parents and their grandparents. This may include a commitment to family life and to the work ethic, and a belief in the inherent value of education (Jeffs and Smith, 2004).

One way to theorise this continuity is to view kin groups as providing networks within which assets flow. Social and economic changes alter the mix of resources needed to secure advantage; however, their value continues, albeit in different forms. For example, the 'obsolescence of old social networks and family influences on the transitions to work' has been associated with an increasing importance of formal education (Fevre, 2000, p. 107). In this respect, the introduction of user pays in higher education may have reasserted the importance of the intergenerational transfer of financial resources (Ahier and Moore, 1999). In addition, the development of mass higher education means that the role of social networks in gaining quality information about qualifications and the institutions from which to obtain these has also become more important. Instead of being freed by such changes, we are witnessing different strategies employed by families and individuals to secure advantage, essentially a process that is being structured by the state. We are seeing the development of new dependencies, for example, the financial dependence of young people on their parents; new freedoms, for example, the introduction of greater choice in education; and demands for new forms of information, for example, on what credentials are of value. These changes are forcing a reconfiguration rather than a transformation of transition to work.

Before exploring the relationship between educational credentials, the labour market, and social networks and situating access to employment-rich networks as a form of intergenerational asset transfer, it is necessary to explore further the importance of educational credentials in the process of individualisation. If technological change and modernisation of the economy have reduced the role played by friends, families and communities in the reproduction of social class and in the creation of worker identities, how do young people make transitions into work? This is an important question, as how young people obtain work and the kind of work they do are likely to play an important role in influencing future patterns of advantage and disadvantage (Crompton, 1993).

As noted above, the conventional view is that young people make transitions into work by competing in the open labour market on the basis of their educational credentials. This suggests that new and trustworthy forms of information about individuals have been developed by the state that 'speak for' young job seekers and transmit useful information to employers. How trust that facilitates transition into work is produced and maintained, if at all, goes to the heart of the state's search for a solution to disruption.

Economic Change and the Production of Trust

According to Zucker (1986), in earlier times the creation of trust, obligation, and expectation were based on repeated informal interpersonal exchanges. These exchanges and negotiations created process-based trust or reputation based on past exchanges. In this context, trust is not an abstract entity, rather it is an outcome of repeated exchange between people. Individual 'reputation', for example, signalled to employers whether one had the skills required to be effective in the workplace. Where reputation became associated with a particular ethnic or family grouping, membership of these various groupings were used as a proxy for other skills and attributes. An outcome of this was the reproduction of existing social class groups and creation of categorical inequality (Tilly, 1998). Zucker (1986) argues that the creation of reputation was possible in traditional societies as labour was not highly mobile and the skills necessary for production could be obtained through informal methods of skill transference. Accordingly, new workers learned the skills and attributes necessary to be successful in the workplace by working alongside existing employees in an apprenticeship-type relationship (Cohen, 1983). Importantly, skill should not be limited to something passed from worker to worker in a kind of direct training model: rather, skill and reputation are properties that reside in relationships between individuals; they had collective properties. Collective skill was a result of interdependencies within a social group, which were heightened when work was of an intermittent nature (Grieco, 1996). Individual workers did not have all the knowledge required to complete tasks and could not build reputations on their own. Consequently, workers relied upon the knowledge of other workers in order to complete tasks and build reputation. Thus, although knowledge could be the property of an individual, it was often the property of a group. In such settings, faith in individual skills and abilities to meet the required standard was not established by impersonal means, such as educational credentials. Rather, it was based on repeated exchanges and was embedded in the social relationships, communication structures and labour cultures that exist within groups.

The collective character of skill explains why hop-growers in eighteenth century Kent recruited teams of hop-pickers rather than individual workers. In addition to reducing the cost and difficulty of negotiating employment relationships on a one-to-one basis, employing teams of workers offered advantages to employers because they were natural 'skilling' organisations (Grieco, 1996).[3] This is just one example of similar processes occurring in many ways in different settings. In the later 1800s and early 1900s, American factories subcontracted much of their production to Italian entrepreneurs who hired their own workforces and produced the required goods for an agreed price. The padrone, as the labour contractor of the day, had access to an indefinite supply of willing workers and could exercise great control over the fate of these workers (Tilly, 1998, p. 165). Similar claims are made in a study of craft labour markets, which showed that by the beginning of World War I the labour supply and training of new workers in both the printing and construction industries in the United Kingdom was controlled by the relevant unions (Jackson, 1984). Employers benefited from the arrangement as they gained access to a dependable supply of skilled labour without paying the costs for training or running a labour hire service. However, social relationships such as those described by Grieco (1996), Jackson (1984) and Tilly (1998) do not last indefinitely. Rather, ongoing economic change means that relationships die out and new relationships are established (Waldinger, 1986).

Zucker (1986) argues that in the contemporary period high levels of labour mobility, rapid changes in technology, the related constant changes in skill demand, and globalisation of the economy mean that process-based trust no longer facilitates economic relationships efficiently. Institutional-based trust, for example, educational credentials, has now assumed a greater role in facilitating employment relationships. As a result, the role of the VET system in transferring skill and reconfiguring identities has increased in importance. Thus, although the processes captured by Grieco (1996), Jackson (1984) and Tilly (1998) are useful historic accounts of employment relationships, they lack relevance in modern economies in which institutional-based forms of trust are of utmost importance. In other words, 'reputation' as described by Zucker (1986) is no longer sufficient to maintain economic relationships in modern economies in which competitive pressures have emphasised the need for businesses to maximise profit margins, and markets now function globally across contrasting cultures.

Industrial development has produced a number of other changes that have also disrupted the production of process-based forms of trust. For example, contemporary workers are more geographically mobile and a measure of skill and motivation is necessary to facilitate employment over long distances and between unfamiliar people who have had no opportunity to create process-based trust. In addition, geographical mobility has increased ethnic and social diversity and there exists a need to facilitate employment relations between individuals from diverse cultural and social backgrounds. The increasing cultural heterogeneity that resulted from increased levels of migration between and within nations meant the loss of 'a world in common' (Zucker, 1986, p. 70).

Facilitating economic relationships between these different worlds requires the development of new trust-producing mechanisms. This task has largely fallen upon institutions within the state. For example, the state maintains the legal system that is designed, amongst other things, to facilitate commerce. Similarly, institutional-based forms of trust have been developed to replace social networks in the allocation of labour power, for example, the recognition of competence by educational credentials. Indeed, major educational interventions have been developed to increase the level of trust employers, learners and parents have in credentials. For example, the Qualifications and Curriculum Authority (QCA) in the United Kingdom, the New Zealand Qualifications

Authority (NZQA) and similar organisations in Australia and elsewhere have been developed to 'guard standards'. In an attempt to ensure high standards and signal to users of education, such as employers, that credentials offer trustworthy assessments of student abilities, quality assurance procedures for universities and schools have been developed. The Qualifications and Curriculum Authority accredits credentials and monitors the administration of national tests to enhance confidence in the credentials and national testing system. By developing an educational system that attempts to provide employers with trustworthy information, in the form of educational credentials, about the skills and abilities of job seekers, the state has attempted to institutionalise trust.

Credentials and the Labour Market

The centrality placed upon the role of credentials or institutional-based forms of trust in the recruitment process, by functionalist sociologists, politicians and others, is useful as it provides a way to test the validity of the claim that the significance of social networks has declined. The notion held by proponents of the technocratic/meritocratic perspective, in which credentials assumed a central and defining role in the allocation of labour power, rests upon a number of inter-related and widely held assumptions about the relationship between education, the economy and the role of credentials. It is assumed that the technological change and innovation, which saw the number of professional, technical and managerial workers in the United States increase by 68 per cent between 1950 and 1960 while the overall workforce grew by just 8 per cent, would continue (Trow, 1977). Eventually economic modernisation means all members of society would become middle class, as young people increasingly take positions in the rapidly expanding ranks of technical, scientific and professional workers. Hence, economic change means that all workers will need to be highly skilled and credentialed leading all workers to engage in ongoing periods of training. Governments, policy advisors and others have widely and uncritically adopted this view. For example, in the United Kingdom the Department for Education and Skills argue:

> More people need to be better educated than before. To improve economic competitiveness and promote social justice we need to develop the skills and talents of young people across the full range of abilities. Young people need to continue their education and training past 16, and must be challenged to reach their full potential. (Department for Education and Skills, 2002a, p. 1)

Similarly, in New Zealand a former Minister of Education argued that 'it is impossible to overestimate the importance of the credentials young people aim for while they are at school' (Creech, 1998, p. 1). The perceived link between credentials and employment is so embedded in state policy that solving the unemployment problem is often considered to rest in skill development and skill recognition (Skill New Zealand, 1999a; Wolf, 2002). The emergence of skill development and recognition, referred to by Swift (1995) as the 'training gospel', is believed to be a solution to youth unemployment and has provided impetus for the state in New Zealand, the United Kingdom, Australia and the United States to develop and promote training systems. The idea is to use a form of institutional-based trust to 'speak for' young people who, in the context of economic change, no longer have someone who can do this for them in the workplace. For example, in New Zealand and the United Kingdom, national qualification frameworks and related systems of competency-based assessment have been introduced. Initially, policy-makers saw these systems as a short-term response to the sporadic vagaries of the business cycle and its depressing effects on labour market activity. These systems have since assumed central importance as defining components of macro economic policy. However, as elucidated in subsequent chapters, the 'training gospel' has legitimated the development and introduction of training systems but the universally high wage/high skill economy has yet to eventuate. Whilst there has been some growth in the proportion of people in professional and managerial positions, growth in the low skill segments of the labour market, where employers demand little by way of formal education and training, has been strong in the United Kingdom (Wolf, 2002) and New Zealand (Statistics New Zealand, 1998). Thus, we are witnessing a polarisation of the labour market between jobs that require high levels of training and credentials and that attract high levels of remuneration and jobs that do not require skills that are formally recognised through educational credentials. Given this, it is not surprising that employers are not making unequivocal demands for school-leavers to have higher levels of technical competence and school credentials. This is especially true in situations where credentialed skills may lead to demands for increased remuneration. Instead demand is strong for basic workplace disciplines or the so-called 'soft skills', for instance, punctuality, reliability, communication, and attendance (Colmar Brunton Research, 1994; Spours and Young, 1990; Wolf, 2002).

A central aspect of the technocratic/meritocratic perspective and its close relation, institutional-based trust, is that credentials accurately measure individual potential and signal to employers what skills and qualities school-leavers have. However, this claim has proved questionable as it is not clear that credentials can accurately report information about the range of skills and qualities employers require. For example, much formally 'unskilled' work requires high levels of tacit skill and efficient performance in the workplace requires new workers to gain these and get along with co-workers (Manwaring, 1982). Formal school credentials poorly measure such 'skills' or qualities. Given the difficulty in creating institutional-based trust, it is not surprising that when recruiting work-bound school-leavers, employers tend not to use basic school credentials. Indeed, there is little evidence to suggest that they refer to basic school credentials when making hiring decisions (Rosenbaum, 2002; Wallace et al., 1993), Results of a survey of range of public, private, manufacturing and service sectors indicates that 93 per cent of employers of labourers in the UK did not require qualifications. The proportion of employers in service, sales and clerical occupations requiring minimum levels of qualifications was also low, as was proportion of employers looking for National Vocational Qualifications (Millar et al., 2002).

Arguably, the movement to a technologically-advanced economy in which credentials play a key role in allocating labour power is proceeding more slowly than first envisaged and, in time, it is likely that credentials will assume a far greater role in the allocation of labour power as a universally high wage/high skill economy is realised. However, this is only likely to occur if areas of the labour market where the skills required are accurately measured by school credentials expand and areas in which credentials are not required decline. No one really knows what the future holds in terms of skill demand, but it is unlikely that economic development will create a universally high wage/high skill economy in the mid-term at least. A reason for this is that a greater proportion of young people are entering the service sector today than has traditionally been the case. Service sector occupations typically rely more heavily upon 'soft skills', such as interpersonal skills, than on technical skills. Unless credentials systems can accurately measure 'soft skills', it is reasonable to expect that employers will continue to use other methods to select workers. Moreover, even if employers commonly use school credentials as an initial screening device when making recruitment decisions, as some researchers argue (Holzer, 2000; Livingstone, 1999), massive increases in high school participation have increased the New Zealand and the UK completion rates. Therefore, most work-bound school-leavers hold qualifications whether or not employers require them. As the number of people who hold credentials increases, the usefulness of the information conveyed to employers decreases (Breen and Goldthorpe, 2001). In such circumstances, employers are likely to rely more heavily upon process-based trust in the form of social networks.

In turn, this is likely to have a negative effect on school achievement and motivation. Students are told that credentials are important but, through watching their peers obtain employment without them, they soon learn that high-school grades do not effect labour-market outcomes (Rosenbaum et al., 1990). The tendency for employers to ignore school-based signals, such as school grades, suggests that the behaviour of employers may be partly to blame for problems of poor student motivation and for the mismatch between what schools offer and what employers require by way of skills (Rosenbaum, 2002).

Employment and Social Networks

There is a growing literature that theorises labour-market failure among work-bound school-leavers as a function of labour-market transactions that are embedded in a social infrastructure (Granovetter, 1995; Miller and Rosenbaum, 1997; Rosenbaum, 2002). If this infrastructure, including social networks, is absent, then labour markets will not function efficiently. If employers cannot easily receive information about the level of skill school-leavers have to offer, the credentials awarded by schools are of little use to either party.

There are at least two explanations for the apparent inefficiencies of school credentials that have to date limited the ability of institutional-based trust to function as predicted. Firstly, as suggested above, school credentials appear not to transmit the kind of information employers require to make selection decisions. Rosenbaum (2002) argues that this is likely in the United States where a high school diploma only indicates that a student has satisfactorily attended high school. Secondly, it is possible that employers do not trust the information provided by schools about leavers. For instance, researchers in the United States report that employers do not seek more detailed information about student performance by requesting grade transcripts from schools (Rosenbaum and Binder, 1997).

If credentials do not function as predicted by functionalist theories, how do work-bound school-leavers find employment and obtain the skills needed in the workplace? There is evidence that social networks continue to play a role in regulating the labour market today despite economic change and modernisation of the economy. Although postmodern theorists such as Beck (1999) and subscribers to the technocratic/meritocratic thesis base claims on a decline in the value of social networks, researchers have established the importance of familial and group resources in securing employment despite technological innovation and the spread of mass education. Thus, just as membership of kin groups proffered advantages in the past and was a form of intergenerational asset transfer, so too does membership confer benefits and advantages in the contemporary period. One reason membership of networks proffers advantage, thus comprising a form of intergenerational asset transfer, is that recruitment through networks makes economic sense from an employer's perspective. That is, it reduces the cost of recruiting new staff, reduces the likelihood of making hiring errors, and increases worker compliance. For example, networks provide a conduit through which trusted employment-related information can flow. For workers, networks provide a means of obtaining information about job vacancies not advertised in the mainstream media and information about the quality of particular forms of work. In addition, networks can convey information about the labour market that is specific to a given location. For job-seekers, recruitment through social networks offers advantages. For example, networks provide access to information about job vacancies not advertised in the open labour market, they provide reliable information about the quality of particular jobs, and they provide information about the credentials needed in the labour market. In many contexts, the information that is conveyed through networks is far better than that conveyed through formal means.

Existing workers know what is required of particular positions and whether the contacts they have in their social networks will make good workers. Such information is poorly measured and conveyed by formal school credentials. Existing workers are unlikely to recommend contacts who are likely to prove poor workers for fear of damaging their own relationship with their employer. By the same token, new workers often appreciate the value of the networks that have helped them get a job and do not want to damage those relationships. Indeed, they may well help friends get a job once they are established. Moreover, existing workers are likely to want to protect the value of their social networks and thus they have an obvious interest in ensuring the workers they have recommended perform. They do this, for example, by training new workers and policing the behaviours of those they have recommended. Thus, networks are better placed than bureaucratic training systems to reproduce local labour markets by ensuring young people have a good understanding of the skills and qualities needed to be effective in particular workplaces.

Given the economic advantages of recruitment through social networks to employers and to job seekers, it is not surprising that throughout the 1980s and 1990s qualitative and quantitative research has consistently shown the key role of networks in allocating labour power (Grieco, 1987a; Heath, 1999; Jenkins et al., 1983; Lin, 1999; Miller and Volker, 1987; Miller and

Rosenbaum, 1997, 2002; Montgomery, 1992; Newman, K., 1999; Okano, 1995; Rosenbaum et al., 1990; Stone et al., 2003; Wallace et al., 1993; Wong and Salaff, 1998). Similarly, the development of employee referral programmes in the United States speaks of the power of network recruitment within the ranks of middle class occupations (Lachnit, 2001) and in lower-level service occupations (Fernandez et al., 2000). Indeed, Benner (2003) sees the functions completed in matching employers and employees as an emerging business opportunity. This means that access to employment networks plays an important role in reproducing patterns of advantage and disadvantage. For instance, in the United States, young workers who have connections with employers are advantaged ahead of those who do not, irrespective of their level of credentials (Newman, K., 1999). Similarly, a study of inner city youth showed how young people who have access to employment rich networks are advantaged over those who do not (Sullivan, 1989). The advantage enjoyed by those with access to valuable social networks was not just that they were able to get employment but they were then able to build their human capital through experience on the job.

Importantly, access to social networks, which may initially lead to labour market advantage, may become a source of labour market disadvantage over a longer term. For example, it is possible that those who obtain employment in declining sectors of the labour market through their social networks may experience some disadvantage relative to those who, through lack of valuable network capital, go on in education to obtain credentials that enable them to secure a place in expanding sectors of the economy. In the United Kingdom and other European nations, research in rural areas found that young people often relied on parental social networks to obtain employment (Burnett et al., 2001). Burnett et al. (2001, p. 269) suggest that those with 'enabling networks' may be able to pursue their life-plans, while for others following the footsteps of friends and family may be the safest but not necessarily the best option. The importance of networks in securing employment holds both prior to and after the process of formal schooling has taken place. For example, individuals that have access to valuable social networks gain information about the kinds of credentials needed to obtain particular employment and are better positioned to choose to obtain these at institutions that offer links to desired employers. In sum, the importance of social networks has remained intact despite modernisation and technological change in the economy (Granovetter, 1995).

Networks and Credentials

As the foregoing discussion shows, the relationship between school credentials and the labour market is less strong than is often assumed. While more highly qualified work-bound school-leavers are less likely to be unemployed and are more likely to use productive job-seeking activities than their less qualified peers (Rosenbaum, 2002), the precise relationship between obtaining credentials and labour market outcomes remains unclear. For example, research shows that students who achieve in school are more likely to come from work-rich backgrounds and are thus better placed to access employment-rich networks. Related to this is the notion that credentialism may simply delay the use of network strategies, rather than destroy them altogether. In this respect, accounts that link credentials to labour market destinations are likely to hide important network processes. For example, how do young people obtain the work experience and create the networks that subsequently give them an edge in the labour market? As the number of young people entering higher education increases and obtaining a degree no longer guarantees access into middle class careers, the value of networks is likely to increase. Indeed, obtaining the right credentials from the 'right' universities is likely to become all-important as the middle classes battle for positional advantage (Brown, 2000).

The need to secure the right qualifications from the right institution highlights an additional problem for the technocratic/meritocratic perspective and for policy-makers. It is assumed that credentials of equal face value, for example Bachelors degrees from different universities, will convey equal amounts of information and will be of equal value. Indeed, much effort has been made to ensure standards of achievement are recognised by different institutions in the same way. However, homogeneity created by mass higher education is overcome by other strategies in the face of intense competition for middle class jobs (Brown and Scase, 1997). Middle class parents may seek access to elite universities for their children in order to gain an edge. That is, they purchase process-based trust in the form of 'reputational capital' or credentials that signal a superior educational experience compared to that provided to the masses. Thus, as the supply of highly credentialed job-seekers increases, so too does the importance of social networks as a source of information about valuable credential. In this way social capital is converted into better forms of human capital; a process similar to that reported by Ball and Vincent (1998) and Reay and Lucey (2003) in which informal information networks aided parents and students in choosing schools. Further supporting the notion of intergenerational asset transfer is an earlier quantitative study that found higher status individuals were embedded in better networks to gather information about schools (Schneider et al., 1997).

The following unpublished data was gathered as part of earlier research and demonstrates the relationship between social networks, employment, and credentials. The data were gathered in a series of semi-structured interviews. The point of presenting this data is to illustrate the inter-relationship between networks, credentials, and experience that may be combined to produce patterns of advantage and disadvantage.

Donald Smart (high achieving, male, secondary school student): Dad was at a meeting just the other day and he was telling me what credentials the people at the meeting had. Where they were coming from. So he can give me information. Also my father has a wide network. He works with accountants and lawyers and that sort of thing and he can say well this guy is a barrister, this guy owns 90 per cent of his firm practically. And he's doing such and such and he just went to Fiji. Do you want to do the same kinds of things as this man? And he would be interested in giving me work experience and that sort of thing. ... [M]y dad has given me information from law firms and barristers and [asked me] 'do you think that this is something that you would like to do?'

Mr Smart (senior manager in a large metropolitan council): I used to employ personally 50 staff in a variety of teams. So I looked over a huge range of disciplines as part of my management role. And I am in close contact with a whole range of professionals in my workplace over a vast range of disciplines anything from the city solicitor, there are about four or five solicitors. Heaps of accountants and of course that's Donald's focus. So as part of every day chit chat, in the smoko room over a cup of coffee in a meeting, I will ask questions. And they just come as part of a repertoire of questions along with hundreds of other things. So I network. I am also a member of the Institute of Management and Accountants, which I typically don't use them because we have so much information at work. So, well, I was having a game of squash at the squash club and the guy beside me was John, who is a principal of a law firm in town. He is the major partner, the senior partner. So I had a chat with John. And he said to me, 'I have a mate who is in charge of the law school ... at Monash, if you want a bit of advice on that I will sort it out for you .... And one of the elected reps on the council in the same [political] party is principal of another law firm and so he and I are good buddies and we discuss issues.

Interviewer: So you will go and find out what credentials Donald needs to obtain?

Mr Smart: Well to a degree, at the same time I don't claim to have exclusive knowledge, so I simply source ideas and thoughts and we have opportunities to see jobs that appear all over the country because I get to see management magazines and adverts for jobs. I try to keep as much of a feel for the market place as possible. It has interest to me as well as to Donald. ... I could probably get him a job with a law firm. If he completed his degree I think I could just about get him a job. I have enough contacts and I could surely hit one of them right. People already know about him. They know about his motivation and one or two of them would be interested.

The data show how Mr Smart's contacts provided high quality advice about the credentials David would need to obtain and suggests that David may obtain work through these networks should he gain a degree. This data illustrates ways in which resources are transferred across generations. Although the argument requires further empirical research and testing, the data suggest that networks and credentials interact and that credentialism does not diminish the importance of networks.

Social Networks and Skill Development

Recently social capital theorists have adopted the arguments of social network theorists by emphasising the importance of process-based trust in facilitating skill transmission and development. In this context, discussion of the difference between information and knowledge is useful as it highlights ways that social relationships remain vital to the process of skill transference (Winch, 2003). Accordingly, no matter how efficient formal educational and research institutions are at creating information and theoretical knowledge, relationships between people are required to transform theoretical knowledge into applied knowledge for practical settings. Thus, as Grieco (1996) says, knowledge is embedded in social relationships and the quality of these will have an important impact on how nations compete in global knowledge wars. For example, in the case of French cuisine the maintenance and transference of knowledge depends upon numerous interdependencies between people and institutions directly and indirectly involved in food production (Winch, 2003). The knowledge needed to produce cuisine is not embodied in a single individual but rather is a property of the group. Generalising from this single instance to national economies, the quality of the relationships that exist between individuals and institutions has an important impact on how nations react to the pressures of global competition. This idea is important as it goes to the heart of current debates about how best to organise not just the VET system but society more broadly. Economies where knowledge is distributed throughout the society and is a collective property are thought to be best placed to compete effectively in the global economy (Brown and Lauder, 2001). Importantly, the way social relationships are embedded in and produced by the social infrastructure is context specific and how production is organised is critical. In the Grieco (1996) example of hop picking, it made economic sense for growers to outsource labour recruitment and labour training services leading to the development of trust between growers and hopping teams through repeated exchanges. In what can usefully be considered an example of intergenerational transfer, membership of kin groups helped workers secure access to resources in the form the training and reputation needed to gain employment. On the other hand, although certain industries continue to function in the manner described by Winch (2003) in his example of French cuisine, such practices are dying as new, more efficient technologies are developed. Indeed, the recent debate over the impact of McDonalds' restaurants, globalisation and the loss of traditional cuisine in France illustrates the revolutionary impact of economic modernisation on tradition.[4] However, a case can also be made that today context specific social relationships in the workplace are in fact growing in significance. For example, although the extent to which 'high performance' organisations are going to dominate the future is open to question, it is the case that some forms of work require particular social skills that are poorly transmitted and competence that is poorly measured, by VET systems. The rise of teamwork, project-based work and other measures designed to improve workplace efficiency, such as short-term contracts increasing job turnover, has increased the need for context-specific social and cultural skills, that is, those skills and practices that are embedded within particular institutions and practices. Gaining the information that allows an understanding of these practices and the development of these skills is only likely to come from individuals that have participated in such settings and can instil job seekers with skills and qualities needed to be effective. This observation applies to certain segments of the labour market, such as in the rapidly growing service sector employment where 'aesthetic labour' is increasingly important (Nickson et al., 2003) and in new knowledge-based sectors of the economy such as biotechnology (Simmie, 2003).

Conclusion

At first glance, the continuing significance of social networks seems incongruent with a major claim of this book that the value of social networks to the state has declined. However, the findings of the social network theorists do not necessarily refute this. The literature shows that, at least in the short term, poorly qualified young people without access to social networks leading to employment are disadvantaged in the labour market in relation to those who have networks. This suggests that, for work-bound school-leavers, access to valuable social networks can mean the difference between employment, further training, or unemployment. Consequently, social networks may be of value to some, whilst those who do not have any access may remain in education as discouraged workers. On the other hand, the value of social networks as a source of information about particular credentials is likely to have increased as the number of people engaged in education and training grows.

The significance of familial and community-based resources in the employment process continues to generate much concern from educationalists and politicians. Networks are viewed by some negatively in the sense that they play a central role in reproducing patterns of advantage and disadvantage and efforts should be exerted to erase their impact on egalitarian grounds. For example, young people who grow up in work-poor families are disadvantaged in that they may lack an employed person who can 'speak for' them in a place of employment. From a related perspective, the continuing significance of networks in the allocation of labour power is seen to be a result of flaws in the schooling system. This means that schools do not provide useful and trusted information to employers about the skills and attributes of their students and thus, the technology is not effective. For example, selective assessment systems that do not fully report the skills held by school-leavers, such as the A-levels in the United Kingdom, are part of the problem, as they do not allow employers to make properly informed decisions about the skills and attributes of job seekers. As a result of inadequacies in the level of information provided, employers are forced into making employment decisions on the basis of ascribed characteristics and through their social networks. Accordingly, the creation of a society that is meritocratic and effectively competitive in the global economy rests in the development of new forms of educational technology that more accurately measure what students can actually do and can transmit this information to users, such as employers and teachers.

The purpose of this chapter has been to describe the relationship between economic change, educational qualifications, and social networks. For economic and social reasons, educational reform has been designed to separate individuals from the influence of kin and community. Modern variations on this theme argue that school-to-work transitions have become individualised. However, rather than being separated from their influence, evidence suggests resources that help reproduce patterns of advantage and disadvantage continue to flow to individuals through kin and community. Evidence from social network theorists, which shows that networks play a vital role in allocating labour power, suggests that economic change and educational reform have yet to separate young people from the influence of kin and community. Concurrently, in areas of the labour market where employers require education credentials, the relationship between education, social networks and employment has arguably become more complex. Although the thesis awaits firm empirical research and testing, it is likely that as the attainment of credentials, especially at higher levels, becomes more common, the kind of credentials obtained is likely to become increasingly important (Brown, 2000). Gaining high quality and trustworthy information about the kinds of credentials needed is likely to mean that the role played by networks in the allocation of labour power will not diminish despite the expansion of higher education. Indeed, it is highly likely that a student's decision to pursue particular study rests upon important network processes. The broader issue of how social networks have declined in value to the state is pursued in greater detail in the next chapter.

Notes

1   From a different perspective, neoconservatives agree that individualisation is the result of state intervention. In education, neoconservatives argue that the state is acting in *loco parentis*. Low-ability students and those from poor socioeconomic backgrounds rely heavily upon the state and the education system as credentials hold the promise of social mobility. From this perspective, the current imbalance in student choices that has seen too many young people reject vocational education in favour of study leading to university is a result of the schooling system. In turn, this has eroded the value of family and community-based forms of social capital for young people who perceive the jobs available to them through their social networks as undesirable (Okano, 1995). Thus, state intervention has undermined the ability and desire of individuals to solve their economic and social problems by, for example, being more self-reliant (Apple, 1993).

2   Debate continues regarding the impact of social origins on subsequent destinations (Aldridge, 2001). Evidence from the United States, for example, suggests that although the influence of origin on subsequent destination remains, its influence has weakened. Growth in access to higher education is seen to represent an important vehicle for expanding opportunity (McMurrer et al., 1997).

3   Although further research would enrich our understanding of these processes, the collective character of skill is apparent in contemporary settings, for example, design teams, medical response teams and financial teams (Grieco, 1996).

4   Businesses devote a good deal of effort creating institutional based forms of trust. In the case of McDonalds' restaurants, reputation is created and protected through detailed quality

control systems that enable products of similar quality to be produced irrespective of the restaurant location. In such settings, the knowledge needed to produce food has assumed an institutionalised form. It is embodied in the quality control systems and other technology used by McDonalds' restaurants that ensure consistent and reputable production in diverse settings.

Chapter 3

Disrupted Labour Markets

The previous chapter showed that social networks provide an important mechanism for helping young people make the transition into employment. The presence of these networks enhances the effectiveness of the labour market by facilitating employment relationships. For example, they provide mechanisms for enskilling young workers, for connecting young people with recruiting employers and for regulating the supply of labour. This chapter briefly reviews recent changes in the labour market in New Zealand and the United Kingdom brought about by the continued introduction of new technologies, workplace reform and credential inflation. It is widely agreed that these pressures have disrupted employment relationships by, for example, reducing the value of manual labour power, increasing unemployment and increasing the level of credentials needed in order to gain employment. Existing studies in this area (Brown and Lauder, 2001; Callister, 2001; Gallie et al., 1998; Statistics New Zealand, 2003) provide detailed accounts of labour market changes in New Zealand and the United Kingdom. This chapter draws on these to support the argument that changes to the labour market and to households have reduced the effectiveness of social networks in regulating transitions into employment. Thus, the chapter argues that for the state, familial and community-based networks no longer comprise a valuable source of intergenerational resource transference. Moreover, the evidence presented regarding the labour market supports the view that though networks leading young people to employment remain, labour market changes mean the quality of jobs available is lower than that obtained through similar means in the past. Thus, for young people making the transition into work and for the state, the value of social networks that lead to employment has declined in terms of quality and the availability of jobs. Arguably, this has reduced incentives for job seekers to make use of social networks, which are now more likely to be linked to downwards social mobility.

Before proceeding, it is important to note three caveats to the discussion that follows. Firstly, there is a dearth of published research into the factors affecting the labour market participation of poorly qualified young people. Although research shows that those with poor levels of school qualifications are more likely to be unemployed, there is little evidence suggesting that lack of qualifications is the primary cause of unemployment. As Wolf (2002) suggests, it may be that holding qualifications signals other qualities employers desire, for example, motivation and perseverance. Secondly, it should be stressed that although evidence clearly points to intergenerational transmission of disadvantage, there is a dearth of empirical research into the precise cause of this. While research suggests network effects, these may be the result of unobserved factors, such as the quality of local schools (Bertrand et al., 2000). Thirdly, although the evidence presented in this chapter demonstrates the declining employment conditions of young people making transition into employment, this does not comprise firm proof that networks have declined in value. Whether or not social networks have declined in value compared to the earlier period is a question that awaits research. Addressing this issue would be difficult, as one would need to compare the experiences of similar individuals across time and assess changes in the relationship between qualifications, social networks, and employment. It is also important to be aware that networks function in different ways. For instance, networks may help young people break free of their social setting and promote social mobility. On the other hand, as previously noted, networks may initially help young people obtain employment, perhaps in declining sectors of the labour market, which may lead to disadvantage in the longer term.

Although the central argument of this chapter – that social networks have declined in value to the state – resonates with functionalist accounts of economic and social change, it differs in terms of its explanation of the cause and its impact. Unlike the dominant view, in which the erosion in the value of social networks is considered to be a result of economic and social change that has increased the proportion of jobs and requires higher levels of credentials, the present account is based on three arguments. Firstly, a decline in the value of manual work and increases in the proportion of part-time and temporary employment means that, where young people are able to obtain employment through their networks, the quality of employment is likely to be comparatively poor. This reduces the incentive for young people to take up opportunities that might become available through their social networks. Young people might also reject job opportunities offered through their social networks and stay on in school in the hope of securing qualifications that hold the promise of more desirable employment (Okano, 1995). Secondly, credential inflation means that work-bound school-leavers who leave school without qualifications are less able today to draw on their social networks to enter forms of employment which require credentials, for example, some forms of apprenticeship training. Thirdly, as Mizen et al. (1999) suggest, the erosion in the value of social networks is a result of increases in adult unemployment, which means unemployed parents are less able to aid their children's transition into employment compared to previous generations. This means that some young people lack access to employment-rich networks within the communities in which they live. This resonates with the position promoted by neoconservative perspectives of 'workfare' in which it is argued that work-poor families and their immediate community are generating welfare pathologies. By implication, work-poor families and their immediate community have lost the ability to be self-regulating. In such settings, social networks are not viewed by the state as a resource; rather, they are viewed as a liability.

However, in contrast to the neoconservative position, in which welfare dependency is a major reason for unemployment and a form of learned helplessness transmitted through social networks, the thrust of this chapter is that the erosion in the value of social networks available to poorly qualified school-leavers is more usefully conceived as a 'secondary effect'. In other words, networks have eroded in value as the jobs on offer through such methods have declined in quality.[1]

Economic Change and Work

The post-war economic boom and the increasing use of bureaucratic methods of production, created numerous new middle class jobs. Like the existing blue-collar jobs, these new jobs were linked to rules and norms that provided certainty about some aspects of employment. For example, in New Zealand and the United Kingdom, the principal of collective bargaining was buttressed by legislation that made union membership compulsory for all workers and wage rates were linked to national award systems. In addition, internalised career structures meant that progression through the levels of remuneration was linked to years of service not performance. In Northern Europe, as was the case in New Zealand, a settlement was formed between employers, the state, and unions. In what became known as the 'social partnership', powerful trade unions cooperated with employers in return for income redistribution and other egalitarian measures. However, important differences existed in the way work was organised in different contexts. For example, in the United States, International Business Machines was aggressively non-union, wages were more closely linked to individual performance and job descriptions more flexible than those found in the majority of corporations at the time (Osterman, 1999).

Despite some important differences within and between nations, in general terms career stability was a key feature of the post-war labour market and policies were adopted in order to secure the long-term commitment of workers (Brown and Lauder, 2001). An important effect of this and the strong employment growth that characterised the post-war period was that up until the mid-1970s, young people making the transition to school faced better labour market conditions than those experienced by previous generations. As Doeringer et al. (1991) note that, in the United States context in the 15 years preceding 1973, the earnings of young men improved almost continuously. During this period, young people in developed nations could make successful transitions into work through utilising resources available through their social networks and could enjoy social mobility. Significantly, young people could enjoy this mobility without having gained educational qualifications and indeed many did not obtain them.

However, changes in the economy since the mid-1970s, particularly the introduction of new technologies and greater globalisation of the economy, have led to increasing unemployment in New Zealand (Blaiklock et al., 2002), the United Kingdom (Barrell and Genre, 1999) and declines in the relative wages of poorly qualified school-leavers (Brown and Lauder, 2001; Murnane and Levy, 1993). An important reason for this is that employers addressed competitive pressures by evaluating their own cost structures. An outcome of this evaluation was that the bureaucratic paradigm, upon which modern corporations were founded and which led to the creation of many middle class jobs, came to be seen as a major source of inefficiency (Brown and Lauder, 2001). In turn, this led to a shift in management away from an 'industrial relations' to a 'human resource management' perspective (Gallie et al., 1998). A distinctive feature of the industrial relations model is that unions and collective bargaining played key roles in establishing employment conditions. The role of unions in securing improvements in the working conditions was aided by compulsory unionism, passive welfare systems, and minimum wage legislation, which effectively created a benchmark below which wage rates could not fall. This benchmark was important as the presence of high wage rates helped regulate the labour market by creating economic incentives for young people to take up work.

In New Zealand and the United Kingdom, the industrial relations model or social partnership first came under attack from Conservative administrations in the late 1970s and 1980s. For example, in the United Kingdom, the Conservatives in Britain under the leadership of Margaret Thatcher argued that a lack of labour market flexibility contributed to declining profit margins and increased unemployment. As a result, during the next 20 years or so, collective industrial relations were weakened through such measures as the removal of legal support for collective bargaining and statutory wage setting and the removal of employment rights generally. In New Zealand, the Employment Contracts Act of 1991 had the same effect. It has been estimated that, in the United Kingdom and the United States, the decline in unionisation in the 1980s increased income inequality by about 20 per cent (Blackburn et al., 1990; Gosling and Machin, 1993).

New management techniques were also brought to bear on production to reduce labour costs. An example of this is the creation of so-called 'hollow' organisations in which flat management structures are adopted and the actual production of goods is outsourced to on- and offshore producers. Outsourcing has reduced the cost of providing services, particularly in areas of low-skill employment, such as cleaning. Savings come from a range of sources, including imposing additional market discipline on workers, reducing the size of a firm's core workforce, reducing the cost of staff training, reducing union influence, reducing rates of pay, and by intensifying work (Australian Industry Commission, 1996; Hall et al., 2000; King, 1994; Quiggin, 1994). Employing workers on a temporary basis has also increased in recent years. Unlike in the past, where layoff was followed by 'recall', in the contemporary era laying off workers permanently or downsizing is an accepted management strategy that is typically greeted positively by stockholders. A need to reduce stock inventories and to better match labour supply to production, especially where demand for product fluctuates, has led to the adoption of 'just-in-time labour'. Consequently, the use of temporary workers has increased in Australia (Hall et al., 2000), the United Kingdom (Trades Union Congress, 2001) and the United States (Osterman, 1999). A lack of data means this claim cannot be advanced in relation to New Zealand (Tucker, 2002). Like its close relation outsourcing, the use of just-in-time labour is a strategy designed to reduce labour costs by reducing rates of pay, overtime costs, and by making it easier to lay off workers. Employing temporary workers may also be a mechanism for better disciplining existing workers. However, whatever the strategy settled on, the overriding consideration is to increase profit margins by creating flexible organisations that can respond quickly to changing consumer demands for goods and services.

Concurrently, new technologies have been brought to bear on the production process in an attempt to increase profit margins. This too has had a deleterious impact on some segments of the labour market. The standard argument is that globalisation and the introduction of new technology have contributed to economic specialisation (Aronowitz and De Fazio, 1994; Doeringer et al., 1991; Reich, 1991). Economies that have particular human, material, and technical resources tend to support particular kinds of employment. For example, economies where low-cost labour is readily available tend to support labour-intensive industries, whilst economies where the cost of labour is comparatively high tend to support industries that rely more heavily upon mechanisation in order to reduce labour costs. For example, advances in new information technologies and investments in human capital and economic capital in developing nations means that many commodities can now be produced much more cheaply in countries such as China and India.[2] In response to changing technologies and globalisation, employment in manufacturing declined in the United Kingdom in freestanding cities by about 60 per cent in recent decades and conurbations by about 75 per cent since 1961 (Rowthorn, 1999). However, productivity in manufacturing increased massively as fewer workers used new technology to produce more commodities.

In New Zealand, the global recession and changing production processes resulted in job losses in manufacturing industries as demand for exports decreased. As a result of such shifts, it is estimated that in the six years between 1986 and 1991 about 100,000 jobs were lost (Prime Ministerial Task Force on Employment, 1994). These were mostly in manufacturing, where many companies shut down or moved offshore and in the state sector, which was reorganised by a government committed to New Right policies.[3] In the United States, employment in manufacturing also declined. For example, it has been estimated that between 1981 and 1991 the number of young people aged between 16 and 26 years employed full-time in manufacturing declined by 4 per cent – the loss of 1.65 million jobs (Zemsky, 1998).

Although blue-collar and craft workers were initially identified as surplus to requirements, by the 1990s white-collar workers also came under pressure as management sought to increase profit margins by cutting out middle management and supervisory staff and by introducing new computer-based technology. A result of this has been a decline in internal labour markets in which career progression and job security were maintained with an increase in temporary employment and job insecurity (Osterman, 1999). It is important to note that this view is contested. In terms of job security, recent evidence from the United Kingdom challenges the view promoted by Osterman (1999) and others (Castells, 1996; Sennett, 1998) that the emergence of 'new' forms of capitalism have reduced job security. This new evidence shows job stability has actually increased, as reflected in a rise in long-term employment. For example, between 1992 and 1999 the number of people working for the same employer in the United Kingdom increased by approximately 4 per cent to reach 33 per cent of the workforce (Doogan, 2001). As Doogan (2001) shows, tenure varies from sector to sector. In manufacturing, for example, between 1992 and 1999 almost 500,000 jobs were lost in the United Kingdom, yet the rate and the level of long-term employment rose, suggesting that those able to keep hold of a job while their peers were laid off are not moving to other jobs. In contrast, employment fell in the mining industry during the same period by 77,000 jobs and the rate of long-term employment fell from 49 to 43 per cent. Qualitative research also raises questions about the connection between changes in the way work is organised and increased insecurity. Subjective insecurity appears to be higher in an organisation with standard forms of employment. The lowest level of subjective insecurity was found in an organisation which had non-standard employment (Charles and James, 2003). Thus, important differences exist in the type of insecurity experienced, gender differences exist and other factors of work organisation, such as male and union hostility, can contribute to increased feelings of insecurity.[4]

As a result of the changes described, unemployment has increased. Since the end of the post World War II economic boom, the average rate of unemployment has increased. For example, in New Zealand 376 men were registered as unemployed in 1961 (Department of Statistics, 1972). By the early 1990s the percentage of the population registered as unemployed peaked at 14 per cent (Blaiklock et al., 2002). In recent years a number of factors, including economic growth, the introduction of active labour market policies, and changes to the rules of entitlement, such as increasing the age of eligibility for receiving welfare, have seen the recorded level of unemployment reduced from its highs in the early 1990s. In Australia, New Zealand, and the United Kingdom, unemployment has moved into a range of approximately 6 to 10 per cent, whilst at the time of writing the rate in the United States is slightly lower. However, when considering the level of unemployment, it is important to recognise that differences exist in the concentration of unemployment in particular locations and that the proportion of people classified as 'inactive' but not officially classified as unemployed has increased. In the United Kingdom, unemployment is concentrated in northern regions, in former coalfields (Webster, 2000) and in some housing estates, where a rate of unemployment of 25 per cent is common (Dickens et al., 2000). In most regions in the United Kingdom the number of men classified as inactive is more than twice the number classified as unemployed. In regions that were formerly industrialised, such as Merseyside, the rate is even higher, with three times the number registered as unemployed being inactive (Rowthorn, 1999).

A reason for the increase in inactivity in the United Kingdom is that financial incentives to take up work are not strong (Dickens et al., 2000). For example, although they treat the figures with caution, Brown and Lauder (2001) report data from the United States that shows approximately 43 million people were laid off between 1979 and 1995. In this case, most displaced workers were able to find new jobs, but two-thirds of these jobs were offered at lower wages and with poorer conditions of employment. In Britain, it seems that where the unemployed do manage to find employment, they too accept jobs that pay less than the level they previously received and wage mobility rates are currently low (Gregg and Wadsworth, 2000). In Australia, Borland et al. (2002) show that growth in full-time work has collapsed, with permanent full-time work being replaced en masse by casual and part-time employment. Significantly, most of the new jobs have been remunerated at relatively low rates despite a period of strong economic growth.

Importantly, young people and ethnic minorities are more likely than older people and whites to be unemployed in the United Kingdom (Dickens et al., 2000) and New Zealand (Statistics New Zealand, 2003). For example, approximately 40 per cent of those registered as unemployed in New Zealand are aged 25 years or less. Furthermore, although New Zealand, along with many other western nations, has been experiencing sustained levels of employment growth, young people have yet to benefit from this growth. For example, between 1986 and 1998, employment increased significantly for those aged 25 to 64 years. However, this coincided with a fall of 50,000 in the number of jobs held by teenagers (Statistics New Zealand, 1998). It seems unlikely that this reduction resulted from increasing numbers of students staying on in education, as evidence suggests that the holding power of New Zealand's secondary schools has declined slightly since 1993 (ibid.). It is more likely that young people are simply at the end of the hiring queue and must watch from the sideline, whilst older and more experienced workers take up new opportunities in the labour market. The unemployment rate for young Maoris is even higher. For example, in 1992, when unemployment peaked, 48 per cent of young Maoris aged 15 to 19 years were unemployed compared to a rate of approximately 23 per cent for all people in this age bracket (Blaiklock et al., 2002). Since then, the rate has declined, but still remains approximately twice the rate for non-Maoris. Changes such as increasing the age of eligibility for the unemployment benefit and strong economic growth have reduced the proportion of young people on welfare. However, inactivity, as measured by the proportion of young people NEET, has remained constant for the last decade.

Work-poor Households and Communities[5]

One result of increases in the rate of adult unemployment has been an increase in the proportion of young people who grow up in 'work-poor' households in Australia (Miller, 1998), New Zealand (Callister, 2001; New Zealand Ministry of Social Development, 2002), the United Kingdom (Gregg and Wadsworth, 1996), and the United States (O'Regan and Quigley, 1991; Reingold, 1999). In New Zealand, for example, one in four, or 26 per cent, of children are dependent on welfare (New Zealand Ministry of Social Development, 2002) and in 1996 36 per cent of work-poor households in New Zealand contained children (Callister, 2001). The polarisation of work between households also speaks of a further problem for social reformers, namely that new opportunities for employment created by economic change are likely to be concentrated within households where an employed person already resides and within particular regions. For example, although employment growth in service sector occupations has created new opportunities for employment, in the United Kingdom, most of these jobs have been taken by people in the south (Rowthorn, 1999) and by people living in households where an adult is already in employment. These factors have reproduced social divisions. For example, evidence from Britain points to a:

> ... clear intergenerational transmission of 'poverty' through unemployment. Those people raised against a backdrop of unemployment are approximately twice as likely as the population in general to end up with a substantial history of unemployment themselves. (Johnson and Reed, 1996, p. 135)

A similar conclusion has been reached by Dex and Taylor (1994) and by Peck (1997) in Australia where about one in six children of the most disadvantaged and welfare-dependent parents were highly dependent on welfare between 16 and 18 years of age. An explanation for this is that the socially disadvantaged link with other disadvantaged and there are few mechanisms through which individuals can bridge barriers to social mobility and create the process-based trust needed to find jobs (Kelly and Lewis, 1999). Contacts may supply better information about welfare eligibility than about employment and training opportunities. Other commentators have suggested that social norms and work ethics, such as the motivation to work, have an important impact on the work patterns of solo parents, and joblessness seems more related to individual decisions than to lack of opportunity (Buckingham, 2000). There is some evidence to support this position, with Clark (2003) finding in his study of the impact of unemployment on personal well-being that 'unemployment always hurts, but it hurts less when there are more unemployed people around' (p. 346). The main policy implication that arises from his study is that prompt labour market intervention is required to avoid a newly unemployed person acquiring a social norm of unemployment.

Sociologists and politicians agree that growing up in work-poor households and families is linked to subsequent disadvantage. For example, the Performance and Innovation Unit (2002c) see a lack of access to employment networks as an important contributor to the reproduction of patterns of disadvantage and advantage. Similarly, Wilson (1987) is convinced that cultures of poverty are reinforced through 'work-poor' social networks. Conservative commentator Lawrence Mead argues that policy-makers have allowed the poor to become separated from the mainstream society and to adopt social mores that reduce the obligation to work. For Mead, the welfare state is a major source of the problem, as it has sanctioned worklessness in the face of a growing impatience with the demands of low-paid work (Mead, 1986). He argues that social policies that discipline the poor in such a way that they are prepared to accept low wage work may rectify this, but wage subsidies will be needed to keep the poor out of poverty (Mead, 2003). From a left-wing perspective, Mizen et al. (1999) argue that young people who grow up in work-poor families and communities are likely to lack someone to help them obtain employment by 'speaking for them' at their own places of work. Mizen et al. speculate that for:

> ... children largely working in sectors of the economy notorious for informal recruitment procedures and a high turnover of labour, the absence of a parent or older sibling to 'ask around', 'put a good word in' or 'keep an eye out' for a vacancy is likely to constitute a real barrier to work. (1999, p. 430)

Despite difficulties in demonstrating that labour market changes have caused networks to erode in value by examining the effects of economic change, a strong case can be made that the value of social networks to the state has declined. Arguably, the erosion in the value of social networks has contributed to the discouraged worker effect, to the intergenerational transfer of inequality and, according to New Labour and the Labour-led Coalition, to the development of welfare pathologies within work-poor families and the communities in which they live. Even where young people have someone who can speak for them, labour market changes mean that the kinds of jobs on offer are likely to be of poor quality. This argument is pursued below.

The Decline in the Value of Manual Labour

Increased economic competition and the introduction of new production strategies have also contributed to changes in the distribution of people employed in the various industrial sectors, which has had a deleterious impact on the youth labour market and reduced the incentive to take on work. Of particular significance have been a decline in the proportion of workers employed in blue-collar and craft occupations and growth in the proportion employed in service sector occupations. In 1951 the service sector in New Zealand accounted for 46 per cent of people employed full time. By 1991, the proportion employed in the service sector had increased to 63 per cent, an increase of 17 per cent on the 1951 figure (Department of Statistics, 1993, pp. 10–11). Although minor changes to the New Zealand Standard Classification of Occupations make direct comparisons problematic, more recent figures show that these trends have continued (Statistics New Zealand, 1998). Similar trends have been identified in Australia (Borland et al., 2002), the United States (Hendel, 2000) and the United Kingdom (Gallie et al., 1998; Wolf, 2002).

The increase in the proportion of people employed in the service sector, and the corresponding decrease in the proportion employed in the blue-collar segments of the labour market and as craft workers, is an important shift as service sector jobs are more likely to be part-time and less highly paid. These factors have contributed to a reduction in youth incomes. In New Zealand, between 1986 and 1996 the median incomes of young people aged between 15 and 25 years fell in real terms from NZ$14,700 to NZ$8,100 per annum. For those aged 25 and over the decrease was smaller, with incomes declining from NZ$19,600 in 1986 to NZ$18,100 in 1996 (Statistics New Zealand, 1998). The decrease in annual median incomes in the younger age group partially reflects the high number of young people remaining in education and working part time. In 1996 three in four young people employed in the wholesale and retail trade and the restaurants and hotels industry were also in education of some kind. In the past the majority of school-leavers left school and directly entered full-time work, but this is no longer as common. In 1951 approximately 70 per cent of those aged between 15 and 19 years were in the labour market. By the early 1990s, this had reduced to 53 per cent (Prime Ministerial Task Force on Employment, 1994).

The reduction in demand for labour in sectors of the labour market that have traditionally paid highly has been offset by growth in service sector industries, such as retail trades. However, jobs in the service sector tend not to be as highly paid as those in the declining secondary sector, such as manufacturing.

To give an example of the effect on male wage rates, Doeringer et al. (1991) showed that in 1986 male workers employed in manufacturing in the United States had incomes that averaged US$17,830 per annum. This exceeded the average income of males employed in the retail trade by 49 per cent.

The changes described above mean that in contrast to the post-war boom period of the 1950s, 1960s, and early 1970s, today there are comparatively few well-paid jobs for poorly qualified male school-leavers (Murnane and Levy, 1993), and such school-leavers making the transition into work can no longer reasonably expect to enjoy social mobility. For example, there is evidence in many households that one well-paid factory job has been replaced by two marginal service sector jobs. As a result of the increase in the proportion employed in the service sector and other changes, it is estimated the wages paid to male workers declined in the United States by 19 per cent between 1973 and 1987. Hewlett (1993) notes a similar trend in Australia, where average real earnings declined by A$29 a week between 1984 and 1989.

Labour market restructuring can be seen to have impacted most heavily on poorly qualified school-leavers who have found their wage rates shrinking as they compete for the comparatively few semi-skilled and unskilled jobs available today. For example, after adjusting for inflation, Doeringer et al. (1991) showed that the average annual incomes of high school dropouts fell by 37 per cent between 1973 and 1986. In contrast, in the period between 1979 and 1986 college graduates were the only group of young males to improve earnings. Wilson (1996) supports this, arguing that an oversupply of youth labour in the United States has meant that real wage rates paid to young people reduced by approximately 30 per cent between 1970 and 1989. In other research in the United States, Hewlett (1993) reported a drop of 19 per cent between 1973 and 1987 for male workers, whilst Zemsky (1998) noted a decline of 10 per cent between 1981 and 1991 for all young workers aged between 16 and 26 years. Similar research conducted in New Zealand supports these findings as part of a global trend. Podder and Chatterjee (1998) suggest that technological change and greater globalisation of the world economy have contributed to increased inequality of the earned component of income by redistributing the total wage bill in favour of skilled labour. One result of this shift is that, while the bulk of the population became poorer between 1984 and 1996, the poorest segment of the economy – that is, unskilled workers and the unemployed – fared the worst. Only the very rich enjoyed increased incomes.

Another cause of the decline in wage rates paid to semi-skilled and unskilled male workers has been the entry of large numbers of women into the labour market. Hewlett (1993) argues that in the United States and Australia a decline in the rate of pay for male workers relative to inflation led to large numbers of women entering the labour market to prop up the family wage. This means that poorly qualified male workers are increasingly finding that they must compete with a wider segment of the population for a shrinking number of quality jobs. In New Zealand, similar trends are apparent. In 1951, women constituted approximately 25 per cent of the labour force (Prime Ministerial Task Force on Employment, 1994 p. 28). Overall, male labour market participation in New Zealand has been decreasing, whilst female participation has been increasing (Blaiklock et al., 2002).

For young poorly qualified males the expansion of the service sector and the contraction of the secondary sector is significant, as many of the low level and part-time jobs in the expanding service sector are typically taken by women (Walby, 1991; Wilson, 1996). In New Zealand, Stuart (1995) estimates that between 1981 and 1991 women's employment expanded by 15 per cent, or approximately 80,000 jobs, whilst men's declined by 8 per cent, or approximately 72,000 jobs. Evidence supporting this shows that the distribution of young men and young women in the labour market varies markedly between industrial sectors (Statistics New Zealand, 1998). For example, young women are more likely to find employment in the expanding service sector, with 84.4 per cent of women aged between 15 and 25 years employed in this sector. This compares with 57.6 per cent of men in the same age group. Young working men continue to be attracted to contracting segments of the labour market, such as the trades, where about 94 per cent of all workers are male, plant and machine operators and assemblers, where about 80 per cent are male, agriculture and fishery, where about 75 per cent are male, and elementary occupations that are defined as low-skilled, manual jobs, where about 70 per cent are male (Statistics New Zealand, 1998).

Credential Inflation

Labour market restructuring, which has reduced labour market demand for semi-and unskilled labour, has seen an increase in secondary school retention rates in New Zealand (Statistics New Zealand, 2003) and the United Kingdom (Wolf, 2002). For example, in New Zealand between 1986 and 2001, retention rates for male students continuing schooling until the age of 16 increased from 66.6 per cent (Statistics New Zealand, 1998) to 79.8 per cent (the figure for females is 83.2 per cent) (Statistics New Zealand, 2003). The increase in secondary schooling retention has been mirrored by a decrease in the number of students leaving school without qualifications. For example, between 1974 and 2001, those leaving school with no qualifications decreased from 39 per cent to 17 per cent over the same period. In 2000 about 36 per cent of Maori students left school without qualifications (Statistics New Zealand, 2003).

Evidence from a variety of sources shows that students are remaining in education longer and leaving school more highly credentialed than in the past. A reason for this is that a lack of suitable opportunities in the labour market has encouraged young people to remain in education. Concurrently, as described more fully in the following chapter, changes in assessment and curriculum have increased young people's training options. These have made it easier for young people to get their learning recognised and to remain in education, even though, as the discouraged worker effect suggests, they may not be particularly motivated towards achieving. At the same time, many young people and their parents see education as holding the key to individual future prosperity. Indeed, those with few or no school credentials are more likely to be unemployed and where such school-leavers are employed, they are likely to be receiving lower rates of pay than those who are credentialed. Whether or not credentialism reflects the exclusionary tactics of professional enclaves (Collins, 1979) or real changes in demand for skill (Gallie et al., 1998) will continue to be a source of debate. It is clear, however, that a good deal of over-education exists (Green et al., 1999). Nevertheless, as Wolf (2002) clearly establishes, the personal benefits in terms of income from obtaining an education are substantial. Thus, Marginson (1997) argues that the massive rise in credentialism has increased the punishing consequences of not having educational credentials. Pye et al. (1996) support this, asserting that the political legacy of the 1980s for low-achieving working class males is a low expectation of finding 'real work'.

Conclusion

This chapter has described some of the factors that have arguably led to the erosion in the value of social networks. Firstly, the quality of jobs available to poorly qualified young people today has declined in terms of pay and conditions, in relation to those obtained by previous generations. Secondly, unemployment is concentrated in particular geographical locations and households have become polarised between work-rich and work-poor. Thirdly, there is evidence that disadvantage is transmitted between generations, although the precise mechanisms through which this occurs remains unclear.

While this evidence does not provide firm proof that networks have declined in value, declining pay rates and growth in the proportion of work-poor families mean that work-bound school-leavers are likely to find it more difficult than their parents to make the school-to-work transition through utilising network resources. As Okano (1995) suggests, would-be school-leavers stay on in school as discouraged workers because they perceive the jobs available to them through their social networks to be undesirable.

These arguments do not decrease the importance to individuals of social networks in the recruitment process. Indeed, given the decline in the number of quality jobs available to young people making transitions from school into work, networks that lead to quality jobs have become relatively scarce and, hence, increased in value. However, for the state, the fact that networks do not yield jobs of the quality they once did, nor appear to regulate labour as efficiently as they once did, is problematic. By the same token, the disengagement of young people from mainstream society as represented by the discouraged worker effect and the pool of young people NEET indicates that networks no longer effectively regulate the labour market. Whether social problems, such as youth unemployment and the discouraged worker effect are the result of dependency cultures or a lack of economic incentives to take up employment will continue to be a subject of debate. However, for the state, the emergence of these and other social and economic issues is problematic as it indicates that neither social networks nor other mechanisms are sufficient to reproduce the social relations of production amongst certain segments of the population. Although researchers will continue to debate the precise mechanisms through which advantage and disadvantage are transmitted across generations through social networks, policy-makers and politicians in the United Kingdom and New Zealand are convinced that they exist. How policy-makers are responding to this is the subject of the next chapter.

Notes

1   Of course, the conservatives are correct when they maintain there is no shortage of work. The problem is that the price that employers are willing to pay and the kind of work they expect people to complete does not match the needs, wants nor expectations of the unemployed. In this respect, the observation that labour market change has reduced the incentive for unemployed people to take up 'dirty' jobs is salient (Mead, 1986).
2   It is important to note this view is contested (see Auhion and Howitt, 2000).
3   In the United States context, Osterman (1999) notes that firms have historically dealt with competitive pressures by, amongst other strategies, laying off blue-collar workers, whilst white-collar workers were 'nearly inoculated' against layoffs. In the recession of the early

1980s, it was blue-collar workers who bore the brunt of the changes. As Thurow (1992) argues, 90 per cent of the firms in the United States that laid off blue-collar workers did not lay off any white-collar workers.

4   Doogan's (2001) perspective is that, in the United Kingdom and the United States, insecurity has been manufactured by governments in a conscious attempt to 'increase the productivity and competitiveness of the economy' by increasing perceptions of personal employment insecurity. Recent research suggests that New Labour has been successful in creating this risk. Burchell et al. (1999) show that insecurity is created by a broader range of anxieties and fears than those created by actual job losses. When broader measures are considered, insecurity has increased, particularly amongst professional workers.

5   In addition to an increase in the proportion of young people who grow up in work-poor families and communities, social capital theorists argue that other important changes to the social infrastructure have occurred. These changes include a decline in community associations and declining rates of civic, political and religious participation. Although further research and testing is needed, the implication of social capital theorists, such as Putnam (2000), is that broader changes in the social infrastructure, among which is participation in work-rich networks, have already occurred in society.

Chapter 4

The Third Way and the Search for Solutions to Disruption

Gordon Brown, the Chancellor of the Exchequer, concluded that where markets work best and where they do not is a key issue for the next phase of Third Way policy in the United Kingdom (Brown, 2003). Third Way governments maintain that the selective use of market strategies can improve policy outcomes and provide a solution to the disruption described in the previous chapter. They aim to do this through harnessing market forces. However, as Brown (2003) indicates, decisions must be made about when, where, and under what circumstances this can be achieved.

To properly situate the Third Way within recent approaches to political and economic management, it is necessary to understand that the First Way refers to the approach to economic management found in England prior to the election of Margaret Thatcher in 1979 and prior to the election of the fourth Labour Government under the leadership of David Lange in New Zealand in 1984. This approach was characterised by high levels of state control and regulation of the economy. The Second Way refers to free market or neoliberal approaches to economic management, which emerged with the election of Thatcher and Lange. In this approach, the objective was to free the economic system from all unnecessary regulation, to embrace economic globalisation by exposing domestic markets to international competition and to generally allow competitive market forces to exert a greater influence in the economy, for example, by reducing the influence of labour unions in the wage-setting process. The Third Way aims to adopt what are believed to be the strengths of Second Way methods without losing sight of core First Way values. Consequently, a defining feature of Third Way governments is a belief that the judicious use of both market and non-market strategies can strengthen and empower communities and help them to develop solutions to their own social and economic problems. Third Way governments argue that the Second Way's wholesale and uncritical adoption of free market policies has destroyed the fabric of local communities by constructing an economy and a society on an individualistic and competitive model of human behaviour. In turn, this has created individualistic and competitive modes of behaviours. A related reason offered for the erosion in the bonds of community life and related social changes is that the moral codes created and encouraged by free markets are not conducive to the creation of social capital (Cox and Caldwell, 2000; Hazeldine, 1998; Szreter, 1998; Wolfe, 1989). Similarly, Pusey et al. (2003) argue that economic rationalism is antisocial, that it attacks civil society and has led to the 'weakening of community'. However, through such initiatives as the Stronger Communities Action Fund[1] in New Zealand and the National Strategy for Neighbourhood Renewal[2] in the United Kingdom, this capacity can be replenished and social capital can be rebuilt.

Through a focus on recreating communities and refashioning of interpersonal bonds, Third Way governments arguably look backwards and romanticise a past in which communities were perceived to have been more trusting and the bonds between individuals to have been stronger. They also look forward to the power of social capital in the form of networks and trust to increase economic competitiveness in the global economy. The concept of social capital has proved to be a useful concept in the Third Way's policy armoury as it offers a way for Third Way governments to broaden their appeal. Those on the Left are attracted to the concept as it provides a tool through which some of the deleterious impacts of neoliberalism can be better understood and because it provides a way to legitimate state interventions designed to counter these. For those on the neoliberal Right, the concept is attractive as it suggests that communities and not the state, can take greater responsibility for their social and economic problems. For those on the Conservative Right, the concept provides a way to legitimate reforms designed to strengthen the role played by families and the community in regulating social life. Thus, the 'community' is viewed as both the source of the problem and the key to its resolution.

The main purposes of this chapter are briefly to establish the relationship between Third Way approaches to political management and social capital and to introduce the contrasting solutions to the disruption caused by the economic and social changes outlined in the previous chapter. The chapter begins by briefly describing the central features of the Third Way. Following this, the relationship between the Third Way and social capital is assessed in order to properly situate the concept of social capital within contemporary debates. This provides the basis for the next section, in which the emergence of 'poor' social capital is described. Brief outlines of the contrasting solutions to disruption follow this.

The Third Way

A defining feature of the Third Way is a belief that the judicious use of market reforms can contribute greatly to the state's social objectives.[3] 'Old' labour was ideologically opposed to the creation of markets. Neoliberals believed that markets could be created in almost every sphere and 'deregulation, marketisation and the withdrawal of the state' was the standard prescription (Brown, 2003, p. 6). However, New Labour and the Labour-led Coalition believe the ability of market forces to do good should not be dismissed since market strategies can be harnessed in the pursuit of social goals. Brown (2003, pp. 5–6) expresses that New Labour rejects 'the left's old, often knee-jerk, anti market sentiment, to assert with confidence that promoting the market economy helps us achieve our goals of a stronger economy and a fairer society'. Like New Labour in England, Labour argues that policies can be developed to promote social connectedness and reduce the social exclusion and inequality created by neoliberal marketisation without creating the bureaucracy associated with previous forms of social democracy. Like their neoliberal predecessors, Third Way governments believe globalisation is inevitable and that greater free trade can be positive. Increasing employment rates is a key policy objective. Consistent with this aim is the belief that the best way to overcome social exclusion and reduce economic dependency is through strengthening the wage-labour relationship. Thus for New Labour and the Labour-led Coalition placing as many people as possible into 'sustainable' employment as quickly as possible is a key policy objective. In addition, like their neoliberal predecessors, Third Way governments believe that able-bodied individuals should be self-supporting and those dependent on welfare must take responsibility for getting themselves off welfare. To help achieve this active welfare systems have been strengthened.

At a basic level, the Third Way is a response to perceived inadequacies in the neoliberal policies introduced by Margaret Thatcher in Britain and by Roger Douglas in New Zealand. For example, in his Ruskin speech, Tony Blair argued that neoliberal reforms had failed to deliver higher standards of achievement particularly in state schools and they had failed to address the century old tradition of low educational expectations (Blair, 1996). Rather than proving a panacea to Britain's social and economic woes, neoliberal reforms had contributed to them by increasing unemployment and by increasing social polarisation. Although neoliberal policies may not have caused the disruption described in the previous chapter, their uncritical use by Second Way administrations clearly exacerbated it. Similarly, in New Zealand the

Labour Party argues that the neoliberal or market-led policies have contributed to falling incomes, increased unemployment and declining economic growth (Clark, 2002).

Intervention to improve the quantity and quality of VET is an important area of Third Way policy. This policy is subjected to a fuller critique in the following chapter. However, it is worth noting that by investing in the capacity of individuals and lifting overall levels of achievement, New Zealand and the United Kingdom plan to become magnet economies, attracting multinationals that create high-wage/high-skill forms of employment. Moreover, in some educational settings, free market approaches to the creation of human capital are seen to be ineffective. In settings where labour market signals are likely to be weak, or in situations where the signals that exist do not support the state's goals, government intervention is required.

In the area of human capital development, government intervention is also appropriate where the 'levels and types of training produced by the free market will be sub-optimal' (Blunkett, 2001, p. 9). It is worth noting that:

> Today, we see that demand can be stimulated through supply-side investment, whether in cutting-edge sectors such as information and communications technology or simply by making greater local and national economic activity viable through provision of the skills and education required to facilitate increased market demand. This is very much a 'post-Keynesian' approach, yet it retains the principle of investment for growth. And we have invested in teachers and in schools, in helping the unemployed and in upgrading the skills of the workforce. This investment pays a long-term dividend for the individuals concerned and for the performance of the economy. It is investment which will increase people's productivity and their wages, and hence the output of the economy and the demand created within the economy. It begins and supports a virtuous circle of economic success and increased economic activity. Crucially, this 'post-Keynesian' approach achieves these results in a long-term sustainable fashion, serving as a bulwark against the boom and bust that the free marketeers so conspicuously failed to address. (ibid.)

A similar position has been adopted in New Zealand with the Labour-led Coalition arguing that the previous neoliberal administration's market-led training strategy failed to deliver the promised economic and social outcomes (Office of the Prime Minister, 2002). To rectify the situation, the Labour Government has set about transforming the New Zealand economy and its education system in order to grow more talent. A central aspect of this is reforming the 'competitive model in tertiary education [that] had led to unsatisfactory outcomes in terms of both the quality and the appropriateness of the skills produced' (Office of the Prime Minister, 2002, p. 5). In this respect, a key difference between Third Way administrations and their neoliberal predecessors is that it is seen as possible to promote economic growth through supply-side interventions, particularly in VET and education broadly. However, this does not signal a return to state planning. Rather, it is an acknowledgement that where governments invest taxpayers' funds, it should be to promote economic growth. Underpinning this investment is the view that those displaced by disruption can also benefit from the relatively strong rates of economic growth enjoyed in New Zealand and England. However, the benefits of economic growth can be shared if those adversely affected by disruption are given an opportunity to adapt to the changed economic conditions. If people are willing to work hard and learn new skills, then according to proponents of the Third Way they deserve good jobs. To date, the benefits of economic growth in England and New Zealand have been captured by relatively few. In no small measure, this is due to the way Margaret Thatcher and David Lange, in England and New Zealand respectively, introduced neoliberal approaches to economic management. It is not that market strategies are flawed; rather it is the manner in which Second Way governments introduced them that is the root of the problem.

To date, neoliberal policies have allowed economically powerful individuals and groups to use their superior market power to increase their wealth. This meant that economic elites were advantaged by Thatcher and Lange's versions of neoliberalism because it cemented their economic advantage. Third Way governments aim to alter this situation by allowing those from economically disadvantaged backgrounds an opportunity to benefit from economic growth through creating 'ladders of opportunity'. For example, New Labour proposes doing more to support entrepreneurs who lack access to financial support from their families or from banks. By allowing those from disadvantaged backgrounds who show initiative, dynamism, and entrepreneurship access to resources, including management expertise and capital, New Labour aims to enable markets to work better and 'to widen economic opportunities irrespective of background' (Brown, 2003, p. 13). The view is that a pool of entrepreneurial potential exists within the working classes but this has remained trapped by conservative banking practices and lack of access to 'old' money. This locates the source of disadvantage and social exclusion in processes that have excluded working class people from engaging effectively in the market. Moreover, where such individuals engage in market processes they do not do so on an equal footing. New Labour argues that neoliberal policies, as introduced by the Conservatives, were primarily concerned with increasing private ownership of the economy, not increasing competition (Brown, 2003). Free markets, as opposed to privatised markets of the kind created by Thatcher's version of neoliberalism, are perceived to be free of class, race, or other such social and economic divisions, and all individuals are able to compete freely as equals. To date, the superior ability of elites to access and process market information and to access the financial resources needed to put this knowledge to use has enabled them to enjoy unfair advantage in the market.

As this suggests, New Labour and the Labour-led Coalition believe that some individuals need help to allow them the freedom to participate in the labour market. Their view on the provision of social welfare is encapsulated in the phrase, 'a hand up, not a hand out'. Accordingly, maximising freedom involves the provision of direct resources in the form of 'seed finance', the provision of quality careers advice, and the creation of quality education and training systems. Strategies are also needed to increase the capacity of individuals to access and decipher labour market and training information. These are needed to enable individuals to participate fully in labour market processes. Thus creating the conditions under which all participate in market relationships is the key to increasing personal incomes, reducing social exclusion, and eradicating poverty. Consistent with this view is the notion that state intervention is legitimate only if it contributes to the creation and maintenance of free markets and if it helps support the wage-labour relationship.

While New Labour and the Labour-led Coalition claim to be pursuing a Third Way, it is debatable whether or not this is occurring in practice. For example, in Australia, politicians from the right of the political spectrum have welcomed the Third Way, in one instance describing it as 'Thatcher without the handbag' (Vanstone, 2001, p. 2). In England, commentators observe that New Labour's approach is not markedly different from that adopted by the previous conservative government generally (Elliott and Atkinson, 1998) and more specifically, in education (Hyland, 2002). The leader of the Australian Labour Party, Mark Latham, offers a different perspective. Latham argues the Third Way represents a departure from neoliberalism and that instead of letting global capitalism and the underlying market forces operate unchecked, Third Way policies can civilise it (Latham and Botsman, 2001).

However, when considering this issue, it is important to look at Third Way reform in particular areas, because important differences exist. In the area of welfare reform, for example, it is clear that New Labour has built on the workfare system developed by Thatcherism (Peck and Theodore, 2000). It has gone much further than its neoliberal predecessor in regulating the reserve army of labour in order to lower inflationary pressures by reducing wage pressure amongst low-paid workers and to seek out new sources of labour power (Grover, 2003). For example, through its New Deal range of initiatives, New Labour has been more active in encouraging the unemployed to enter the labour market. In contrast, in the area of employment legislation, Rhodes (2000) argues that New Labour's approach represents a departure from that adopted by the Conservatives. Moreover, New Labour and the Labour-led Coalition have introduced many new educational policies, some of which demonstrate an attempt to promote greater equality of opportunity. However, in general, critics argue New Labour is building on 'Conservative reforms to increase marketisation and diversity between schools' (Muschamp et al., 1999, p. 120). A recent strategy used to achieve this is the development of new specialist secondary schools. In higher education, New Labour is allowing universities to increase their fees. These measures suggest a greater influence by the market in determining what is considered valuable knowledge. More recently, more fully nuanced analyses have been developed. For example, Patterson (2003) argues that the mainstream view, which sees New Labour as a continuation of Thatcherism, is inadequate and in reality three strands of Labour policy exist in education.[4]

A distinguishing feature of the Third Way is the recognition that making markets work efficiently requires the state to do much more than merely deregulating and privatising the economy in order to let capital and goods flow freely. Making markets work effectively requires the creation of an infrastructure through which market signals can flow. This means that the state needs to do more to create an infrastructure through which information can flow, for example between employers and job seekers. In this way, Third Way administrations have taken seriously the concerns of critics of neoliberalism who have argued that choice policies in education, as well as other areas, reinforced the position of the already powerful who have the material, social, and cultural capital required to succeed in market settings (Ball et al., 1995). In other words, some groups in society lack access to resources that will enable them to compete effectively in market settings. Unless such groups can be provided with a 'hand up', their social exclusion and unemployment will continue. Third Way governments support the Second Way's notion of procedural justice and believe that free markets are ideally placed to create fair processes. However, they believe that without access to resources to enable socially excluded groups to participate in the market, the process will remain unfair.

Improving the fairness of market processes is the main way Third Way governments aim to make the rules of the competition for advancement meritocratic, for example, by providing working class entrepreneurs with access to finance and by providing those not in employment, education, or training with access to quality career and employment information. This social investment, as it is termed by Third Way governments, is given added significance within Third Way literature in the light of the concept of social capital.

The Third Way and Social Capital

The concept of social capital is of great importance to the Third Way as it has provided a platform on which to base its claim that markets can be made to produce better social and economic outcomes. The concept has also proved of great interest to researchers who have used it as a way to renew calls for policies that contribute to the creation of industrial democracy (Winch, 2003). Before offering a critique of these perspectives and situating the view of social capital drawn upon in subsequent chapters, it is necessary to say a few words about the way the concept of social capital is used in the literature.

In the broader debates, social capital is used in different ways and it has different meanings (Winter, 2000). Woolcock and Narayan (2000, p. 225) define social capital aphoristically, that is, social capital is 'not what you know, it's who you know'. Many different conceptions of social capital are derived from the basic principle that who you know comprises an important asset or liability (Portes and Landolt, 1996). For most authors, social capital is generally defined in terms of networks, norms and trust. Within this broad definition, some see social capital as a property of groups in which many, if not all, can benefit (Putnam et al., 1993). Others see it as a property of individuals and groups that may be subject to social closure (Coleman, 1988). For Coleman, social capital is embedded in concrete social relations that permit individuals and groups to access resources. For example, as noted in Chapter 2, ethnic groups have, at various points in history, exerted tight control over the provision of labour in areas of the labour markets, for instance the construction and garment manufacturing industries in the United States (Tilly, 1998; Waldinger, 1986). Moreover, the creation of social capital is context specific and built up through repeated exchange. Thus, social capital can be a product of investment strategies, such as the cultivation of social networks adopted by individuals, by groups and by the state.

One difficulty with the concept is that, unlike economic capital, or to a lesser extent, human capital, social capital writ large is an amorphous concept which can not be easily measured (Stone and Hughes, 2002). However, this is unlikely to pose much of a problem to the value of the concept. As Schuller (2001) points out, the greatest value of the concept of social capital is as a heuristic device that encourages questioning and critical reflection about human relationships. In questioning human relationships, social scientists will continue to draw upon existing concepts, now considered to be part of social capital. For example, social network theorists demonstrated the relationship between social networks and employment long before the concept of social capital became popular. It is important to remain critically disposed to the term. Indeed, Fine and Green (2000) argue that the concept of social capital may simply represent the colonisation of the social sciences by economics.

Within the social capital literature, different perspectives on the relationship between social capital, economic and social development, and the state exist. Although these perspectives are highly stylised and overlaps between them exist, they do, nevertheless, provide a way to better identify the perspective adopted by the Third Way. Woolcock and Narayan (2000) provide a useful overview of the various perspectives expressed in the literature. Four main perspectives exist. The communitarian perspective is that social capital resides in the relationships that exist between individuals and is cultivated by membership of clubs, associations and other groups. Increasing the density and quality of connections between individuals and groups, increases society's stock of social capital. In addition, it is believed that social capital is inherently good and that any increase in society's level of social capital will have benefits for all. The institutional view argues the strength of social capital is a product of the political, legal and institutional environment. It is the quality of the institutions that is most important and, in contrast to the neoliberal view such as that promoted by Green (1996), social capital does not necessarily thrive once the state retreats. The network view posits that social capital can have both positive and negative effects. It exists in the relationships between people and organisations and appears in the form of social networks, civic associations, and levels of trust. Communities with high levels of this form of social capital are seen to be better placed to solve their own social problems and to enjoy economic prosperity (Putnam et al., 1993). On the other hand, tight bonds can lead to downward social mobility. For example, individuals who leave school early after obtaining employment in declining sectors of the labour market through their social networks are likely to find their employment prospects to be lower than those who stayed on in education and training. The final view, the synergy view, combines the network and institutional views. According to this view, communities, the state, and businesses do not alone possess the means to create social capital. An important function of the state is to facilitate relationships or synergies between these sectors. The state is best placed to do this task because it can act as an honest broker, mediating between sectors that may, on face value, have disparate interests and goals. In the literature, this is sometimes referred to as 'co-production'. The synergy view closely resembles the view adopted by the Third Way. For example, the Labour-led Coalition and New Labour see their roles as rebuilding the relationships between the government and the governed and between the state and civil society. New Labour's concern about social exclusion and the effect this has on reducing interpersonal ties and bonds and the Labour-led Coalition's desire to strengthen the social ties and networks that help connect those experiencing social disadvantage to the communities in which they live, are good expressions of this (Maharey, 2000, 2001).

Social Capital and Network Structure

Three types of social capital have been identified, further complicating the picture. Two of these build on distinctions between 'weak' and 'strong' ties (Granovetter, 1995). Granovetter's argument is that the use of 'strong ties' or the networks that are associated with family members or close friends to find employment limits social mobility. This is because it only exposes individuals to opportunities that are at the same level of the labour market as their immediate social class group. In contrast, the 'weak ties' or the networks that are associated with acquaintances, are more likely to promote social mobility. This is because weak ties expose individuals to opportunities beyond their immediate social class group (Granovetter, 1995). From Granovetter's basic distinction, two kinds of social capital have been identified. These are bonding and bridging social capital. Putnam describes the difference between the two, stating 'bonding social capital constitutes a kind of sociological glue, where as bridging social capital provides a sociological WD-40' (Putnam, 2000, p. 23). Like Granovetter's strong and weak tie thesis, the effects of bonding social capital can be positive and negative. For example, bonding social capital might help individuals cope with adversity; however, it might also constrain the formation of bridging social capital that could help individuals escape the circumstance have led to adversity in the first place.

In a position that resonates with that advanced by social democrat, John Dewey, bonding social capital that limits the formation of bridging social capital is not just disadvantageous to those seeking social mobility but is disadvantageous to elites whose strong bonds limit participation in broad networks of people. The more isolated the social groups, the fewer the opportunities for development of social capital. Thus, inequality reduces the production of social capital as it divides citizens from one another. The capacity for community and association to develop is reduced. As Dewey put it, where 'there are rigid class lines preventing adequate interplay of experiences – the more action tends to become routine on the part of the class at disadvantage, and capricious, aimless, and explosive on the part of the class having the materially fortunate position' (Dewey, 1916, p. 85).

More recently a third form of social capital known as linking social capital has been identified. Linking social capital refers to networks and institutionalised relationships between unequal agents. According to Szreter (1998), unlike bridging social capital, which involves interactions between actors horizontally across the social structure, linking social capital operates vertically between actors who have dissimilar access to power and resources. The linking form of social capital has emerged as an important concept because its creation can form a central aspect of the state's role. Indeed, its creation is particularly important for social mobility as it enables the poor access to resources that would otherwise lie beyond their reach. The concept of linking social capital expands the role of the state to include the creation of social capital. However, for social capital theorists and Third Way governments, social capital is more than this as it also involves the creation of relationships built upon trust between individuals and from which all can benefit (Fukuyama, 1995; Putnam, 2000; Szreter, 1998).

Besides the obvious social advantages of creating a more trusting society, the cost of conducting business is thought to be higher than in low trust societies. One reason for this is that high levels of trust reduce transaction costs within the economy. Thus, an absence of social capital is problematic because it reduces competitiveness in the global economy. Those nations that develop strategies that increase trust are better placed to compete effectively in the global economy. In this respect, Brown and Lauder (2001) argue that policies creating high levels of trust in society are a key ingredient in the struggle to create 'collective intelligence'. The claim is that nations that can pool the capacities of all in society will be best placed to compete in global knowledge wars because the productivity of knowledge workers and the capacity of the organisations in which they work to innovate, is improved. The result of this is the creation of a high-wage/high-skill/high-trust society in which all benefit. In this sense skill is seen as a collective resource. By the same logic, some social capital theorists argue that the creation of a society rich in social capital is an important ingredient in competing effectively in the global economy. Proponents of the 'generalised social trust' maintain that nations with high levels of social capital in the form of trust will be best placed to compete effectively in the global economy (Fukuyama, 1995).

A problem with the connection that is drawn between high levels of trust and increased productivity is that the empirical evidence needed to support this contention is weak. While trust is critical to many social relationships, there is little evidence that more or less trust in people in general has any impact on either democracy or economic performance (Foley and Edwards, 1999). Indeed, high levels of trust do not necessarily lead to cooperative behaviour wherever it is present. Similarly, neoliberal economists argue that it is good rules that create good games (Brennan and Buchanan, 1985). In this respect, trust appears to be a helpful but not a necessary precondition for cooperative behaviour. As Fattore et al. point out in their analysis of data generated in the Middle Australia Project, the 'more community' argument appears unrelated to trust.

> Put simply, community-building exercises promoted in the political rhetoric that encourage the 'third sector' or 'more community!' solutions for the disadvantaged (often instead of government interventions or creating employment) may do little or nothing to change the prevailing climate of low trust and pessimism. (Fattore et al., 2003, p. 173)[5]

Research also shows that trust works in different ways and has different effects in different contexts. For example, Cohen and Fields (1999) show that the presence of social capital in the form of 'performance-based trust' helps explain the economic success of Silicon Valley. They argue that this kind of social capital is 'vastly' different to that advanced by Putnam et al. (1993) who argue that networks of civic engagement that were based on a dense civil society propelled development. For Cohen and Fields (1999, p. 112), it is '[u]ltimately, what you do shapes how you do it – all the way back up the value chain, all the way out into forms of social organization'.

Complicating the picture are differences in the sources of social capital within each of these views. Summarising the literature, Adler and Kwon (2000) identify five key sources of social capital. These are networks, norms, beliefs, rules, and trust. Distinguishing between these different sources of social capital is important because each form has different effects. By the same token, the benefits of some forms of social capital cannot be realised without the presence of other forms. For example, the presence of familial networks that lead to employment means little if there is no method of sanctioning the behaviour of individuals. Within the literature, much of the utility of social capital is derived from the presence of shared norms and beliefs. Putnam et al. (1993) for example, emphasise the presence of reciprocity or the notion that doing something for someone now is reasonable because one can expect in the future that the favour will be returned. Reciprocity or the creation of obligation serves to transform self-seeking behaviours into behaviours consistent with shared concerns of communities.

The debate over the relationship between economic efficiency and social capital has highlighted the importance of the network structure in delivering particular outcomes. The structure of social networks plays a critical role in determining which resources, if any, are accessed. In a variation on the notion of linking social capital, Burt (1997) argues convincingly that an actor whose networks bridge groups of actors has more social capital than one whose networks are dense and cohesive, because actors within groups circulate information between one another. Actors whose networks provide a bridge between different groups have access to more information, they are able to broker information between different groups and they can control projects in which different groups are brought together. Thus, considerable positional advantage can be derived by individuals whose networks bridge 'structural holes'. Individuals whose networks are rich in bridges are able to mobilise more resources and are thus able to be more entrepreneurial. Such entrepreneurs are better placed than governments and bureaucracies to monitor and interpret information and can easily shift their attention from one node in a network to another in search of solutions to problems and opportunities.

In contrast, actors participating in dense networks have access to similar information but cannot gain advantage through this, thus no opportunities for individuals to act as entrepreneurs exist. For Burt (2001), an ability to bridge structural holes is a more powerful form of social capital than the capital that resides in closed structures. Although these advantages can be derived from network closure, bridging networks are of greater value, increasing the chances of promotion, financial compensation and of receiving favourable performance evaluations. However, he acknowledges that social closure can also be an important source of social capital. In this respect, Coleman (1993) believed that maximising the effectiveness of social structure incentives needed to be both formal – for example, wages or school grades – and informal – for example, where closure can be created. Although both forms of network structure confer benefits, the precise nature of these, and the best kind of network structure, will vary from setting to setting. For example, new immigrants can derive great benefit from closed social networks to obtain access to finance that can be used to start small businesses in ethnic enclaves. However, once the business is established it may be necessary to access linking forms of social capital in order to expand the business and the social capital that helped the newcomers get established might become a burden as, once established, entrepreneurs are expected to use their capital to reciprocate in supporting newer immigrants.

Similarly, Kenworthy (1997), in critiquing Putnam, points out that trust and cooperation are not mutually inclusive. He asks that if trust has been on the decline in the United States over the past generation, why is it that American firms have only just recently begun experimenting with some important forms of cooperation , such as multi-division teams, employee participation schemes and research and development partnerships? The answer to this question is that firms are simply trying new strategies to increase their competitiveness. To the extent that these strategies succeed, they will become self-sustaining. However, any cooperation that results will be a consequence of these strategies rather than their cause. In this respect, Bowles and Gintis (2002) point out that communities have the capacity to solve contemporary social and economic problems by improving social coordination. In addition, community-based solutions are likely to be more important in the future. A reason for this is that problems of social coordination arise in modern economies in which production is based on quality not quantity and which do not respond to regulation by contracts or by external fiat. In such settings, information-intensive team production and the associated multilateral monitoring and risk sharing comes to replace Fordist 'low-trust' methods of production as they are economically efficient rather than politically desirable.

In their own ways, the perspectives on social capital described above follow Coleman and Bourdieu's lead by viewing social capital as a means of mobilising resources. In this respect, simply having access to networks does not necessarily equate to having social capital. Rather, for 'social capital' to be considered as capital it needs to be connected to resources of some kind. For example, Bebbington (1997) shows that linking social capital plays a crucial role in improving the economic fortunes of the poor living in the Andes. However, a wider 'enabling context', including a high level of consumer demand for the products produced in these regions, is required. Second, like human capital and economic capital, social capital is not equally distributed in society and given its ability to mobilise resources, the resources that some claim will come at the expense of others.

Although the literature has reached a high level of sophistication regarding what may reasonably be considered social capital, less is known about the conditions under which social capital in its varying forms is created. Some researchers believe that policies adopted by Third Way governments have created social capital. For example, Szreter (1998) argues the New Labour policies encouraging citizens to participate in the widest set of 'weak ties', such as their welfare-to-work policies and strategies designed to promote life-long learning cultures, have the capacity to increase social capital through increasing participation and trust in society.

Szreter (1998, p. 1) argues that, should the concept of social capital be successfully integrated into New Labour's understanding of the workings of the market economy, it will provide a 'rigorous and practical analysis of the economy'. His reasoning is that the neoliberal 'experiment' failed as it either did not fully appreciate or ignored the fact that economic relationships take place within a social infrastructure. This infrastructure has an important influence on the information-processing capacities of individuals. In societies characterised by high levels of inequality, the ability to process information is also highly unequal. For example, the elite move in networks in which quality information is exchanged. By attending elite educational institutions they are able to build networks with tomorrow's leaders and through a complex process involving human, social and economic capital, they are better able to process information.

By focusing attention on the critical issue of how an individual's capacity to process information is distributed across an economy, the concept of social capital makes an important contribution to contemporary debates about why free markets increase economic inequality and social exclusion. It also provides a way for social reformers to reverse this situation. The implication for policy-makers from Szreter's analysis is simple – the capacity for individuals to process information needs to be improved. In practical terms, this means that an individual's ability to obtain information needs to improve, hence the concern with basic skills.

Although Szreter (1998) believes that New Labour policies have increased social capital, the conditions under which social capital is created remains unclear as does the impact of government policy on social capital. Indeed, identifying the conditions under which the state creates social capital is a critical area of research (Woolcock and Narayan, 2000). When considering the impact of Third Way governments' policies on social capital, it is important to note that although the concept of social capital has captured the imagination of policy-makers due to its perceived link with economic prosperity, underpinning the Third Way's use of the term is a concern that particular kinds of social capital are not conducive to the promotion of economic growth.

Emergence of 'Poor' Social Capital

An important reason social capital has captured the imagination of policy-makers is that 'poor' forms of social capital which do not support the Third Way administrations' desire to make markets work better have been identified. Thus, unlike some accounts in which social capital itself is seen as a good thing, Third Way administrations do not support social capital writ large. An important reason for this is that social capital might reduce economic competitiveness by increasing voice over exit. As Hirschman, (1970) showed, neoliberal approaches to economic management emphasise adjustment to economic change through individuals exiting or threatening to exit the market. Competitive market pressures reward those willing to adjust to new economic conditions and punishes those who do not. Put another way, an aim of free markets is to promote enterprise culture by increasing the ability of individuals to exit the market. Interference by the state or other agency into market processes can only reduce the sovereignty of the individual consumer or worker in the market and slow the process of adjustment. There is an important legitimatory aspect to exit because the outcomes of market processes are deemed to be the result of individual choices and therefore just. Thus, the market itself is the source of legitimation. A major difficulty with this perspective, however, is that the outcomes of market processes have yet to be accepted as legitimate. For example, we have yet to accept unemployment and poverty, or the massive salaries and profits 'earned' by the rich, as simply the just and legitimate outcomes of market processes. For Hirschman (1970) an alternative means of facilitating change is through voice, or the notion that economic agents are influenced by persuasion, negotiation and mutual education. Adjustment through voice is only likely to succeed if enduring bonds of mutual obligation and loyalty hold economic agents together. The institutions of post-war boom such as comprehensive education, the welfare state and trade unions encouraged collectivism and thus strengthened voice. This limited the ability of individuals to understand the moral requirements of the market (Marquand, 1997). Enhancing the legitimation of the economic system depends on reducing voice and strengthening exit. This can be achieved through distancing individuals from institutions that increase voice, for example, trade unions. A central aspect of the neoliberal campaign to enhance exit in the labour market can be seen in measures that reduced the power of trade unions, such as the Employment Contracts Act in New Zealand, which made union membership voluntary. Hirschman's (1970) analysis suggests that although Third Way administrations might support the creation of social capital in theory, in practice support is likely to be limited because, by strengthening voice, the creation of social capital is likely to reduce the legitimation of market outcomes.

For this reason, support from the Third Way is likely to remain limited to particular kinds of social capital operating in particular contexts. For example, the creation of linking social capital is supported where this helps an individual to find employment and creating bonding capital is supported where this enables the elderly and the sick to be looked after by families and friends. On the other hand, where it leads to socially and economically undesirable outcomes, the role of government is to destroy social 'capital'. For example, where the presence of strong ties reduces engagement in the labour market or where strong ties prevent enforcement of the rule of law, the role of government is to develop strategies to destroy such ties.

As shown in the previous chapter, there has been an increase in the proportion of young people who grow up in work-poor households. Young people who grow up in work-poor environments are seen to be more likely to become 'dysfunctional' as the institutions and the families in the areas in which they live are less able to enforce a work ethic and to build labour market attachment. Lawrence Mead (1986) argues that welfare systems that support the unemployed have been permissive in nature in the sense that they have not expected individuals to do anything in return for their welfare payment. The notion that passive welfare systems are a key cause of welfare dependency has been widely adopted by Western governments. In the United Kingdom, Tony Blair has argued that rights come with responsibilities and that the creation of a 'stakeholder society' requires that a much tougher and more hard-headed approach be taken with the unemployed (Deacon, 2000).

Sources of social capital like the networks that enforced norms of behaviour, such as those described by Young and Willmott (1957) and by Grieco (1987b), no longer exist in some settings. Indeed, creating a social infrastructure that effectively facilitates transitions into work requires a lot more than simply connecting individuals with recruiting employers or placing them in appropriate training programmes. It requires a means of nurturing norms of behaviour supportive of the wage labour relationship. Ways of encouraging the development or enforcement of particular behaviours is also required. In this respect, Streeck (1989) argues that it is the moral obligations and close community bonds found in Germany that have led to a commitment to vocational education which is transformative rather than instrumental. In certain crafts, where training, examination, and admission are a focus for communal life and collective identity, moral obligation plays an important role in industrial training.

The importance of obligation, both as a significant source of social capital in itself and as a means of maximising the usefulness of other forms of social capital, raises interesting questions about how the state can enforce and encourage young people to make use of the opportunities made available through the provision of networks. As will be described later in the book, creating obligation is a key problem faced by policy-makers as they grapple with problems thrown up by disruption. In the area of welfare services, there is little effort to increase the value of networks through creating obligation. Rather, the thrust of the policies is to create 'commitment' through economic sanctions for deviant behaviour. Similarly, in the area of VET and in the Connexions service, policy-makers are driven by a commitment to human capital theory. Accordingly, simply increasing the number of people in learning is seen to hold the key to solving problems created by disruption. Relatively little attention is given to creating an obligation either on the part of young people to work hard or on part of employers to upgrade their production processes thus increasing the demand for credentialed school-leavers.

Closely related to the view that enough work exists and that poor forms of social capital exist is the notion that resolving unemployment is simply a matter of making markets work better. For example, HM Treasury argues that unemployment is in part a spatial problem in that 'pockets of high unemployment' lie within travelling distance of labour markets that have high vacancy rates (2000, p. 1).[6] This means that ways need to be found to encourage the unemployed to travel to employment. This view underpinned the development of the New Deal range of policies which, according to New Labour, aim to tackle the growing underclass in the United Kingdom by getting more people into paid employment by. Increasing the employability of people in 'deprived' areas is one such aim.

Blair's sentiments have been echoed in New Zealand where successive Labour-led governments have built upon the previous neoliberal administrations' so-called 'active' welfare policies by encouraging individuals to do more themselves to move into work. Recent moves to tighten the eligibility for welfare support by non-indigenous people who move into areas of low employment is the latest instalment of a series of policies introduced by the Labour-led Coalition to 'encourage' the unemployed into work. In Australia, the Conservative Liberal Government has adopted a similar position. The former senator responsible for welfare services in Australia, Senator Newman, maintained that the welfare system allowed young people to turn down jobs and remain on welfare as a lifestyle choice. As she put it:

> ... where there are jobs available even though they might fall short of the
> initial expectations of the jobseeker, it is neither fair nor moral to expect the
> hard working men and women of this country to underwrite what can only
> be described as a destructive and self indulgent welfare mentality. (Newman,
> J., 1999, p. 3)

In a similar vein, Newman argues that some families do not transmit attitudes
and values consistent with the need to be self-supporting through working.
In sum, the unemployed have apparently failed in their moral duty to be
self-supporting. This argument illustrates the belief that poor forms of social
capital exist. In the United States social reformers have also sought to explain
the rise in the proportion of individuals on welfare by developing a moral/
psychological discourse. In the 1960s, when poverty was rediscovered in the
United States, social scientists and politicians argued that a culture of poverty
existed and drew upon this to explain why poverty was transmitted from
generation to generation. For some, poverty has become a way of life or a
learned behaviour which is transmitted from generation to generation (Katz,
1989). The development of the culture of poverty is seen as a product of the
welfare state, which has made unemployment comfortable and has encouraged
men to renege on their responsibilities to their families.

In this context, the role of government is to help individuals adjust to the
changing economic circumstances by altering their practices. For example,
New Labour believes that sufficient work exists; it is just that individuals lack
the incentive to take up job opportunities. Accordingly, income support for
sole parents is seen to encourage family breakdown, increase the incentives
to have children out of wedlock and erode the values upon which decent
communities are founded. In addition, the provision of welfare benefits has
reduced the obligation of young people to be self-supporting. Young males
do not need to take responsibility for their actions and can easily avoid the
civilising influence of raising a family. Thus, men who do not have a family
to support, 'do not have to stay in work, do not have to keep up to date with
the payments of bills, and generally they do not have to think of anyone else
than themselves' (Buckingham, 2000, p. 76). Not only does this weaken the
communities in which such young males live, the lack of incentive to obtain
employment means there is little need to stay on in education, and this reduces
employability. In such contexts, the provision of passive welfare support
no longer comprises an effective mode of regulation. Indeed, according
to conservatives, the provision of welfare encourages the development of
dependency cultures. As a result, new modes of regulating the poor are required
in order to ensure that the wage-labour relationship is maintained.

Although they adopt differing perspectives on the issue, those on the Left and the Right, such as New Labour and their Conservative predecessors, agree that these trends have important implications for the value of social capital in the form of social networks because they are likely to affect the ability of young people in such households and communities to access information about labour opportunities. According to the Third Way, in such settings there is too much bonding social capital, which has limited participation in markets, and too little of the bridging and linking types of social capital, which would enable people to access quality employment information. New Labour wants to strengthen communities that support market relationships and self-sufficiency and want to 'weaken' communities which they do not.

Third Way administrations have settled upon three key solutions in order to open markets up and counter the problems created by disruption as described in the previous chapter. These are: to improve the provision of VET; to increase incentives to work and engage in training; and to provide better employment and training information to young people, particularly those not engaged in education, employment or training. Each of these solutions is described in the following sections.

The Third Way and the Problem of Provision

In the early 1980s the emergence of the New Right under Thatcher in the United Kingdom led to a sustained critique of comprehensive education. Critics pointed out that comprehensive education had failed to deliver on its social and economic objectives; indeed, overall standards of achievement had been lowered, which led to falling incomes and increasing unemployment. This critique has been maintained by New Labour, which also argues that comprehensive education has failed to achieve high standards or to promote equality of opportunity. As the official spokesperson for Tony Blair stressed, New Labour's plan to overhaul secondary schools signalled the end of 'bog standard' comprehensives (Wintour and Smithers, 2001). Similarly, in New Zealand, schools were criticised for being too academic in orientation and for delivering an 'academic' education when most people were not progressing on to study at a university. This contributed to inequality because it meant individuals lacked both the skills they needed to obtain employment and the tools they needed to decipher labour market and training options.

In the current era, the strategies adopted, such as that encapsulated in the 14–19 educational reform in the United Kingdom, broaden what schools offer by introducing new forms of vocational education and new ways of assessing learning. These include motivating young people to learn through developing new methods of assessment, expanding the number of young people entering higher education through developing new pathways, and increasing the communicative competence of learners through investing more in education. The extent to which the education system limits the ability of individuals to process information and communicate effectively with others is the extent to which it limits the production of social capital. This is because it limits the ability of individuals to participate in networks and, therefore, limits the likelihood of social capital increasing. By the same measure, it is implied that skill is a collective attribute. As noted, including measures designed to improve the quality of VET and increasing participation in higher education as part of the general strategy to create social capital, sees the ideas of Third Way administrations and some researchers (Szreter, 1998; Brown and Lauder, 2001) resonate with those of Dewey (1916), who saw the provision of education as an essential ingredient in the creation of a society characterised by the free exchange of ideas between people of different social origins.

A number of strategies have been adopted to achieve this. The first involves the development of new, more motivating forms of assessment. As is the case with earlier functionalist accounts, the argument underpinning this reform is that rapid economic change, high levels of migration and increasing demand for skilled labour are defining features of modern industrial economies. Securing employment in such economies is dependent on individual engagement in intensive and on-going periods of training and on securing the educational credentials demanded by employers. Accordingly, the expansion of higher education and VET is a result of increased labour market demand for skilled workers. Put another way, the aim of VET is to remanufacture intelligence in ways conducive to the labour markets of deindustralised economies. For those growing up in work-poor environments, the creation of qualifications that enable them to break free from their social environment is both economically necessary and socially progressive.

The notion that schools are not equipping school-leavers with the skills demanded by the technologically-advanced labour market locates the source of the discouraged worker effect and related social problems in the education system. It is widely believed that the education system is attempting to organise and structure school-to-work transitions in accordance with the demands of an outdated method of production. To rectify this, it is believed that state intervention is required to increase participation, create a lifelong learning culture, increase overall levels of achievement, and align the status of vocational and academic learning (New Zealand Qualifications Authority, 1991). In effect, New Labour and the Labour-led Coalition claim that obtaining and retaining a place in the post-industrial economy requires students to remain at school for longer periods and to learn different skills.

The critical questions asked of this strategy in Chapter 5 are to what extent measures in the area of VET are likely to create new ladders of opportunity in which all learners are able to achieve highly and are motivated towards obtaining qualifications employers find meaningful. To what extent do the measures defuse the domestic competition for positional advantage? Do the measures increase the communicative capacity of learners from all walks of life? A critique of the likely ability of Third Way policies to achieve this is provided in the next chapter. For the moment, discussion turns to the second strategy, that is, reform of the welfare system.

The Third Way and the Problem of Incentives: Welfare Reform

Although the provision of VET remains a key strategy, Third Way governments in New Zealand and the United Kingdom have lost faith in the ability of VET alone to solve contemporary social and economic problems. For example, both the Labour-led government in New Zealand and New Labour in the United Kingdom have continued the previous neoliberal administrations' welfare reform agenda and their so-called 'active labour market' policies. Accordingly, while the Labour-led Coalition and New Labour agree that networks have declined in value, this has less to do with the erosion in the value of manual labour than it with the development of the welfare state and the associated development of 'welfare pathologies' which have reduced the incentive for individuals to be self-supporting (Peck and Theodore, 2000). Third Way administrations believe that welfare systems should be reformed to increase the punishing consequences of being on welfare. Not only is this thought to reduce the development of welfare pathologies and increase the incentive to learn new and transferable skills, it is also thought to strengthen families and the role they ought to play in transmitting pro-work attitudes and values. Where families and the communities in which they live do not support forms of social capital that support the state's goals, state intervention is required to destroy such social 'capital'.

The weakening of labour market attachment created by the emergence of welfare dependency has led to a growing acceptance of unemployment. Young people have apparently adopted unemployment as a lifestyle choice and seem to lack a work ethic. For Third Way governments, one strategy designed to resolve this problem rests in reforming welfare systems by manufacturing risk. Thus, welfare systems have been reformed to increase the incentives for individuals to attach themselves to the labour market. Not only is this thought to reduce the development of welfare pathologies and increase the incentive to learn, it is also thought to strengthen families and the role they ought to play in transmitting pro-work attitudes and values.

A similar set of arguments is advanced in relation to those who deliver welfare-related services. According to the neoliberal critique, social democratic methods of service provision had been subject to provider capture. As a result, the cost of providing services had been driven up. Concurrently, the quality of the services delivered had suffered from a lack of clear direction and specification of performance targets and from welfare sector workers who pursued their own interests. To change this culture of underperformance, Third Way administrations have followed in the footsteps of neoliberal predecessors by adopting 'modern' public sector management techniques. Of critical importance in the new methods of delivery is the development of performance targets and the increase use of private sector companies to deliver social welfare related services through competitive tendering. Thus, the new measures in the area of welfare reform are designed to better regulate the practices of those receiving welfare services and the practices of those who work with them. Along with increased incentives to take up work, Third Way governments are attempting to provide better sources of information about career and training solutions. This is the third solution.

The Third Way and the Problem of Information: The Connexions Service

The third solution to problems created by the erosion in the value of social networks amongst those from disadvantaged backgrounds is the development of new careers advisory services. The development of the Connexions Service in England is an example of Third Way policy which is designed to provide young people with quality information about training and employment opportunities. Connexions illustrates the New Labour belief that economic markets do not provide the level of information required to enable young people and employers to make efficient training and employment decisions. Instead, additional information is needed in order to enable training markets to be effective. The creation of the Connexions Service is recognition that individuals vary in terms of their ability and level of motivation to access useful training and employment-related information. In addition, it is a recognition that economic relationships, such as those which provide access to quality information about training and employment options, are embedded in a social infrastructure and that not all have access to this. It is an attempt to liberate young people from work-poor backgrounds in networks that are likely to be poorly endowed with social capital of the kind needed to support the wage-labour relationship. By providing quality information at little or no cost, the Connexions Service is designed to facilitate employment by reducing transaction costs.

The introduction of the Connexions Service is a good example of how policy-makers are attempting to replace functions formerly completed by social networks by providing young people with good quality careers advice. It is an attempt to replace forms of social capital that are no longer effective. In effect, New Labour is acting on the belief that in some settings markets do not provide the level of information required to allow young people to make useful training and employment decisions. Connexions is designed to change this and allow markets to function better by providing young people, particularly those in the category of NEET with quality information. As Blunkett (2001, pp. 6–10) makes clear:

> [The Connexions service] will make explicit for individual children the link between what they are doing at school and the options open to them for further education and in the labour market, including through work experience. It will also provide youngsters with the support they need to help them achieve their goals. ... for individuals, information problems are often daunting. It is hard for them to know what skills are likely to be required and what the costs and benefits to them of acquiring those skills will be. ... We are not in the business of manpower planning. We are not in the business of replacing or paying for the specific training that firms themselves ought to be doing. But, through the new LSCs [Learning and Skills Councils] and the new Connexions Service we will be putting huge emphasis on providing people and employers with information.

Part of the solution to problems created by disruption rests, therefore, in providing better information to young people about their training and employment options. It aims to devalue forms of social capital that have to date perpetuated patterns of advantage and disadvantage. As Lin (1999) suggests, well-connected parents can enhance the ability of young people to obtain more valuable credentials through their superior ability to gather information about the labour market and training options. Underpinning Connexions is an attempt to decommodify knowledge and challenge advantage, which is derived from the elite's access to superior forms of labour market information. Consistent with the technocratic/meritocratic perspective, it is essential that this is achieved, because competing effectively in the global economy depends upon drawing on the widest pool of talent (Brown, 2003).

Conclusion

In the introduction to this chapter, it was shown that a defining feature of Third Way governments is their belief that the judicious use of both market and non-market strategies can assist governments to meet their social objectives. Third Way governments such as New Labour and the Labour-led Coalition believe that their policies can strengthen communities and empower them to develop their own solutions to their social and economic problems. For example, in New Zealand, the Labour-led Coalition argues that the previous Conservative government's policies have destroyed the fabric of the local community. They believe that their policies can restore this and thus create social capital. The purpose of this chapter has been to briefly establish the relationship between Third Way approaches to political management and social capital, and to introduce the contrasting solutions to the disruption described in the previous chapter. Three key strategies were identified. The first is that New Labour and the Labour-led Coalition believe that the creation of better VET systems, the development of new qualifications, and new ways of delivering knowledge will help reconnect people with the labour market and liberate them from poor networks. Put another way, the aim of VET is to remanufacture intelligence in ways conducive to the labour markets of deindustrialised economies and to build ladders of opportunity for all young, working class people. The second strategy revolves around New Labour and the Labour-led Coalition's support of the previous neoliberal administrations' welfare-to-work policies. Welfare systems should be reformed to increase the punishing consequences of staying on welfare. Not only is this likely to reduce the development of welfare pathologies and increase the incentive to learn, it is also likely to strengthen families and the role they ought to play in transmitting pro-work attitudes and values. The third solution is the provision of better careers guidance services for young people. An evaluation of these three strategies forms the basis of the following chapters.

Notes

1   The Stronger Communities Action Fund provides local communities with funds to deal with social and economic policies. The government argues that the Fund encourages communities to identify their own needs and to develop strategies to meet these (Maharey, 2002b).
2   Strategy for Neighbourhood Renewal was launched by Tony Blair on 15 January 2001. It is designed to reduce socioeconomic differences between deprived neighbourhoods and the remainder of the United Kingdom. Through the National Renewal Unit, New Labour funds strategic partnerships with local communities that involve genuine community participation.
3   Although important differences exist between versions of the Third Way in the United Kingdom (Thrupp, 2001), New Zealand and elsewhere, in general terms a number of core values are shared.
4   These are a 'renovated version of social liberalism, a form of weak developmentalism and a type of new social democracy that is in the mainstream of European thinking on the left' (Patterson, 2003, p. 165).
5   Muntaner et al. (2000) make a similar point in reference to claims that 'more community' arguments favour an idealist psychology, rather than a psychology based on material resources and social structure.
6   This does not mean that networks lack density in employment-deprived areas. Indeed, as Stack (1974) points out in her study of a black community, unemployed people have dense networks, though these are not rich in employment opportunities.

Chapter 5

Replacing Social Networks through Vocational Education and Training

A central theme of this book is that devising solutions to social and economic problems created by disruption, such as the discouraged worker effect, has formed an important part of the state's work in the UK, New Zealand and elsewhere. In the past, employment relationships were facilitated by social networks deeply embedded in the social infrastructure and little, if any, state intervention was required to ensure that young people made transitions into work. However, economic development and technological change has disrupted these relationships thereby necessitating state intervention. In this chapter, intervention by the state in the area of vocational education and training is evaluated on the basis of its ability to replace the functions previously achieved by social networks.

The dominant view from policy-makers and politicians in New Zealand and the UK is that the development of forms of human capital that better meet the needs of employers will provide a solution to disruption. The idea is to improve the responsiveness of training systems to the needs of the labour market by making them employer-led; that is, employers elect the skills to be developed. The resulting increase in the relevancy of training will contribute greatly to the creation of an innovative workforce able to respond quickly to changing demands for particular skills. The development of types of qualifications that improve information to employers about the skills individuals have will also facilitate employment. In turn, the development of training systems that produce workers with the skills demanded by employers and the development of qualifications that better signal an individual's capacity or level of competency will increase the incentive for young people to engage in training, lift overall standards of achievement, and help create pro-learning identities. In sum, these measures will better regulate labour.

In New Zealand and the UK, the method settled upon to create more transparent, useful and motivating VET systems, in which learning identities are created, is the development of national qualifications frameworks, with the related introduction of 'employer-led' systems of curriculum development and competency-based assessment. The view is that by more clearly specifying the actual skills and abilities job seekers have obtained, employers will make better informed, and therefore meritocratic, recruitment decisions (New Zealand Qualifications Authority, 1997). By providing employers with a means to drive the development of curricula, through their representative bodies (Skill Sector Councils in the UK and industry training organisations in New Zealand), it is believed that more relevant and meaningful qualifications can be developed. For students, the development of clearer pathways into employment or further training is thought to contribute to the creation of more motivating VET experiences. For these reasons, the introduction of competency-based education and training (CBET) is ideally placed to connect those most affected by disruption with the labour market.

The historical roots of this solution go back, at least, to the performance-based education movement which enjoyed prominence in the United States from the early 1960s to mid-1980s (Matlay, 2000). The performance-based movement rose in concert with the growing significance of bureaucratic selection methods, in which the economic necessity to recruit the best person for a given position necessitated the development of assessment techniques that more accurately identified the skills people had. The view is that conservative systems of assessment which ranked learners against one another and methods of developing curricula that were not employer-led had not kept pace with changes in the nature of work and the development of scientific recruitment procedures. It cannot be claimed that these systems and methods caused the problems associated with disruption, but they have certainly exacerbated the severity of such problems. Although proponents of CBET seldom make this case, it can be argued that it will modernise the education system and replace the role played by social networks in the recruitment process where such networks exist, and complete such functions where they do not. As such, they offer the possibility of liberating young people from poor forms of social capital which limit labour market opportunities and restrict the creation of pro-learning identities. The aim is to use CBET to develop forms of institutional-based trust to create meaningful and motivating pathways into employment for young people and to contribute to the creation of pro-learning identities.

Recently critics have built upon these arguments, claiming that meeting the challenges thrown up by globalisation and the introduction of new technologies requires more than simply increasing the number of people who are highly skilled and qualified and providing better measures of an individual's capacity. The critical issues concern how to encourage employers to create high-wage/high-skill forms of employment and how to utilise better the skills that exist. In this respect, evidence indicates that educational reform has driven up the proportion of people in training and the proportion of those with qualifications, such that Scotland has a more highly qualified workforce than the rest of the UK. However, this has yet to lead to gains in labour productivity, which lags behind the rest of the UK (CBI Scotland, 2000). As Banfield et al. (1996) argue, unless a range of personal and organisational issues which prevent and disrupt the use of newly-acquired competencies are dealt with, the job-competency approach or CBET will not lead to the expected increases in productivity. Creating a mix of policies which maximise skill utilisation and skill development within organisations and the economy more broadly is seen as a vital ingredient in creating vibrant, innovative economics that can compete effectively in the global economy and which can attract investment in high-wage/high-skill employment (Brown and Lauder, 2001).

In this context, social capital theorists and others argue that close attention should be given to creating a social infrastructure that maximises skill development, skill utilisation, innovation, and skill diffusion. The social infrastructure is of great importance, as the weight of evidence suggests issues of motivation, commitment and identity formation are closely bound to cultural, economic, and social issues (Brown and Lauder, 2002). Remaking identity through the creation of lifelong learners, creative thinkers, problem solvers and entrepreneurs does not simply require a political commitment to creating relations of trust, but requires their institutionalisation (Baron et al., 2000). If the social infrastructure does not encourage or reward the development, utilisation, and diffusion of skill then there is little reason to believe that the VET system will have the desired outcome. For example, if individuals are unable or not encouraged to use creative potential and the skills developed in the VET system in their places of work, this potential will remain untapped, innovation will be stifled and talent will be underutilised.

This chapter begins by briefly restating the nature of the solution to disruption in the area of VET as introduced above and by detailing how it is intended CBET will provide this. It is argued that despite its many flaws, to date the use of CBET has offered the best possibility for remanufacturing intelligence in ways conducive to the needs of advanced industrial economies. The main reason for this is that it embodies an optimistic view of intelligence and human potential in which the capacity to learn is neither limited by one's social class of origin or the level of peer achievement in a given examination. However, it is argued that despite its positive aspects, CBET has yet to create an effective form of institutional-based trust or provide a solution to disruption. A number of reasons for the failure of CBET to replace functions completed by social networks are identified here. Firstly, the new ways of measuring learning are yet to be widely adopted by employers and problems exist with the ability to signal that potential recruits have the skills and abilities employers require. For example, the expansion of forms of employment in the service sector has increased demand for young people to 'look good' and to 'sound right' (Nickson et al., 2003). Currently, such aesthetic qualities are poorly captured by competency-based assessment. Secondly, and partly due to this weakness, competency-based assessment and training have yet to motivate all young people to learn in the way desired by policy-makers. For example, the proportion of young people who leave school without the qualifications needed to gain a job remains high and the dropout rate from various forms of training remains unacceptably high. Thirdly, as noted, how or whether skills are utilised is a result of a range of issues and not just about increasing the supply of skilled labour. In this respect, politicians in the UK have recently acknowledged and researchers have explained that New Zealand and the UK are locked into a low-wage/low-skill equilibrium. The availability of cheap sources of labour encourages the adoption of production techniques which require workers to have only basic levels of skill. As skill development and utilisation are a result of wider social processes, which include identify formation, the social context in which individuals become workers is of critical importance. According to Brown and Lauder (2001), it is much more difficult for market societies, with their weak sense of interpersonal obligation and tenuous community bonds, to create high levels of skill and positive attitudes towards training. Such societies are unable to tap the level of commitment or the degree of cooperation within their workforces which is needed to create innovative organisations. High levels of inequality compound problems of low commitment and low trust. In such settings, workers come to understand that the rewards of their efforts are not equally or fairly shared. In addition, market societies are likely to lack the 'communities of practice' where offering training to young people is seen as a social obligation.

Consistent with this analysis, Third Way governments claim that the failings of the VET system are due to the previous neoliberal or market-led training systems and that reform can reverse this situation. For example, in New Zealand the Labour-led Coalition has been highly critical of the previous administration's 'market-led' VET strategy. The Labour-led Coalition argues that this strategy had led to unsatisfactory outcomes in terms of the appropriateness of the skills produced and the quality of training delivered and this had led to falling incomes (Office of the Prime Minister, 2002). Similarly, New Labour has been highly critical of the previous administration's VET strategy (Blunkett, 2001).

Although it is possible to identify some areas of VET in which Third Way governments in the UK and New Zealand have made a difference, changes introduced are unlikely to alter the picture and the basic thrust of the previous neoliberal administrations' policies have been retained. For example, in England, although National Vocational Qualifications (NVQs) and the Scottish equivalent (SVQs) have yet to enjoy widespread support from employers, they remain a cornerstone of New Labour's VET strategy. Moreover, as the social capital perspective illustrates, maximising the development and utilisation of skill requires policy-makers to take a broader perspective than is currently the case. In particular, it requires policy-makers to break the low-wage/low-skill equilibrium. This means a shift away from investing in individual human capital and towards investing in the collective capacity of the workforce and the adoption of a product strategy that requires high-skilled workers (Keep and Mayhew, 1999).

To date, however, policy measures introduced by Third Way administrations, such as the introduction of new 'elite' qualifications, and the continuation, if not strengthening, of the previous neoliberal administrations' welfare-to-work policies, have fuelled competitive pressures in the domestic market. These policies contribute to this by increasing the supply of low-skilled workers and ensuring that qualifications which provide entrance to selective university programmes remain the gold standard. These measures encourage the continued development of an hourglass economy.

Within nations, the creation of unified qualifications frameworks and the eventual creation of a global framework is seen to play a critical role in addressing weaknesses in the VET system. For example, it is hoped that a unified qualifications framework will create parity of esteem in the eyes of learners between academic and vocational qualifications and drive up demand for VET. According to policy-makers, increasing the status of VET is essential if ways are to be found to motivate all learners to obtain economically relevant credentials. Recently, Hodgson and Spours (2002) called for the development of a unified qualifications framework in the UK, partly on the grounds that motivational pathways into work are needed for all 14–19-year-olds.

Importantly, although the historical evidence supports the claim that government interventions in the area of VET are yet to have the desired impact, it does not mean they will necessarily fail in the future. Unless stated otherwise, to improve the readability of this chapter, CBET is used to refer to the new vocationalism and competency-based assessment. Although these are theoretically different aspects of current moves to modernise VET, in practice they are two sides of the same coin. In this respect, competency-based assessment provides a vehicle for the introduction of new forms of 'employer-led' VET.

The Critique of Education

Since the 1970s, the provision of VET has been subject to a sustained critique in New Zealand and the UK. Much of this critique is based upon the premise that production in the late nineteenth and early twentieth centuries was primarily reliant on unskilled labour. Young people did not need to be highly educated as demand for unskilled labour was strong. Under this system of production distinctions between academic and vocational learning and the development of strategies that limited participation and achievement in higher education were valid, as they reflected the demands of production. These strategies were legitimated by conservative theories of intelligence, which maintained that intelligence was not equally distributed amongst individuals and that only the economic and intellectual elite had the ability to benefit from extended periods of education (Brown and Lauder, 2002). However, the introduction of new technology and the emergence of the 'knowledge economy' means that all people need to learn and conservative assessment techniques need to be dismantled. If the economy has changed as the critics maintain, then what is taught in our educational institutions and how learning is assessed should also change.

Critics focused particularly upon assessment techniques, which were seen to promote unnecessary failure and reduce the development of pro-learning identities. For example, the critics successfully argued that selective or norm-referenced examinations, such as the 11-plus in the UK and University Entrance in New Zealand, were specifically designed to limit participation and achievement. Such selective assessment systems promoted the failure of predetermined proportions of learners irrespective of their overall level of achievement and reflected a kind of class-based logic in which only the elite were seen to benefit from a university education (Hughes and Lauder, 1990). It was also argued that such systems only measured a narrow range of skills, many of which were not directly related to the employment situation where the skills would be used and did not convey to employers information that was useful or trustworthy. Poor information flows are believed to have contributed to credential inflation, particularly during periods of high unemployment. This has occurred as credentials have tended to serve as simple selection devices rather than indicating exactly what skills potential recruits can demonstrate. One consequence is that employers demand credentials far beyond those that are necessary for particular jobs in the hope that recruits will have the actual skills they want (New Zealand Qualifications Authority, 1996b). Another consequence is that students remain in education for longer periods of time than necessary and are more likely to obtain skills that are in poor demand in the labour market.

Just as strategies which limit participation and achievement came to be seen as outdated, so too have distinctions between academic and vocational knowledge. Today, academic and vocational knowledge should have parity of esteem, not just because viewing them differently reflects outmoded class distinctions, but, more critically, because skill shortages exist, particularly in the area of intermediate skills (Department for Education and Skills, 2003). Thus, there is an urgent need to increase the proportion of people undertaking VET by increasing its status. Indeed, divisions between academic and vocational learning are invalid, as most learners in 'academic' programmes are in training for particular vocations. Creating a knowledge economy requires that a greater proportion of young people see vocational education as a 'positive choice, not a second-class fall back' (Blunkett, 2001, p. 6). In this way, parity of esteem is seen to address problems associated with what is known as 'tracking', or the notion that vocational education locks working class students into courses of study that lead to lower status and poorly paid employment, relative to the employment outcomes of academic courses (Shavit and Muller, 2000). As American educator Dale Parnell explains:

> I tell people in the US that vocational education was born with a very fundamental birth defect called 'prestige deficiency' and we've never really been able to change that. I see it changing just now, in the last couple of years. I'm optimistic that we are beginning to see a shift and probably that's due to the changing nature of work. We've shifted in our economy from manual labour to mental labour and that takes a different kind of training and background to the old manual labour. You used to be able to go to work in our steel mills for a pretty good wage and you didn't even need a high school education. You just did what you were told. Today that's not true. Today you've got to think. (New Zealand Qualifications Authority, 1996a, p. 9)

When announcing the introduction of new vocational General Certificate of Secondary Education, the Education and Employment Secretary expressed similar sentiments.

> In the future, vocational and technical education will be a positive choice, not a second-class fallback, with as much status and esteem as academic

education. ... These are historic reforms. For the first time, we will have in place a vocational and technical education system that secures high standards, status and esteem. Breaking down the barriers between academic and vocational education will also be helped by an emphasis on employability and high quality work experience for pupils of all ability. ... Academic success may enhance your future prospects but it does not shield you from the world of work or the need to make a meaningful economic contribution. The extension of vocational and technical education represents an important modernisation of comprehensive secondary education. (Blunkett, 2001, p. 6)

Progressive educators had also long called for educational reform on social grounds. For example, in New Zealand a range of interested parties, including educators and academics, called for educational reform on the grounds that selective assessment techniques had tended to reproduce existing social divisions (New Zealand Qualifications Authority, 1996b). In a position that strongly resonated with the neoliberal critique of comprehensive education, one explanation concerned the lack of quality information about the kind of skills young people had obtained. In addition, the lack of relevance to the workplace was seen to have limited the ability of young working class people to enjoy social mobility and the content and assessment systems of the schooling system appeared to reflect the needs and aspirations of the elite who were destined to attend university and were intentionally prepared for this by their middle class teachers.

Critics point out that the need to select students for higher education has driven assessment policy and as a result the information provided in basic school credentials is geared to meeting the needs of universities not employers. This means that even if working-class students know what skills are demanded in the labour market, they cannot obtain them. Those lacking access to valuable social networks could not compensate for a lack of social capital by obtaining useful qualifications that could 'speak for' them in employment situations whilst those with access to social networks were forced to rely on them even though these may not have led to employment that was of high quality. For example, while there is a range of non-academic courses available in secondary schools, particularly at higher levels, the majority of students are faced with a lack of choice over their courses of study. This leads them to study towards achieving 'academic' credentials. Although the proportion of young people entering university has increased over recent years, this academic bias clearly ignores the needs of the majority of school-leavers whose post-school destinations are either in the labour market or in non-academic forms of post-compulsory education and training. Similarly, assessment practices are seen to have been captured by schools, meaning that the validity of current methods of recognising and rewarding achievement has not been sanctioned by market forces. This may contribute to inequality and economic inefficiency by suppressing or underrating information about student learning.

> Attempts to suppress information about students arising from the process of certification or study in schools, will increase the transaction costs of job seekers and employers and lead the latter to rely more on external signs such as the school attended by a job seeker; thus imposing both equity and efficiency costs beyond the world of education. (New Zealand Treasury, 1987, p. 146)

Although progressive educators had been calling for reform for some time, political support for reform was given decisive impetus by neoliberal and neoconservative critique of education in the late 1980s and early 1990s.[1] The basis of this critique was that economic change has increased demand for highly skilled forms of labour power and that the creation of educational markets, in which the consumers of education drove the development of curriculum, provided the best solution in bridging the so-called skills gap. Moreover, as economic change is rapid, demand for particular skills changes rapidly. As a result, attaining and retaining employment depends upon obtaining the skills demanded by employers and engaging in lifelong learning to ensure these remain current.

Vocational Education and Training and Social Capital

Recently, academics from a social capital perspective have added to the debate over VET by arguing that meeting the challenges created by the global skills auction requires the creation of a high-trust, cooperative and egalitarian society. They also argue against the conservative view of intelligence and of human potential, claiming it is too narrow and that it reflects the needs of an outdated method of production and the interests of a small elite. Although the conservative view is abhorrent on social grounds alone, competing effectively in the global skills auction through creating a magnet economy, for example, has rendered such narrow views of human potential, intelligence and policies related to these views ineffective on economic grounds. Indeed, education and economic reform is needed to maximise human potential and release the pool of talent that has, to date, remained trapped within the working class by conservative economic and educational policies (Brown and Lauder, 2001).

A central and distinguishing feature of this position is the belief that the struggle to create a more open and fair society requires recognising that the individualism and competition inherent in human capital theory has given rise to educational policies which are able to unlock human potential. Elite groups are likely to see any extension of opportunities to less privileged groups as a threat to their status and will be reluctant to support policies that challenge this (Brown, 2000). In this context, an essential part of creating a high-skills/high-trust society is investment in VET as a means to improve the communicative competence of learners such that they are enabled to participate in the widest set of social networks (Szreter, 1998). Without this investment, the privileged will continue to create distance between themselves and the rest of society through their access to quality information and their superior means of analysing this. Thus, following Dewey, the provision of quality VET is seen to challenge positional advantage based on access to information obtained, for example, through social networks and the means to analyse such information. Similarly, the provision of education is an essential ingredient in the creation of a society characterised by the free exchange of ideas between people of different social origins (Dewey, 1916). Not only is challenging positional advantage – which is derived from the elite's superior access to better forms of social network capital – necessary on grounds of social justice, it is required in order to maximise economic competitiveness in the global, knowledge economy. In a position that echoes the technocratic/meritocratic perspective, competing effectively in the global economy requires the utilisation of the talents and potential of all. It is only through harnessing our potential that innovation which creates high-wage and high-skill forms of employment will flourish. In different ways, Brown and Lauder (2001) and Szreter (1998) believe that the economic benefits derived from social capital are such that we will either see the benefits of working cooperatively or face poorer economic conditions. In other words, the aim of VET is to remanufacture intelligence and create identities conducive to the labour markets of deindustralised economies. To the extent that the education system limits the ability of individuals to process information, communicate effectively with others and participate in society, it also limits the production of social capital. This is because individuals are limited in their participation in bridging social networks and therefore this kind of social capital cannot increase.

As noted, an important aspect of the struggle to create high-wage and high-skill forms of employment rests upon the idea of a magnet economy. Accordingly, although the UK and New Zealand may currently be experiencing labour market polarisation, investment in VET is needed to lift overall levels of achievement in order to attract investment in high-wage and high-skill forms of employment. In this context, CBET plays a critical role in signalling to multinational investors the competencies held by a nation's working population and the nation's skill base becomes a factor of production considered by investors, along with other factors such as access to markets, in a global skills auction.

Remanufacturing Intelligence and Identity

The perception that CBET would provide a solution to disruption goes back to the mid-1970s in the UK and New Zealand, and earlier in the United States, when it was seen by policy-makers as a short-term strategy to address youth, and later, adult unemployment. In New Zealand and the UK, CBET has been incorporated into VET systems. In the UK, the National Council for Vocational Qualifications (now the Qualifications and Curriculum Authority) and the associated National Vocational Qualifications (NVQs) and their Scottish equivalent (SVQs) were created.[2] A central role of the Qualifications and Curriculum Authority is to establish standards of occupational competence which are employer-led and to accredit these into a national qualifications framework. Arguably, as NVQs and SVQs are based on clear competency-based standards, they present strong evidence of a person's ability to do a job. Moreover, as NVQs and SVQs are developed and regularly reviewed by independent bodies designed to represent the interests of employers (the Sector Skills Councils, formerly known as National Training Organisations), the standards of achievement are believed to be based on a thorough understanding of each industry and the needs of users.[3]

Developments in New Zealand mirror those that occurred in the UK. In the early 1990s, moves to increase the significance of VET, not just in formal schooling but in the economy broadly, was typified by the introduction of the National Qualifications Framework (the Framework) and a form of competency-based assessment (known as standards-based assessment). The New Zealand Qualifications Authority (NZQA) established the Framework under the Education Act of 1988 (Government of New Zealand, 1995, p. 242). The main aim of the Framework under the legislation is '[t]o develop a Framework for national qualifications in secondary schools and post-school education and training'. To create a framework in which 'academic' and 'vocational' learning was to be measured in the same way and to have parity of status, policy-makers devised a new measure of learning. These are known as unit standards. Unit standards can be grouped together to create different qualifications. They vary in size depending on the amount of work needed to complete them and are placed upon the Framework at different levels depending on their difficulty. However, all learning is expressed in terms of outcomes or standards of achievement.[4]

The creation of a qualifications framework in which all learning is recognised distinguishes the situation in New Zealand from that in the United Kingdom. As such, New Zealand offers the best example to date of an attempt by policy-makers to create a unified qualifications framework. As is the case in the UK, standards of achievement in the area of VET are developed and reviewed by employer and industry groups known as industry training organisations (ITOs) in the case of industry-related standards, and by standards-setting bodies in the case of school-related standards. It was intended that the unit standards-based Framework would replace existing qualifications by 1997 and by 1995 thousands of unit standards had been written and were appearing in schools.

Policy-makers in the UK and New Zealand hope that by clearly defining what skills young people have achieved and by accrediting the providers of educational qualifications relevant to employers, trustworthy measures of an individual's abilities will be developed and new ladders of opportunity will be created. In contrast to norm-referenced assessment, which is designed to limit participation by establishing predetermined pass rates irrespective of the overall standard of achievement, under CBET, all students who reach the described standards can be rewarded. In this way, CBET removes a structural barrier to advancement and achievement. This is seen to be more motivating for students, particularly those students who have traditionally performed poorly in schooling and also for the teachers, who know that all who reach the required standards will be rewarded. Students can be set clear learning targets, be rewarded more frequently for learning, and repeat failed sections of a course without having to repeat the whole course. Finally, CBET qualifications can be obtained in schools, tertiary institutions and workplaces, they can be accumulated throughout one's working life, and they are portable because they are registered in a comprehensive framework of qualifications. Individuals need not complete all of their studies in one institution. In these ways and others, CBET is promoted on the grounds that it will increase equality in education, increase achievement, enhance the status of VET, and create the learning identities needed in order to compete effectively in the global economy.

In addition to making the training systems market-led by increasing the influence of employers in curriculum development, CBET contributes to the creation of educational markets in other ways. Firstly, CBET provides learners with a means of moving from provider to provider whilst working towards a single award. Thus, CBET provides a common educational currency which, like money in the economy, helps create market relationships. Secondly, the role of the QCA and the NZQA in accrediting providers of education has opened the training market to a range of providers. This means training providers can now compete. Public and private sector providers of CBET in New Zealand now compete for 'clients' (see Chapter 6). In the UK, New Labour is also moving to give employers greater choice and control over publicly-funded training and how this training is delivered (Department for Education and Skills, 2003).

By providing new systems of assessment and new methods of developing curricula designed to create more motivating and meaningful learning pathways, CBET is an attempt to replace recruiting functions which were formerly completed by social networks. In effect, CBET aims to motivate all students to obtain relevant educational credentials sought after by employers. It is designed to replace process-based trust with an institutional-based form of trust through increasing the signaling capacity of credentials. Where process-based forms of trust continue to facilitate transitions, they are seen to be unfair and inefficient. They are unfair as they function as a form of social closure being based on membership of particular social class groups, which limits the labour-market activity of those without access to those groups (Murphy, 1988). They are also inefficient as they do not ensure the most effective match between skill and employment level and may actually reduce economic competitiveness.

The challenge of promoting economic growth and the solutions to social problems such as youth unemployment and the discouraged worker effect are seen to rest in perfecting the methods through which individuals are skilled and improving the instruments that recognise and reward skill. By replacing process-based trust, CBET aims to reorganise and restructure education through new management and administration systems in the expectation that these will replace those traditions and practices which had previously made school-to-work transitions efficient. The critical question asked of this strategy is to what extent the measures in the area of VET have created new ladders of opportunity in which all learners achieve highly and are motivated towards obtaining qualifications employers find meaningful? This question is addressed in the following sections.

Competency-based Education and Training as a Solution to Disruption

Although reforms in the area of VET have created a large training market in New Zealand at least, evidence suggests that in terms of providing a solution to disruption CBET has delivered comparatively little. Despite many years of reform in CBET and great expense, youth unemployment remains high, particularly for certain groups. The proportion of young people NEET also remains high and the proportion of workers lacking basic levels of skill is unacceptably high. The continuation of youth unemployment and other social problems suggest that policy-makers in New Zealand and the UK have struggled to establish a training culture in all segments of society. Indeed, the inability of the CBET systems to provide solutions to disruption have been acknowledged by Third Way governments (New Zealand Labour Party, 1999; Performance and Innovation Unit, 2002b). The failings of the CBET systems in New Zealand and the UK are widely known and there is little need to set these out in great detail. Nevertheless, it is necessary to establish briefly what they are, as this provides a way to better assess the likely impact of changes introduced by New Labour and the Labour-led Coalition in the area of VET as they search for a solution to disruption. It is important to stress that VET has benefited individual students (Shavit and Muller, 2000). However, it remains unclear just how CBET will benefit learners as a group. The literature identifies a number of reasons why, in New Zealand and the UK to date, CBET reforms have failed to achieve the aims of its supporters.

Firstly, despite being 'employer-led' there is little evidence to show that employers as a group have embraced the new training arrangements. At a political level, employers in England have been criticised for being 'lazy', for investing too little in training and for failing to appreciate its benefits (Performance and Innovation Unit, 2002a). In a similar vein, one explanation for the apparently low uptake of CBET in New Zealand is that employers appear to be 'ambivalent' about the government's industry training strategy in general and industry training organisations in particular (Long et al., 2000). In New Zealand, less than 10 per cent of young people aged 15 to 19 years received training linked to the Industry Training Strategy. In contrast, 35 per cent of those aged 50 years and over received training. The amount of training varies markedly across different industries in New Zealand. Approximately 30 per cent of trainees are in the building services and contractors ITO whilst other industries are not represented at all (Office of the Associate Minister of Education – Tertiary Education, 2001). Despite being employer-led, 45 per cent of all employees in New Zealand were not covered by an ITO. Reasons for the reluctance of employers to adopt the ITS include a belief that the ITO model does not meet the employer/occupational group needs, qualifications and necessary entry requirements have been established through other means, for example via the university system, and a reluctance on the part of industry to be involved in training that may lead employees to demand increased remuneration (Department of Labour, 2000).

In the UK, major evaluations of the VET system have also revealed serious problems with the performance of National Training Organisations (now Skill Sector Councils) (Siora and Chiles, 2000). Problems include a poor understanding on the part of employers of the role of the National Training Organisations. Employers were 'arguably ... quite apathetic towards the role of NTOs ... [and] very few had had direct experience of or use of their services to date' (Questions Answered Ltd, 2000, p. 1). In another survey of employers, Matlay (2000) found that although a relatively high proportion of employers were aware of SVQs and NVQs, two-thirds of respondents were sceptical of their relevance and questioned the potential impact upon the competitiveness of their businesses. A reason identified by researchers for this is that, despite being employer-led, NVQs and SVQs are too narrow in scope to be of use (Smithers, 1993; Wolf, 2002). Recent evidence indicates that in fact, although the cumulative number of NVQs awarded continues to increase, the number of people awarded NVQs has begun to fall (Unwin et al., 2004). The uptake of NVQs varies between framework areas, with 75 per cent of all NVQs being awarded in three of the nine framework areas (ibid.). An important influence driving up the completion of NVQs in some areas was state intervention. The fastest growing framework area for the year ending 2002 was 'Providing Health, Social and Protective Services', where a legal requirement that a proportion of workers in care homes be working towards an NQV (level two) drove up participation by 13 per cent over the previous 12 months (ibid.).

A related reason for the poor uptake of CBET is that demand for skilled workers has not been universally high and low skill routes into employment exist. This is not to suggest that demand for workers with high levels of skill has not grown in some sectors; indeed, there is evidence that it has (Felstead et al., 2002). Rather, consistent with the bifurcated labour market or 'hourglass economy', in which low-skill employment grows alongside high-skill employment in New Zealand (Labour, 2003) and the UK (Nolan, 2001), significant growth has also occurred in forms of work that only demand low levels of skill and pay relatively poorly (Learning Skills Council, 2003). This is particularly true for the rapidly-expanding service sector occupations that make few, if any, demands for new recruits to be highly qualified. Indeed it appears that employers in New Zealand and in the UK place high value on basic workplace discipline, for instance, punctuality, attendance, and reliability (Colmar Brunton Research, 1994; Skill New Zealand, 1999a); and on 'aesthetic' labour, for instance looking and sounding 'right' (Nickson et al., 2003).

A related problem is that simply increasing the supply of skilled labour will achieve relatively little if work practices and organisational structures do not allow these skills to be properly utilised. It is widely accepted that some segments of British industry are locked into a low-wage/low-skill equilibrium in which the availability of cheap sources of labour encourages the utilisation of production techniques that do not require people to be highly skilled (Finegold and Soskice, 1988). Meeting the challenges posed by globalisation and the introduction of new technology not only rests upon increasing the skill base, but also on creating workplaces in which these skills are utilised effectively. The basis of Finegold and Soskice's (1988) argument is that policies are designed to increase the supply of skills and relatively little attention is being paid to increasing demand. Increasing demand for labour and creating good jobs requires more than simply increasing the supply of skilled labour. At present, research suggests that, in the formulation of production strategies in the UK, skill is a third or fourth order issue and considered after the competitive and product market strategy, the organisational structure needed to deliver this, and work organisation, job design and people management systems (Keep and Mayhew, 1999). The adoption of a product strategy in which the production of high-specification goods is emphasised may not in itself lead to more high-skill jobs (Keep and Mayhew, 1999). It may soon be feasible to produce high-specification goods with low-skill workers.

A consequence of growth in occupations that make few, if any, demands for all young people to be highly skilled is that not all learners see an incentive to engage in training. Evidence suggests demand from young people to engage in CBET has been disappointingly low in the UK (Wolf, 2002). A reason for this is that it is seen by learners as a low status, low reward route into employment. For example, limited qualitative evidence suggests that at a senior school level CBET under the NQF in New Zealand has yet to be widely understood by students (Fitsimmons, 1997; Strathdee and Hughes, 2001). Moreover, despite claims to the contrary, policy-makers in Britain have yet to convince young people that vocational qualifications have parity of esteem with academic qualifications (Wolf, 2002). Similarly, in New Zealand the lack of demand from employers means that Framework qualifications are seen to be of low status and have met with poor market demand in schools. In addition, the reforms do not appear to have challenged the status of academic learning and most prefer academic qualifications such as the recently abolished University Bursary in New Zealand, which hold the promise of high incomes and social mobility (Strathdee, 2003). An important reason for this is that academic and professional qualifications lead to jobs that pay more highly (Harkness and Machin, 1999; Learning Skills Council, 2003; Robinson, 1997). On the other hand, in the UK the economic incentives to invest in human capital below the NVQ level three are not strong (McIntosh, 2004; Steedman, 2002), except for those with limited prior attainment (Learning Skills Council, 2003).

Evidence also suggests many employees are already overqualified for the work that they do. For example, Felstead et al., (2002, p. 11) report that there are '6.4 million people qualified to the equivalent of NVQ level three in the workforce, but only 4 million jobs that demand this level of highest qualification'. Similarly, '... there are 2.9 economically active people aged 20–60 who possess no qualifications [and there] remains 6.5 million jobs for which no qualification would be required to obtain them'.

Finally, a central message from policy-makers, politicians and some social capital theorists is that young people lack information about the skills employers demand, which something CBET and market-led training systems are designed to change. The provision of better labour market information is thus seen to provide a key means for increasing achievement and aligning skill demand and skill production. However, there is debate about the extent of young people's understanding of the relationship between qualifications and the labour market (Rosenbaum, 2002). In this respect, Steedman (2002) argues that the decision on the part of young people not to invest in VET is not purely a cultural lag, rather it reflects an understanding that VET qualifications below level three are not highly sought after. She adds that in the case of VET courses for 16–19 year olds, individuals are acting rationally by using further education as a 'waiting-room' for labour market opportunities. This suggests that young people are able to cut through the ambiguity created by policy-makers and politicians regarding the notion of skill and its impact on the labour market.[5] In contrast to the dominant view, in which young people are seen to lack information about their employment and training options, it seems that young workers have a good understanding of the kinds of skills they need to secure employment. In addition, it is important to recognise that the majority of British children are involved in paid employment at some point before they reach the minimum school-leaving age. This suggests that much of this understanding is developed through their participation in wage labour (Mizen et al., 1999). Similarly, Rosenbaum (2002) states that young people understand that employers recruiting school-leavers do not use school qualifications when making hiring decisions. As a result, students remain poorly motivated towards achieving these qualifications.

In sum, the weight of evidence from the UK and New Zealand indicates that, to date, policy-makers have failed to create the desired learning cultures in order to compete effectively in the global economy. Moreover, although the introduction of CBET has removed a structural barrier to advancement in education and embodies a more optimistic view of human potential and intelligence, it has yet to create new ladders of opportunity in which all young people are able to and are sufficiently motivated towards obtaining qualifications they can cash in for employment.

The Third Way and VET Reform

As noted, Third Way governments in the UK and New Zealand have been highly critical of the previous neoliberal administrations' policies in the area of VET and acknowledge that, to date, policy-makers have failed to establish training cultures and remanufacture identities as planned. Since taking up office, New Labour and the Labour-led Coalition have acted on their concerns by providing more financial support for VET and by adopting a more strategic approach to VET. In order to 'grow more talent' the Labour-led Coalition has reformed the Industry Training Strategy (designed to provide quality VET for those in work), reformed the pre-employment programmes for people with no or few school qualifications (youth training) and introduced a new school-leaver qualification (the NCEA (National Certificate of Educational Achievement)). In addition, a number of new programmes have been introduced, including the introduction of a modern apprenticeship scheme and a scheme to promote school–business links and workplace training (gateway). The NCEA is a new qualification designed to credential vocational and academic learning undertaken in a diverse range of settings and is registered on the NQF at levels one, two and three. In addition, in contrast to the previous government's free-market VET system, ITOs are now required to take a leadership role and identify training needs. Key government departments are required to work more closely with one another and to place greater emphasis on multi-industry generic skills (Office of the Associate Minister of Education – Tertiary Education, 2001). Ambitious training targets have also been established. For example, in New Zealand's

2003 Budget, the Labour-led Coalition announced that it was investing an extra NZ$84.3 million over four years into the Industry Training Fund to increase the number of workers participating in industry training programmes. The government wants to increase the current figure of 106,000 workers to 150,000 workers by 2005 and to 250,000 workers by 2007. The logic underpinning this investment is that market incentives to invest in work-based training are currently not strong. Consequently, state intervention is required to stimulate the participation of employers and workers in work-based training. In addition, Maharey (2002a) argues that the training sector needs to get better at predicting future skill shortages. To help the sector achieve this, a new body, known as the Tertiary Education Commission (TEC) has been given responsibility for identifying future skill shortages and is charged with producing a biannual report on changes in supply and demand for particular skills, conducting a survey on job vacancies, and surveying the employment and earnings outcomes for tertiary graduates.

In Britain, New Labour has also adopted a more interventionist approach in the area of VET (Hyland, 2002). Policy-makers have established ambitious training targets and hope to have 50 per cent of those aged 18 to 30 years participating in higher education by 2010. A skills strategy has been developed by the Learning and Skills Council.[6] An important aspect of this strategy is the establishment of Skills Sector Councils to replace the 73 poorly performing National Training Organisations.[7] Skills Sector Councils are a new network of UK-wide councils comprising employers, professional bodies, and trade unions working with government to develop the skills UK businesses need. Amongst other tasks, they are designed to develop occupationally relevant standards of achievement and qualifications and to work with employers to broker skills agreements across sectors. In sum, they are designed to create a truly employer-led VET system. Numerous other measures have also been implemented but it is impossible to describe them all here.[8] However, as stated in the guiding report, '21st Century Skills: Realising our Potential, presented to the British Parliament in 2003', the 'strategy is not predominantly about new initiatives. It is about making more sense of what is already there, integrating what already exists and focusing it more effectively' (Department for Education and Skills, 2003, p. 12).

New measures, such as the Modern Apprenticeship Schemes, new levels of state planning, and the commitment of more state financial support for VET, will create new learning pathways for some in New Zealand and the UK as they have done elsewhere (Shavit and Muller, 2000). It is possible to identify ways in which the approach adopted by New Labour and the Labour-led Coalition differs from that of the previous neoliberal administrations. However, there are grounds to question whether the new measures will transform the New Zealand and the UK VET systems in the manner required. In this respect, there are a number of critical issues that are left unresolved.

Firstly, the policies remain wedded to increasing the supply of skilled and unskilled workers but the 'missing level' that would increase demand for skilled workers still appears to be missing in nations such as Britain (Brown and Lauder, 2001), which has adopted neoliberal approaches to economic management. As acknowledged by New Labour, the strategy is not predominantly about new initiatives and it remains unclear how the creation of the Skills Sector Councils will succeed in developing a solution to disruption through VET where National Training Organisations failed. Moreover, whilst it is intended that the Skills Sector Councils will be employer led, their core activities will be funded by the state, they will operate under licence from the state, and their key objectives are established by the state.

Secondly, although changes such as gathering better information about skill demand through conducting surveys of employers suggest that a more strategic approach to VET has been adopted, the basic thrust of the previous administration's market-led strategy has been retained. For example, the system remains firmly market-led in the sense that the standards of achievement and the skills developed are designed to meet the needs of employers. Changes that would have signalled a clear break from the neoliberal VET system, such as compelling employers to invest in training as promised by the Labour-led Coalition in its pre-election strategy, appear to have been quietly forgotten.

Thirdly, much of the discourse calls for a high-skill/high-wage, value-added training strategy, but in practice many of the programmes are aimed at developing basic workplace skills such as communication and social skills. This is clearly evident in the New Labour and Labour-led Coalition approach to welfare reform where a 'work-first' approach has been adopted (Fergusson, 2002). As will be discussed more fully in the following chapter, work-first welfare has a conscriptive effect that encourages the creation of low-wage/low-skill forms of employment. The focus upon employability is a result of the New Labour and the Labour-led Coalition's adoption of neoliberal funding models. These encourage private training providers to produce training outcomes as efficiently as possible. The result is a proliferation of short-term work, focused 'training' programmes that do little, if anything, to produce sustainable, high-quality employment. Performance-based management strategies, such as outcomes-based funding, can have perverse and unintended outcomes (Gray, 1997) and their ability to improve the performance of the public sector remains unclear (Propper and Wilson, 2003). New Labour and the Labour-led Coalition have a strong high-wage/high-skill discourse. However, some of their policies actually help lock in low-wage/low-skill forms of employment by ensuring a supply of low-skilled workers. Although the Labour-led Coalition has been highly critical of the previous administrations' welfare-to-work policies, they have taken their policies much further. This is illustrated by the latest Labour-led Coalition intervention, 'Job Jolt'. Job Jolt is a new package to reduce the welfare roll by making it harder for people to receive welfare benefits. As part of the new measures, work tests for people over 55 years of age have been introduced and form what the government calls a 'positive ageing strategy'. Unemployed people who live in areas of low unemployment are being asked to move to areas of higher labour market demand or their benefits will be cut off. In addition, Work and Income New Zealand have drawn up lists of 'no-go areas' or areas of high unemployment for people of non-Maori descent who claim welfare.

Fourthly, the continuation, and in some instances the strengthening, of the previous neoliberal administrations' policies suggests that neither the New Labour nor the Labour-led Coalition approach is likely to create the social infrastructure some social capital theorists deem vital before training cultures can develop. As pointed out, creating such an infrastructure requires the creation of a social context in which a strong sense of interpersonal obligation, high levels of trust, and the presence of strong community bonds will facilitate the development of learning cultures in which identities are transformed. Arguably, continuing support of the Labour-led Coalition and New Labour for the bulk of the previous governments' neoliberal reforms has done little to reverse the declining interpersonal obligation and weakening community bonds (Brown and Lauder, 2001).

At first glance, one area where it seems the Labour-led Coalition has not followed in the footsteps of its neoliberal predecessors is the area of assessment. Where the previous neoliberal administration was happy to let academic and vocational learning continue along separate tracks or to let the value of the various kinds of qualifications be established by market forces, the Labour-led Coalition has tried to integrate the two pathways into a unified system of assessment. Due to its impact on all school students, the NCEA is arguably the most significant educational policy introduced by the Labour-led Coalition. It is intended to address weaknesses in New Zealand's VET system that, to date, have frustrated policy-makers searching for a solution to disruption.

The National Certificate of Educational Achievement in New Zealand[9]

The NCEA is designed to raise standards, increase the length of time students stay in education, create a lifelong learning culture, increase the status of vocational subjects, and convey valuable information to employers. The NCEA is also designed to create flexible learning pathways by, for instance, allowing individuals to study at more than one institution for a single award. Both initiatives are backed by financial support. Until recently, assessment practices were market-led in the sense that schools could choose whether they offered standards-based assessment linked to the NQF or retain the traditional system of norm-referenced assessment which functions outside the NQF. However, under the NCEA all learners are required to work towards a single award and have their learning assessed against predetermined standards. Policy-makers hope that the new award will be a motivating and relevant qualification which will help create pro-learning identities. However, despite its merits, it is doubtful whether the new award will have the desired effects or provide a solution to disruption. To make this case, it is useful to briefly review the NCEA and to assess its likely impact.

As noted, in New Zealand the original plan was to introduce a unified qualifications framework. Academic and vocational learning were to be measured in the same way, a common grading system was to be used, and a single ladder of progression was to be developed. However, although the NCEA was first mooted in the early 1990s as a replacement for the traditional, selective forms of assessment, the election of a conservative administration which supported selective assessment methods and held a cynical view of human potential delayed its introduction. Moreover, the early vision of creating a unified framework was also resisted by elites, universities, and students who favoured selective examinations that held the promise of social mobility. As a result, New Zealand operated a dual system of assessment, limiting the ability of the Framework to assist discouraged workers to become more motivated towards learning (Fitsimmons, 1997; Strathdee and Hughes, 2000). Following the election of the Labour-led Coalition, policy-makers turned their attention back to the NCEA, which was introduced from 2002 as the major school-leaving qualification. The NCEA is designed so that vocational and academic learning will count towards a single award. As a result, the number of young people having learning assessed against standards has increased dramatically.

The Labour-led Coalition deserves credit for tackling the vexing issue of assessment and curriculum reform: however, changes introduced to the

NCEA since its conception to accommodate conservative interests mean that it is unlikely to contribute greatly to a solution for disruption. Although all secondary students, irrespective of the nature of courses of study, now work towards one qualification, the way in which learning is recognised in 'academic' and 'vocational' courses continues to differ. In vocational and academic areas learning is measured against predetermined standards of achievement. However, learning in academic areas is graded so that satisfactory work, good work, and excellent work can be recognised with 'credit', 'merit' and 'excellence' grades. In addition, academic students are provided with a grade point average in each approved curriculum-related subject. This is designed to facilitate selection into competitive tertiary programmes, help employers select new recruits, and provide parents with useful information about the academic performance of their children (Mallard, 2001). Students in VET programmes do not receive a grade point average and are likely to lack the qualifications required for entry into competitive tertiary programmes. The changes mean that VET and academic programmes will lack the parity of status deemed vital by the government if New Zealand is to develop the skilled workforce thought necessary to effectively compete in the global skills auction. As the Organisation for Economic Cooperation and Development (OECD) notes, and experience in New Zealand shows, students will avoid programmes that limit their chances of entering higher education (Lee and Lee, 1992; OECD, 2000). Moreover, although it is compulsory for all New Zealand students in state-funded schools to study towards the NCEA, academically talented students are able to gain additional qualifications through another new award known as the New Zealand Scholarship. The New Zealand Scholarship is intended to be the premier secondary qualification, will be registered at level four of the Framework (the NCEA is only offered at levels one to three) and is designed to challenge New Zealand's top academic students. The result is the NCEA has been reconfigured to emulate previous academic and non-academic divide.

In the initial version of the NQF it was intended that the method of assessment would reflect the nature of the learning being assessed. This meant that in certain areas of the curriculum examinations would not be appropriate, as the learning was not best assessed through this method. This was underpinned by an extensive system of moderation procedures designed to ensure that standards of achievement were comparable across the country. This was a high-trust and professionalising system in the sense that it relied on the educators to make judgements about the standards achieved and the best method to assess learning and to work with other educators, the standards-setting bodies, and the ITOs to ensure consistency. However, the Labour-led Coalition has bowed to conservative interests by mandating the use of examinations to determine at least 60 per cent of the final grade in most conventional subject areas. This is a low-trust, low-cost strategy designed to allay the fears of conservative educators about the ability of educators to make rigorous assessments of students' standards of achievement. These changes mean the NQF is not a truly unified system and shows that policy-makers have departed from their initial vision. It is also worth noting that one advantage of the original vision was that students would be able to have their learning reassessed without having to complete the whole course again. However, the Minister of Education decided to limit students to one reassessment opportunity for each internally-assessed achievement standard. Nevertheless, policy-makers and politicians remain adamant that the NQF will be a major contributor to New Zealand's effort to create a learning society and highly skilled workforce (Mallard, 2000; West, 2001). In New Zealand, it seems that even the Labour-led Coalition, which championed the economic and social benefits of assessment against clearly detailed standards of achievement, doubts that employers will find the more detailed information produced by CBET of use. The move to include a grade point average as part of New Zealand's standards-based assessment system was underpinned by a belief that employers would find a single figure more useful when recruiting school-leavers than more detailed information across a range of subject areas (Mallard, 2001).

The state is creating and supporting a system of accreditation to facilitate youth transitions into employment in the hope that employers will find the new system useful. The introduction of CBET and the development of qualifications frameworks were designed to increase achievement, create innovation, and diffuse skills. Moreover, it was hoped tht they would replace process-based trust in recruitment and training processes. Indeed, replacing such trust was deemed vital if those from work-poor environments were to enjoy social mobility.[10] The evidence presented above shows that policy-makers have, to date, failed in their quest to replace process-based trust.

Networks, Skill Diffusion and Magnet Economies

The notion that investment in CBET is needed to raise overall levels of skill rests upon two views about labour market change and skill. The strong view is that the post-Fordist future, in which high-wage/high-skill employment is the norm, has arrived and that investment in CBET is needed to meet current demand in the labour market for skilled labour (Drucker, 1993). Such claims build upon those that predicted the emergence of a post-industrial economy in which the increasing importance of science would increase demand for educated workers (Bell, 1973). The weak view is that, although the post-Fordist future has yet to arrive, investment in CBET is needed to attract the type of industry that creates high-wage/high-skill forms of employment. The idea is to create a magnet economy in which investment that utilises and generates high-wage/high-skill forms of employment is attracted to nations by their well-developed training systems and high levels of skill workers.

There are a number of critical issues which raise questions about the contribution of CBET to the state's search for a solution to disruption. Firstly, it fails to account for the relationship between global industrial structure and the demand for skilled labour (Brown and Lauder, 2001). Networked production and outsourcing do not necessarily lead to the creation of many high-wage/high-skill jobs in one country. In earlier periods, it was possible to find examples of vertically-integrated companies, such as IBM in the United States in the case of the electronics industry or Daimler-Benz in Germany, where production was undertaken by one company within one country. In the contemporary period, the emergence of network production, which has been facilitated by information technology and skill development in developing economies, means that production is increasingly organised horizontally. Thus, Audretsch and Fritsch (2003) argue that stagnant growth and double-digit unemployment rates in Germany have been associated with a shift away from established firms, which were a source of growth in the 1980s, and towards entrepreneurial firms of the 1990s. They argue that a process of convergence in the sources of growth is occurring between Germany and the United States. Associated with this has been a growth in German firms creating employment outside of Germany and the adoption of 'lean production' methods (Green and Sakamoto, 2001). Secondly, it fails to acknowledge the rise of knowledge workers in Asia, who represent substantially less cost than similarly skilled workers in nations such as the UK and New Zealand. This means that countries like New Zealand and England are competing for investment with high-skill/low-wage nations. Finally, as is the case with domestic employers, there is little evidence that global investors look closely at the competencies of the workers in the manner predicted by proponents of CBET, when making investment decisions.

Case study evidence suggests that critical information about the nature of the workforce is transmitted through social networks. For instance, Saxenian

(2002) argues that, according to her case studies of the information technology industry, transnational communities provide a flexible and responsive mechanism for the transfer of skill and know-how, particularly between different business or cultural environments. Thus, although it is an emerging field of research, there is strong evidence showing that process-based trust operates at a global level. In this respect, recent work in economics has built upon the arguments developed by social network theorists demonstrating that skill diffusion is embedded in networks and that these networks play a critical role in promoting innovation.

Case study evidence regarding the information technology industry in Taiwan, China and India shows how transnational entrepreneurs draw upon their technical expertise and networks to transfer skill across international borders (Saxenian, 2002). In this context the first-generation immigrants such as the Chinese and Indian engineers of Silicon Valley have the cultural capital, the language skills, and the technical skills needed to be successful in both the US and elsewhere. Thus, 'by becoming transnational entrepreneurs, these immigrants can provide the critical contacts, information, and cultural know-how that link dynamic, but distant, regions in the global economy' (ibid., p. 185). Networks fulfilled this function in earlier periods both within nations such as England (Grieco, 1996), and between nations (Bull, 2002). According to Saxenian (2002) networks are far more flexible and responsive than multinational corporations, particularly between different cultures, and when these networks can be harnessed, they can facilitate the upgrading of local economies. It is important to note that the benefits of this are not necessarily widely felt and that high-wage/high-skill employment is created alongside the low-wage/low-skill forms of employment (Finegold, 1999).

In another perspective Simmie (2003) argues that in the knowledge society the most innovative firms have access to a strong local knowledge base and international sources of knowledge. Access to knowledge is a key resource that allows innovative firms to maintain their competitive advantage in the global economy. However, as he points out, knowledge is a complex concept. Drawing on Polanyi, Simmie (2003) identifies two ideal types of knowledge: explicit codified knowledge and tacit knowledge. Although for analytical purposes it is possible to separate codified knowledge from tacit knowledge, in practice tacit knowledge and experience are needed to understand formal codified knowledge. For example, whilst an instruction manual or a circuit diagram represents highly codified forms of knowledge, experience and tacit knowledge are required in order to make sense of these. If firms are limited to formal codified knowledge they will not be in a position to innovate. Thus, access to tacit knowledge is essential. Two common ways of sharing tacit knowledge are through social networks and closely related labour mobility. As Simmie (2003, p. 612) points out, social networks are 'significant for innovation because they act as vehicles for importing tacit knowledge into individual firms'. However, the nature of the knowledge has an important impact on the network structure needed for its efficient transmission. In this respect, Nahapiet and Ghoshal (2000) caution that bridging networks may be efficient as far as transferring information that is relatively unproblematic is concerned, and where the meaning is clear. However, much richer networks are required where the information is unclear and the meaning is ambiguous.

As the work of Saxenian (2002), Kanter (1995) and Simmie (2003) demonstrate, the presence of social networks facilitates the diffusion of skill within and across national borders and is an essential ingredient in transmitting the knowledge required for innovation. Saxenian (2002, p. 201) stresses that in today's volatile and fast-changing economy, personal connections are more flexible and responsive than multinational corporations 'and can facilitate the rapid adaption of domestic capabilities to facilitate the upgrade of the position of local firms in global production networks'. What this suggests is that network creation is needed. As she makes clear, the reason for Taiwan's success is not simply the presence of social capital – for instance, dense social networks, shared identities, and trust within the community – which enabled links to be created between Silicon Valley and Taiwan, although these were vital. Taiwan's success is also a direct result of the support provided by the Taiwanese government for business. Elements of this environment included a well-developed skill base, an attractive physical environment for entrepreneurs, a growing venture capital industry, and a range of fiscal incentives including access to low interest loans and tax concessions. Thus, the value of networks is underpinned by the value of the resources to which networks provide access.

In this respect, China is set to benefit from 'brain circulation' by the linking of US-educated Chinese computer engineers and scientists working in the Silicon Valley with emerging IT regions like Shanghai. Chinese policy-makers actively created this link. An important aspect of the environment is in the provision of access to resources – in the case of the IT industry the availability of cheap sources of labour to assemble IT products. Thus, underpinning the formation of these networks and the resulting innovation is the availability of a resource. Changes in the availability of these resources are likely to have a deleterious impact on the value of these networks. For example, increases in the cost of labour relative to China may mean that Bangalore prices itself out of its current market.

Conclusion

The central argument of this chapter is that, to date, the VET systems in New Zealand and the UK have not replaced functions formerly completed by social networks in the recruitment process. It was argued that CBET was specifically designed to achieve this by creating meaningful and motivating pathways into work for young people. However, evidence suggests it has yet to achieve this and is unlikely to do so in the future. Reasons for this include a lack of demand from employers for qualifications and a tendency for young people to seek qualifications that hold out the promise of social mobility. In general these tend to be those that provide access to the university system. Concurrently, policies that might increase demand for high-skilled workers appear to be absent and policy-makers have yet to find the 'missing lever' that might change this. Indeed, difficulty in stimulating demand from employers for high-skilled workers is compounded by policies in other areas, particularly work-first welfare, which has reduced the incentive for employers to adopt high-wage/high-skill strategies. The presence of a relatively low minimum wage and the creation of active welfare systems mean that supplies of cheap labour are readily available.

The Labour-led Coalition and New Labour attribute the failure of the VET system to provide a solution for the disruption to the previous neoliberal administrations' market-led training strategy. It was argued that reform of VET was needed. However, although it is possible to identify some differences, in general the basic thrust of the previous neoliberal administrations have been retained. This is evident in numerous ways, particularly the move to strengthen the extent to which the VET system is market led and the extent to which Third Way governments have supported and extended the active welfare policies. Although the Labour-led Coalition attempted to increase the status of VET through introducing a new school-leaver qualification, the changes introduced mean that the measures are unlikely to have their desired effects.

In the final part of the chapter, attention turned to the development of global production networks. It was argued that the New Labour and the Labour-led Coalition belief that investment in VET would lead to the creation of a magnet economy is flawed as it is possible to source highly-skilled workers in countries that have low production costs. The creation of global production networks depends upon the presence of social networks through which technology can be transferred and skills dissipated into global production sites. The role played by networks in this process brings into sharp relief the continuing importance of process-based trust in facilitating innovation and skill transference.

Notes

1   Whilst it is important to note that differences exist between the training systems introduced in different nations, there is nevertheless a consensus shared by policy-makers, politicians and others in New Zealand, Britain, Canada, and elsewhere, that CBET is a key component in the search for a solution to disruption.

2   NVQs and SVQs tend to be referred to as is they were the same thing. However, there are some differences. For example, NVQs are viewed as 'employer-led' while SVQs are viewed as being 'education-led' (Matlay, 2000).

3   Trades unions and professional organisations are also represented on the Skills Sector Councils.

4   There are 10 levels of learning on the Framework, ranging from National Certificates which are awarded at all levels but normally found at levels one to four, through to National Diplomas which are awarded at level five and upwards.

5   Payne (2000) argues there is a great deal of confusion within policy debates about the nature of post-Fordism.

6   The Learning and Skills Council is responsible for post-compulsory education and training in the United Kingdom. Its mission is to raise participation and attainment through the provision of high-quality education and training.

7   Although National Training Organisations were created by the previous Conservative administration, they were established shortly after the election of New Labour in 1998.

8   See the LSC's website www.lsc.gov.uk for details.

9   This section draws on Strathdee (2003) by permission.

10 However, recent work in the sociology of economics indicates that the goal of replacing process-based trust with institutional-based trust may be misplaced and that process-based trust and institutional-based trust play important roles in diffusing skill and stimulating innovation.

Chapter 6

Making Social Networks in New Zealand

Third Way governments in New Zealand and the UK recognise that neoliberal policies will not provide a solution to disruption. A key reason for this is that such policies do not always create the kind of infrastructure needed to enable individuals to make good training or employment decisions. To help rectify this the Labour-led Coalition is drawing upon market and non-market strategies in an attempt to engage all young people in training and employment. The Labour-led Coalition funds three major labour market interventions which are designed to create meaningful pathways into employment for young people, with each targeting a different population. These are the Modern Apprenticeship Scheme (MAS), Gateway, and youth training (YT).[1] In the cases of the MAS and YT, public and private sector providers compete largely on the basis of price for the right to manage and place trainees in employment and training. In the case of Gateway, most of the providers are secondary schools and are funded on the basis of a block grant, which is based on the school's roll, and a fee per student placed. However, schools may subcontract private providers to deliver the service if they wish. In all three programmes the government is keen to build capacity across the country and the location of providers is considered when awarding contracts.

The purpose of this chapter is to assess the impact of these programmes on the practices of the tutors or intermediaries who work with trainees. A particular focus is on the way the practices employed by the intermediaries help produce the employment and training outcomes purchased by the state. The first section of the chapter focuses upon the relationship between welfare reform in New Zealand and outsourcing. The second section is a review of the supporting documentation, publicity material, and programme evaluations of the MAS, YT, and Gateway, which shed light on how the various schemes work. Following this is interview data gathered in semistructured, face-to-face interviews which were conducted with 21 intermediaries working within these programmes. The impact of outcomes-based funding on their practices is explored. The final section summarises this chapter.

Welfare and Training Reform[2]

As faith in the potential of VET to solve problems associated with youth unemployment has waned, policy-makers in the United Kingdom and New Zealand have drawn inspiration from the United States, where the passing of The Personal Responsibility and Work Opportunity Reconciliation Act of 1996 dramatically changed the United States welfare system into one which requires work in exchange for time-limited assistance. Evidence suggests that in the United States the policies have yet to lift participants out of poverty (Fremstad, 2004) and they have been criticised for their dehumanising and conscriptive effects (Platt, 2003; Priven, 1998). However, on the back of an improving labour market, they have been very effective in reducing welfare rolls (Loprest, 1999; Shah et al., 2000; White, 1999). The United Kingdom equivalent for young people, the New Deal for Young People, has been in operation for a shorter period than its American cousin. Research suggests that although differences exist in the effectiveness of the various options (Bonjour et al., 2002; Dorsett, 2001), overall the New Deal for Young People has been very effective in reducing welfare rolls particularly amongst the long-term unemployed (Barrell and Genre, 1999; Mcllroy, 2000; Reenen, 2001). The New Zealand version of workfare has also been credited with reducing welfare rolls and the policy has been embraced by the Labour-led Coalition.

The Labour-led Coalition's perspective on reform of the welfare state can be encapsulated in the following formula: skill deficits and passive welfare systems = high rates of unemployment and welfare dependency. This formula has been applied in other nations, including Australia, the United States, the United Kingdom, Canada, and Continental Europe, where active welfare measures have been introduced. Although there are important differences between the strategies employed in these nations, a common underlying theme is that welfare systems need to promote labour market attachment. To effect this the Labour-led Coalition has developed 'work-tests' and outlined new work-related responsibilities which the unemployed must meet to qualify for income support. These responsibilities, or 'mutual responsibilities' as termed by the Labour-led Coalition, are outlined in individualised Job Seeker Agreements and those beneficiaries who do not comply with the agreement are sanctioned through a reduction in the level of state support.

The development of Job Seeker Agreements represents an attempt by the state to create a quasi-legal regulatory framework designed to encourage young people to adopt behaviours and attitudes that support the wage-labour relationship.[3] As the social network theorists show, these behaviours and attitudes were arguably effectively supported within families and the communities in which they lived. However, as shown throughout this book, the development of work-poor families and communities means that some young people do not have the social network capital required to facilitate their transitions into employment. The development of Job Seeker Agreements and their equivalent is an attempt to replace forms of social capital, which have been eroded by economic and social change, with quasi-legal relationships. The contracts are a form of institutional-based trust in which the unemployed agree to participate in activities that improve their employability.

From this perspective, Job Seeker Agreements can be seen as a technology of government designed to engage the unemployed in a process of identity re-formation by encouraging them to act on those 'attitudes, affects, conduct and dispositions that present a barrier to [them] ... returning to the labour market, and [that] alienate them from social networks and obligations' (Dean, 1995, p. 572). Acting on attitudes, affects, and other barriers to employment requires young people to adopt identities as wage workers, to develop a basic work ethic and to acquire the skills associated with the low-wage labour market such as attendance, punctuality, and respect for authority. In contrast to the past, where labour market attachment and work ethics were arguably more readily enforced through forms of family- and community-based social capital, the task of enforcing these aspects of the wage-labour relationship has been increasingly adopted by the state. This process is buttressed by coercion in the form of sanctions, such as reduced income, which are designed to force the unemployed to heed the state's wishes (Peck, 2000). To legitimate such measures the Labour-led Coalition has echoed the views of conservative social commentators who argue that passive welfare support has encouraged the development of dependency cultures in which staying on welfare has become a lifestyle choice (Mead, 1986).

As noted, the work-first approach has been credited with cutting welfare rolls and 'enforcing a vision of the work ethic commensurate with the realities of the (low-wage) labour market' (Peck, 2000, p. 76). Work-first welfare is seen by some within New Labour to be an effective supply-side measure designed to strengthen the economy by creating a culture of employability and increasing the 'pool of employable labour available' (Blunkett, 1999, p. 25). In an economic context characterised by increasing inequality and declining incomes for many workers, it is highly likely that by following rather than leading the labour market, work-first welfare systems will reproduce, if not strengthen existing inequalities through lowering wages (Peck and Theodore, 2000).

The Labour-led Coalition and Outsourcing

The Labour-led Coalition clearly supports outsourcing.[4] However, its use in social welfare-related areas was also actively promoted by the previous neoliberal administration. Harnessing the power of market forces to reform the delivery of social welfare-related services required a shift from the state as a direct provider of services to the unemployed, to that of purchaser of outcomes supplied by the public and private sector organisations which compete with one another for the right to deliver services. In work-focused welfare and training regimes such as those administered by the agency responsible for managing the welfare caseload ((Work and Income New Zealand (WINZ) and the Tertiary Education Commission (TEC)), 'best practice' means that services are delivered through personalised relationships developed between individual case-managers or trainers and their unemployed or at-risk 'clients'.

Outsourcing has been used for many years by governments to provide services such as refuse collection and road construction. However, its use in delivering social services is comparatively recent. Nevertheless, the central aim of outsourcing is to reform the work practices of those who deliver social welfare-related services and to shape the delivery of these so that they better meet the state's goals. This aim remains the same irrespective of the kind of service the state is purchasing. For example, in the United States, Kazis (1999) argues that performance measures built into federal funding for employment and training provide powerful incentives which shape the design and delivery of services. In this respect, an aim underpinning the 'New Deal' range of programmes in the United Kingdom was to the reform the public service through changing the culture of 'benefit claimants, employers and public servants' (Department of Social Security, 1998, p. 23). By clearly specifying performance targets and exposing providers to the discipline of the market, the Department of Social Security hopes to improve the quality of service provided, to encourage innovation and to force reform of workplace practices. The creation of competitive 'league tables' across the public sector, as proposed by the British Treasury, can be seen in a similar light (HM Treasury, 1999).

New Labour and the Regulation of Youth Work

Debate exists regarding the impact on youth workers of the introduction of performance targets. For some, the introduction of performance targets reflects a broader change in the way the state regulates relationships between itself and its citizens. Prior to the development of targets, contacts, and other neoliberal technologies of governance, the relationship between the state and its citizens was regulated through social democratic forms of governance. Accordingly, the state was a provider of services to groups of people and the performance outcomes of state sector workers were poorly specified. In the area of youth work, it was assumed that youth workers would work in the best interests of the state and the young people they served and that they had a relatively high level of discretion over the work undertaken. However, following the neoliberal critique of the efficiency of social democratic methods of service provision, state sector workers were seen as driven by self-interest and the services they offered subject to provider capture. To increase the effectiveness of the state, relationships between the state and providers of services has become governed by contracts and the outcomes tightly specified. In turn, the development of contractual relations has led to the development of new technocratic management systems in which interpersonal relationships are increasingly based on rules and regulations which support particular kinds of practice (Dean, 1995) rather than social capital in the form of a shared social ethic or consensus (Codd, 1998). The introduction of contractualism as a technology of governance can be seen as a form of manufactured uncertainty, in which the creation of risk is a deliberate strategy designed to increase the performance of public sector workers (Giddens, 1998). A result of this process is that the state then sponsors and finances particular practices (Dean, 1995). However, neoliberal funding methods do not always support the aims of policy-makers. For example, Barnett and Newberry (2002) argue that competitive tendering is not well suited for the management of areas of high uncertainty. In particular, they suggest that competitive tendering is ineffective where there is a need for coordination and cooperation between providers. The main reason for this is that outcomes-based funding can reduce the incentive for competing individuals and the agencies they work in to share information with each other and agencies. Thus, it can limit the production of social capital.

The use of performance measures in which the production of training outcomes is an important aspect of the Labour-led Coalition's approach and suggests that it has retained an element of its social democratic heritage. In addition, the Labour-led Coalition has invested more funding into training than the previous neoliberal administration. Nevertheless, unlike human capital approaches and the contrasting approach adopted by old Labour, in which training was somewhat removed from the labour market and did not emphasise entering work as an immediate goal, the Labour-led Coalition has emphasised an increase in those finding sustainable work efficiently as a key policy goal.

The literature shows that outsourcing is increasingly being used by governments to reform the practices of young people and those working with them. However, the impact of the new arrangements on those contracted by the state to deliver welfare-related services remains an area in need of detailed empirical investigation. Before continuing to examine this weakness by exploring the interview data gathered as part of this study, it is necessary to briefly describe the programmes explored in this chapter.

New Zealand's Main Youth Labour Market Interventions

Youth Training

Youth training (YT) is offered to young people aged 18 years or less with low levels of qualifications the chance to gain the skills necessary to obtain employment. The training is both job-specific, offering skills needed for particular industries, and generic, offering skills that can be applied across a range of industries. It is intended that all learning be credentialed and linked to the National Qualifications Framework. The class sizes are small so that all learners can receive individual attention from tutors. YT is delivered by Private Training Enterprises and other state and private sector providers who compete for the right to offer training, and the outcomes of the Programme are closely monitored by the TEC. The programme primarily focuses on obtaining employment and training outcomes, although variations in the precise mix of outcomes exists between courses. Courses funded by WINZ but managed by the TEC are usually shorter in duration and have higher employment outcomes.[5] In the year 2001, more than 12,500 people participated in the YT programme. Forty-four per cent of all learners who left the programme during 2001 obtained employment, whilst 24 per cent went on to further education and training. On average, each student was awarded 20 credits on the NQF. YT was delivered by 313 different providers, the vast bulk of which were Private Training Establishments (Skill New Zealand, 2001b).

A distinguishing feature of YT is that course attendance is one way in which young people can satisfy their obligations under the New Zealand version of workfare. Until recently, people aged 16 years or older could receive welfare payments and support was delivered through bureaucratic and impersonal means. However, changes introduced by the Labour-led Coalition mean that unemployed young people are only eligible to receive the Independent Youth Benefit[6] and support is no longer delivered through bureaucratic and impersonal means. Young people aged 16 and 17 years can receive an Independent Youth Benefit provided they can satisfy their case manager that they are actively looking for work or are attending a work-related training course of not less than 12 weeks duration. Like older people who receive the unemployment benefit, young unemployed people are assigned a case manager by WINZ, whose role is to help unemployed people find work as quickly as possible. Case managers work with the unemployed to identify and treat barriers to employment, for example, by organising a placement in a YT course. They also ensure that young people receive the correct amount of benefit. In addition, those who are deemed by the case manager to be 'work-ready' and not in need of training may be placed with work brokers, who liaise between the unemployed and employers to facilitate transitions into work. In this way, WINZ provides a system of labour exchange. The ability of young people to satisfy their obligations to the state by attending training courses means that, strictly speaking, New Zealand has yet to adopt a fully-fledged work-fare system.[7] Nevertheless, the way the Labour-led Coalition funds its training for unemployed indicates that the work-first approach has been highly influential.

The Modern Apprenticeship Scheme

The MAS is designed to provide young people who have basic school qualifications with training linked to the NQF. The old apprenticeship scheme had been dismantled by previous administrations, which held the view that it lacked flexibility and did not reflect the needs of dynamic workplaces. However, the notion of apprenticeship was deeply embedded in the community, where it continued to be seen as an important means of skill transmission and development. The Labour-led Coalition recognised the centrality of the notion of apprenticeship to the identities of a segment of young males and made modernised apprenticeships a cornerstone of its VET strategy. Unlike the old apprenticeship system, which was available in a relatively narrow range of occupations, the modern version of the scheme has been greatly expanded to include new occupational areas such as hospitality, office administration, public sector services, and sports turf management.

The MAS is administered by the TEC, which contracts the services of modern apprenticeship coordinators to broker apprenticeship opportunities and act as mentors to the apprentices and employers. The government is firmly committed to the concept and increased the number of apprentices from its initial trial of 500 to approximately 6,500 at the end of the 2004 financial year.

Gateway

Gateway is designed to enable schools to offer students access to structured workplace learning. Typically, students are placed on work experience and their learning is recognised through qualifications registered on the NQF. The Labour-led Coalition argues that the programme is designed to make learning relevant to all learners, not just those not achieving school qualifications. In 2003, 63 secondary schools offered the programme. However, the number is likely to expand as the government to attempts to offer it in all deciles 1 to 5 schools by 2007.[8] Through Gateway, structured workplace learning is offered to students in a wide range of occupations including hospitality, automotive, retail, tourism, engineering, and building.

A variety of methods have been used to fund Gateway. The current model is designed to closely tie funding to the number of students being placed into workplaces. This includes a fee-per-student placed component and a block grant determined by the size of a school's senior roll. Although it is not common, schools can elect to employ external contractors to place and manage Gateway students. As the programme is over subscribed, low decile schools compete, partly on the basis of price, for the right to deliver training. However, the government is keen to build capacity across the country and, like the other programmes evaluated in this chapter, a range of factors is considered when selecting providers.

Supporting Documentation, Publicity Material and Programme Evaluations

The three programmes have been credited with facilitating transitions into employment. How do they achieve this? Evidence in the supporting documentation, publicity material and programme evaluations suggests the use of intermediaries is critically important in securing the outcomes purchased by the TEC and WINZ in all three programmes. The three programmes described above function in slightly different ways, target different groups of people and are slightly differently funded. Nevertheless, a theme common to each is the use of intermediaries, whose role is to facilitate school-to-work and welfare-to-work transitions. One way the intermediaries achieve this is by 'shortening the relational chains', thus overcoming weaknesses in the young job seekers' employment networks (Kazis, 1999, p. 2). For example, a recent evaluation of Gateway, completed by the TEC, reported that schools participating in the programme have 'adopted a range of approaches for establishing employer contacts and building relationships with employers' (Skill New Zealand, 2002, p. 10). The positive evaluation of the programme provided the Labour-led Coalition with justification to extend the scheme to include more schools. Similarly, an evaluation of MAS stressed the importance of the extensive employer networks that the apprenticeship coordinators had developed in achieving positive employment outcomes (Skill New Zealand, 2001a). Recently, Max Kerr, the TEC's Manager Tertiary Collaboration, identified the importance of employer networks in securing employment outcomes in the YT (and its equivalent for older people, the Training Opportunities Programmes). He argued:

> There is a long history of programmes such as training opportunities and youth training having a close connection to workplaces. This is a direct consequence of the policy which judges success primarily on the achievement of positive destinations for learners – either work or further training – after they have completed their time on the programme. These destinational outcomes encourage tutors and providers to develop links with businesses, increasing the chances that the training offered is producing the skills that employers need … [P]artly this is astute recognition … that spending time in workplaces as trainees gives them a foot in the door, opening access to contacts and networks that may, and often do, lead directly to jobs. (Kerr, 2002, p. 10)

As well as linking young people with employers, there is evidence in the supporting documentation, publicity material, and programme evaluations suggesting that intermediaries working in these three programmes fulfil a second function. That is, they select new recruits on behalf of employers. As social network theorists clearly document, the value of the social network capital depends upon the value of the resource accessed. In the programmes evaluated here, the value of the resource depends upon the quality of the young people supplied to employers by intermediaries. For example, in a formative evaluation of the MAS, coordinators reported that it is important to select new recruits who best fitted the needs of employers and who were most likely to successfully complete the formal assessments (Skill New Zealand, 2001a). Trainees were selected according to these criteria as it improved the reputation of the coordinators as providers of 'work-ready' young people. Similarly, in the Interim Evaluation of Gateway, schools reported that they:

> [w]ere mindful of the need to select students who will not jeopardise the work placement by their poor behaviour or attitude. Therefore selection criteria

(formal and informal) used by the school include such things as attendance, behaviour, motivation, reliability and commitment to keep up with school studies (Skill New Zealand, 2001a, p. 13)

There is evidence in all three programmes that intermediaries fulfil a third function – workforce development or training. This aspect is apparent through ensuring that all programmes are linked to formal training which is linked to the NQF. Intermediaries in Gateway and the MAS also increase the likelihood that trainees obtain qualifications by mentoring young people and working with employers to ensure that the learning completed is credentialised (Skill New Zealand, 2001a).

Finally, there is evidence of a fourth function fulfilled by the intermediaries which ensures that they can produce the training and employment outcomes demanded by the state. That is, they work hard to make sure the young people placed into employment remain there and complete the training by offering post-placement support. It the case of the MAS, post-placement support is an important aspect of the design and is intended to reduce any disruption employers might experience in employing young people. In practice, this means reducing the cost of complying with the associated programme regulations and managing the behaviour of the trainees to ensure they do not violate the codes of practice that exist in workplaces. The TEC's Max Kerr, states that through the 'practical helping hand' offered by the brokers/coordinators aims to 'deal with hassle [associated with employing and training young people], if necessary by taking over the paperwork, and always being readily accessible for any fire-fighting that may be required' (Kerr, 2002, p. 12). Similarly, in YT, post-placement support is sometimes necessary to ensure that trainees remain in employment until the census date (two months after completing training), at which point the outcome measures are taken. Support of the trainees typically ceases at this point and, although relatively little is known about the outcomes beyond the census date, research into the longer-term impact of a TEC-funded programme for older unemployed people which employs a similar methodology (Training Opportunities), suggests just under 40 per cent of those placed into employment at the completion of their training were still employed 12 months later. Only half of these in employment were considered to be 'stable' (Skill New Zealand 1999b). In Gateway, post-placement support seems to be less important, although some coordinators reported a need to stay in close contact to monitor placements (Skill New Zealand, 2002).

In sum, from the evidence in the supporting documentation, publicity material and official programme evaluations, four aspects of the intermediaries' work seem to be important in securing the outcomes purchased by the state. These involve shortening relational ties, selecting suitable candidates, workforce development and post-placement support. Each of these aspects of the intermediaries' work is evaluated further in the following section where data gathered in the interviews are analysed.

Method

The participants were 21 tutors and coordinators working either as YT tutors, MAS brokers or Gateway coordinators in two major metropolitan centres in New Zealand. The participants were selected so that each programme was represented in approximately equal proportions. Emphasis was placed on recruiting participants who could comment on how their organisations structured their programmes and the practices they employed to produce the training outcomes demanded by the TEC.

A qualitative methodology was employed based on semistructured interviews. These interviews were designed to gather a range of data, including that pertaining to the role played by PTEs in securing employment for trainees. As part of the ethical considerations which underpinned this study, all participants were told that the purpose of the research was to explore the practices and strategies they used to secure the outcome demanded by the TEC. Participants were guaranteed anonymity, informed that they could withdraw from the study at any time without reason and told they could withdraw any data already provided. Pseudonyms are used to protect the identities of all participants and their organisations. The interviews were audiotaped and lasted between 30 and 60 minutes. As soon as practicable after interviewing, relevant data were transcribed. Relevant data were those that were considered central to the PTE meeting the training outcomes established by TEC. Once the data had been transcribed and analysed the transcripts, together with an early draft of the research report, were returned to the participants so that they could attest to their accuracy. No participant suggested that any changes be made. Data analysis involved identifying the key themes and experiences of each interviewee. To improve the readability of the data some text has been removed and some added: an ellipsis (…) indicates text that has been removed and square brackets ([text]) are used to indicate where text has been added. It is important to acknowledge that this study explores the impact of TEC's funding model on the practices of a small number of participants who live in particular locations. These factors should be borne in mind when the study's findings are generalised to other settings.

Making Networks in New Zealand

The literature shows that outsourcing and the use of service level agreements provides the state with a useful way to control the outcomes of policy by better controlling the practices of those who deliver welfare-related services. It was noted earlier in this chapter that an important means of achieving this control is through imposing the discipline of the market so that provider competition improves 'quality' and encourages the development of practices supportive of the state's goals. In the delivery of welfare-related services, 'best practice' tends to be the use of case management where intermediaries work directly on a one-to-one basis with young people. According to one critic of workfare in the United States and Canada, case management involves the use of micro-regulatory frameworks such as job seeker contracts. These are designed to contribute to the creation of new regulatory frameworks that encourage the unemployed to obtain work (Peck, 2001). As the previous section showed, 'best practice' also involves the use of intermediaries who shorten the relational ties between employers and job seekers. Earlier research by Guerin (1997) supports the thrust of the official evaluations of YT and supporting documentation by arguing that an important reason for the relative success of the PTEs compared to the polytechnics in helping young people find employment is that they are more deeply embedded in the social infrastructure. That is, they have closer links with employers and with industry.

Shortening Relational Ties

The need to produce positive training outcomes had created incentives for the intermediaries in all three programmes to develop links with employers. The main strategy used in the YT Programme and the MAS, where many of the programmes offered are industry specific, was to employ people from industry with existing networks with employers. In addition, such individuals had credibility and the knowledge necessary for making new networks. Thus, when recruiting new tutors and brokers to work in the YT and MAS, existing 'social capital' in the forms of industry networks and credibility were seen to be important.

> *John* (MAS): Firstly … [new brokers] have got to have a trade background. They've got to have industry experience and industry credibility. We don't want somebody from the polytechnic or somewhere like that because they are too institutionalised and too bureaucratic.

David (MAS): [John] is a local born person, bred in the industry around this area and knew everyone around this area before he was employed in it. I employ ... [brokers], who are already in the scene. The networks, well they don't even think of them as networks. It's more like, 'I know so and so'. Most of my guys do not actually appreciate the extensive networks they have got and how powerful they are.

Interviewer: Do you look for those [networks] when you're employing people?

John (MAS): Too right. We get them to talk about their knowledge of the industry and what their links have been. There's this one guy that we've got up north who had just worked in one workshop on a machine, but he made a point to know all the customers that came in. They were the biggest engineering workshop in the area. So all the engineering workshops around there knew him and he had huge credibility. So appointing him was a logical and sensible thing to do.

The view is that such individuals have a resource that can be utilised to help produce the training outcomes purchased by the TEC. For example, modern apprenticeship brokers and YT tutors commented that their industry experience and networks meant they already had credibility with employers who they could approach with a view to placing an apprentice or trainee into a workplace. Their credibility lies in their ability to maximise the likelihood of a successful placement through matching the attitudes and values of the young people they work with to the culture of particular workplaces. Facilitating the best possible match depends upon their knowledge of the needs of industry and their knowledge of the skills, attitudes, and attributes of the young people. Thus, when 'speaking for' young people, specific knowledge of the working conditions within particular organisations is important and increases the intermediaries' credibility with employers as a reliable source of suitably skilled labour. For example, in the MAS, brokers reported how, through assessing the culture of a workplace and the skills, attitudes and values of a young person, they could maximise the likelihood of a trainee fitting into the social relations of a given workplace and thus maximise the success of a placement.

Interviewer: So you know the industry, which is important. What about matching the industry with the individual?

John (MAS): You've got to do that with the young apprentice because they don't all fit. Like when I think of some of the ... workshops where there is a lot of mucking around going on. It still carries on in industry. If you put a young fellow in there who is very shy and quiet he doesn't have a hope in hell. It will just destroy him. So you've got to pick the right one. I've got one company like that. This young kid is in there, a 17-year-old, well built and he does not take nonsense from anybody … you've got to match them up.

David (MAS): You've got to read the culture of that company and that takes a number of visits to get the feel and understanding of what the true dynamics are there. Then you've got to spend time with the young kids, getting to know them and that's time and male intuition, which is far better than female intuition. … [It's] old instincts, being there and knowing what it is about. You couldn't bring a salesperson in from the outside because they wouldn't have that credibility, they wouldn't recognise the culture and they wouldn't get the match up right.

* * *

Interviewer: So tell me a bit more about how that matching process works?

Sally (MAS): Well it's building up a relationship with the employers really. I've been going around the countryside talking to nursery managers etc., just finding out what they are wanting. Some might want a young male or female or whatever. It's a matter of matching the right person.

Interviewer: So you have to have a good knowledge of the young people, do you?

Sally (MAS): Yes, you get a feel for what they are like. You sort of gauge it. There have been times when people drop out. It's a hit and miss thing sometimes …

Interviewer: Do you have any strategies for making that relationship and strengthening that relationship, maybe in the way that you match young people?

Sally (MAS): … I've never really thought of a strategy. It's just mainly getting a good feel for the industry … I've done an apprenticeship myself, so you get a feel for what people want.

Maintaining and building upon this credibility through expanding networks was a central aspect of the intermediaries' work in all three programmes. However, building networks was more difficult in Gateway. Unlike YT and the MAS, where the intermediaries tended to focus on one area of the youth labour market, in Gateway it was not possible to employ an intermediary who had all the experience and the networks needed to deal adequately with the broad range of interests held by the young people who participated in the programme. In effect, in Gateway where the intermediaries had industry networks they would exploit these and where they did not they had to make them after becoming a coordinator. Like the other intermediaries, the Gateway coordinators employed a number of strategies to make networks. For example, they would cold-call employers directly or phone them from the telephone directory. However, the intermediaries reported that these strategies were relatively ineffective. A more effective strategy used was to build the networks by accessing the networks of other Gateway coordinators, individuals within Industry Training Organisations, and individuals within PTEs. Reciprocity had developed such that the intermediaries operating within the same programme and between the three programmes came to realise that by working collaboratively they could expand individual networks by tapping into the networks of others.

> *Larissa* (Gateway): I went straight to … the PTE and I said, 'I have a student that would like to become a panel beater'. So they found the employer … I make sure the student gets there with all the right gear and they do the assessing [of the learning]. But perhaps at another time, next year, I could go straight to the panel beaters myself because I know them now … It's going to be easier next year because we are going to have more contacts. We network between the schools, talk, and give each other ideas.

> *Alan* (Gateway): I had two guys that said at the beginning of the year that they wanted to be chefs. It took me about seven weeks of contacting all the major hotels and other businesses. Just rang around and it took them a week to get back to me. The time was just huge. I then rang one place and they said, 'Yes, sure'. So I went down there and did all the paperwork only to have them two days before ring and say they couldn't take them. Then someone gave me the name of a place, I rang them, they said yes and it was done.

> *Interviewer*: … Tell me more about that.

> *Alan*: That was a modern apprenticeship [broker] contact and I rang her and said, 'I'm having a bit of difficulty here [finding a placement]. Can you think of anybody?' She said to me, 'I know such and such. Give them a ring because he is quite open to that'. So I rang the first one up and he said yes.

> *Interviewer*: So how did you present yourself?

> *Alan*: The usual thing, who I was, what I coordinate, the whole idea about Gateway and he said, 'Yes, that sounds just like me. I'm right into doing things like that for young people'.

> *Interviewer*: Did you mention that … [contact's] name?

Alan: Yes, I did. I said, 'So and so told me to give you a ring'. He said, 'Excellent, yes'.

The networks that existed between the intermediaries in this programme were a source of valuable social capital in that they increased the ability of intermediaries to meet their employment objectives. The networks were also important for securing training outcomes.

Petra (YT): I would say that networks are very important. But they aren't solely on the employment side. We also look at other training providers. There is a group called Hotel Training that do the hospitality side of things. When we ring them up they talk to us. There is no coercion. It's a training provider that we have a good relationship with and they are willing to consider that.

Interviewer: What makes a good relationship?

Petra: I think it is largely based on trust. We have a training provider here that gives us one or two trainees a year; we've got four at the moment. They gave us one that was really difficult after three days. The person who sent the trainee to us was around here apologising and saying that he didn't want this to affect our relationship. Of course it wouldn't. Had he damaged the relationship, he would have cut down the number of options he had. There was no way it was going to damage it because the relationship at that point was too long to have one thing wrong end it. If we got seven in a row we would have had a talk. This is too small a place to not have trust.

There is little point to the intermediaries developing and cultivating networks with employers if they do not have young people with the skills, abilities, and cultural backgrounds to 'speak for'. Thus, networking and the production of employable candidates is best seen as two sides of the same process.

Selecting Suitable Candidates and Workforce Development

Before they can 'speak for' young people, the intermediaries needed to be confident they are 'employable'. The intermediaries employ two main strategies to maximise the chances of providing employers with young people with the required skills who are employable and can help build reputation. Firstly, the intermediaries in all three schemes attempt to select young people they perceive already have the skills and attributes required to be successful in the workplace. Typically, this involves interviewing young people prior to offering them a placement in a workplace or in a training course. For example, in all three programmes intermediaries reported interviewing young people to assess their commitment to work and general suitability to respective programmes. A range of subjective signals was used to assess whether a young person was likely to achieve a successful training outcome. For example, intermediaries reported looking at their prior employment history and assessing their 'attitude' and state of dress before forming a judgement about the suitability of a young person for a programme. Often the intermediaries formed 'gut' reactions regarding the potential of young people to be successful in the workplace. Again industry-specific knowledge was important, as the intermediaries knew what employers were looking for by way of new recruits and whether particular aspects attitude, dress, or aesthetics, would be an asset or liability in the workplace. As one MAS broker commented, they looked for the three As: 'attitude, aptitude, and attendance'. This selection process is necessary as the intermediaries want to provide employers with the best possible worker, thus both maximising the chances of obtaining a positive training outcome and enhancing the possibility of repeat business.

Jenny (YT): Our biggest problem is that the outcome requirements are very high. So every time we see someone it is in the back of your mind, 'Can we get this person through the training?' We have to think like that otherwise we'll lose the courses and then we can't help anyone.

Interviewer: So do you have to be careful when you are recruiting the young people?

Sally (MAS): Yes, you do have to be careful because you don't want to annoy the employer. We've advertised [for apprentices] and had quite a lot of response, but only a small percentage of them will be suitable. So you don't want to just send anybody through ...

Interviewer: Why not?

Sally (MAS): It just breaks down the relationship [and leads to a] loss of credibility ...

Interviewer: So you said there is a proportion of people who are suitable. How do you identify those that are suitable?

Sally (MAS): It's more of an attitude that comes through at the interview. It is important to have people with reasonable communication skills, not necessarily academic though. Through their work history, the type of work they have done in the past. They might not have done horticulture. They may have done manual type labour.

John (MAS): If they've got a good attendance that says to us that they're going to turn up on the job and give it a go. The amount of kids the school system has rejected but you put them in a workshop and they just go through the roof. So it's not the actual school reports. It's more the between-the-line stuff about attitude and attendance.

Interviewer: So those are the kinds of judgements you make?

John (MAS): Right and we make those kinds of judgements all the time. But we do come unstuck at times. Some of these kids have absolutely brilliant academic records but their attitude stinks when they get out into the workplace.

Interviewer: So is that bad for business?

John (MAS): Of course that's bad for our business. We can be turned off by an employer who has a bad apprentice. I've got employers who swear by our system but have been let down two, three times by apprentices who started and decided it wasn't for them.

In the case of the MAS, where training was of relatively high status, recruiting suitable young people was comparatively easy. However, recent increases in youth employment were perceived to have reduced the quality of young people participating in the programme. This was perceived to have made the work of the tutors more difficult as the nature of the students entering YT changed, with trainees becoming more 'scruffy'. This created a dilemma for YT tutors who have found it difficult to maintain the numbers of young people needed in the courses to remain financially viable while continuing to produce 'work-ready' trainees. To accommodate what the tutors perceive to be the declining quality of trainees in their programmes and to counter the damaging impact that making a poor placement would have on the value of their social networks, the tutors reported denying some young people access to their networks. In such instances, the young people were told to find their own job.

Nadine (YT): There are sometimes where I say to the tutor, 'Do not recommend that person' and I'll say to the student, 'we could not recommend you. If you want work you'll have to go and find it yourself. We could not recommend you for employment in the industry you are currently training in because of your attitude or behaviour or whatever'. We are upfront with them about that and tell them what the issue is ... We've got a couple at the moment who have been through eight weeks [on the programme] and they are both on [behaviour] contracts but their behaviour is so bad.

Interviewer: What's your logic behind not recommending them?

Nadine: That they would muck it up.

Interviewer: That would hurt your reputation?

Nadine: Absolutely because anyone that we recommend, it comes back on us and it has happened many times [employers say], 'I'll never come back to you again because of last time'. Some employers are more reasonable than that but some aren't. The tutors work very hard to have a good reputation in industry so they can keep working with those people and one student can blow it. I mean we don't do that with many students but with these two students at the moment I have told them that there is no way we would recommend them unless their behaviour changes dramatically. I mean if they want to go and find work that's fine, but I would not let the tutor put her name behind it.

Although selecting individuals perceived to have the skills and qualities needed to be successful in the workplace was their preferred course of action, intermediaries reported that meeting the performance outcomes stipulated by the TEC required them to identify and treat barriers to employment. In this context, the declining quality of new recruits was seen as problematic as it increased the level of remedial action needed to make a young person employable. While it was not unusual for young people to require training to improve their employability, the problem was exacerbated in instances where courses were low on numbers and providers were forced to take all-comers.

Peck (2001) states that improving employability involves the use of strategies that remedy the social 'pathologies' restricting it. The data supports this and shows that intermediaries target and attempt to treat behaviours that reduce an individual's employability. Typically 'best practice' was a form of social work in which the intermediaries worked intensively with trainees to promote pro-work attitudes and values (Eardley, 1997). In YT the social work aspect of the intermediaries' work was very important prior to employment. In this programme, the intermediaries reported working with young people to identify and treat barriers to employment. In some settings, the intermediaries reported using peer pressure to control the behaviour of young people who did not adhere to accepted norms of behaviour in the workplace.

Interviewer: So do you try and match the teaching day to the work site?

Simon (YT): Yeah, definitely. I'm really strict about time. I think time is really important. And we sit down and have a yarn for 10 minutes when we get in the classroom but you're in my classroom on time because that's what the boss expects. If they don't phone when they're not coming in then they'll get a wind-up. I'll ... use peer pressure [to change the behaviour of young people] such as saying 'We're not going out this afternoon [to play sport] because Matt didn't bother to call me yesterday'. That might be something I've learnt from a team environment, but it works. I know it may seem a bit harsh at times but it puts the pressure on them and after a day everyone's forgotten about it, but they'll usually phone in the future. There are some dirty tactics I find I use too, but I'm not doing them maliciously, I'm doing them more for the benefit of the kid more than anything.

The intermediaries reported utilising networks to increase the chances of obtaining a successful outcome through better controlling the practices of the young people in other ways. The human capital approach typically controls behaviour through exchanging consent and attention to studies for educational credentials that hold the promise of employment, higher incomes, and higher status. In the YT programme the approach is quite different. In cases where young people have been compelled to attend training by WINZ, the intermediaries report securing consent through calling on the support of case managers who have the power to withdraw the unemployment benefit in instances where trainees do not act appropriately. In this respect, the data speak of the creation of webs through which different agencies monitor and attempt to police and the behaviour of youth.

> *Sue*: The other side of it is that we also work very closely with the [WINZ] case managers. For instance, if we have a student that we're having some problems with, we may talk to the case manager and get the case manager down here to have a meeting. Sometimes the student will realise that their number is up and they will knuckle down, settle down, and get a job.
>
> *Interviewer*: So what does the case manager do?
>
> *Jan*: Well there was a student that had a meeting with the case manager, tutor, and myself, and we said, 'these conversations have gone on for so long and nothing has really happened. This is the end of the line'. The case manager said that he would be going to army camp for six weeks if he didn't start to behave. That was his option, start to behave or that's where he was going.
>
> *Interviewer*: So the case manager told him to pull his head in?
>
> *Jan*: Absolutely. I said to him that, 'The whole class cannot be disrupted because of one person. It had gone on long enough. This is your last chance. I'm putting you on a contract but don't push me into a corner, don't make me withdraw you because I don't want to' ...
>
> *Sue*: We had another one that did a warehousing course, passed it, Kay got the student into workplace learning and after two weeks the employer rang up and said that he couldn't have him any more because he was dangerous. Well he's done two courses, I consulted with the case manager, the case manager has

got him booked into Limited Service Volunteers [the army] for August and if he doesn't go then he won't have a job. So the pressure is on.

Interviewer: How can the case manager make him go into the army?

Sue: Because they are providing the benefit.

Jan: He cannot live without the money. He has no ability to live without the money ... The minute that they realise they are at the end with nowhere else to go they start to pull themselves together.

The ability of WINZ to increase the pressure placed upon young people to comply was useful in increasing the PTE's ability to produce the outcomes desired by the state. However, the reciprocity that had developed between PTE intermediaries and WINZ was a source of tension, as the PTE intermediaries sometimes felt compelled to take all trainees from WINZ even though they felt the young person would require a good deal of attention before becoming a positive outcome. However, the PTE intermediaries tended to accept the unemployed young people into the courses as they did not want to damage the relationships with WINZ case managers, who are also an important source of trainees, especially when course numbers were low.

Sue: The other course we have is a Youth Warehouse, which took quite a long time to get going, we couldn't get ... [the trainees] in, but we have 10 now.

Interviewer: How did you recruit them?

Jan: Through case managers and schools. Kay goes around to all the schools looking for students ...

Interviewer: How much does gut feeling matter when you meet someone?

Sue: Quite a lot, but if the case manager requests that we take someone then you just have to do it. There is an obligation.

Interviewer: But it's not contractual?

Jan: No, but there is an expectation from TEC that we will give priority to those recommended by our case managers and the majority of ours are now.

Interviewer: How did you become aware of that obligation?

Jan: There's just an expectation.

The role intermediaries play in the process of making social network by, for example, matching young workers to suitable workplaces by assessing their cultural backgrounds and genders, brings in an additional point highlighted in the data; that is the role of qualifications in the recruitment process. Although the Labour-led government actively promote the training gospel in which obtaining qualifications is vitally important to securing employment, the data suggest that although the national qualifications framework (see Chapter 5) provided a basis for the content of the training offered, the qualifications obtained by the students do not matter greatly to securing employment outcomes. It seems employers have greater faith in the word of an intermediary that a young person has the skills needed to be effective in the workplace than in institutional-based forms of trust.

> *Jeremy* (YT): I was getting a lot of young guys work through my contacts. So a lot of my outcomes were coming from 'who you know' more than anything. My mates were looking for young apprentices and I was looking for young guys who would come to me for six months [for training] …
>
> *Interviewer*: … Are they [your building contacts] interested at all in the qualifications that the young people have secured?
>
> *Jeremy*: Certainly if they've picked up a few trade skills it is a bonus.
>
> *Interviewer*: Do they say let's look at … a person's CV and see what … they've got by way of unit standards?
>
> *Jeremy*: No. It's normally a reference, either from myself or someone else that I find gets people jobs in the trade industry.
>
> *Interviewer*: So they might just ask, 'What's he like with a hammer?'
>
> *Jeremy*: More likely to ask, 'Does he turn up at 8 o'clock everyday?' … They want them there at eight o'clock and they want them sitting down at 10 o'clock for a quarter of an hour.

Post-placement Support

To varying degrees, a feature of each of the programmes is a belief that simply placing an individual into work is not sufficient to ensure successful long-term outcomes and effective case management by intermediaries needs to continue long after the initial placement has been made (Kazis, 1999). In the YT programme, post-placement support is a vital aspect of the intermediaries' work until the point at which outcomes are measured (two months after completion of the course). Indeed, the intermediaries reported going to great lengths in some instances to ensure that the young people who participated in the courses remained in the placement until the outcome measures were taken by the TEC. Tutors reported working with the employers and the young people to ensure a successful outcome. When asked about the need to have an individual in employment at the census date and the strategies used to maximise the chances a young person became a positive outcome, a YT tutor responded,

> *Sam* (YT): That's why you have to have good follow up systems. Contact [the employer and trainee], ring around. You've got to make [employment] work. Regularly, every week, or two weeks, depending on the person. If you are quite comfortable with them then you won't ring as often.

Post-placement support is a central feature of the MAS. Indeed, the scheme is specifically designed to provide this support and thus reduce the 'hassle' of employing apprentices throughout the duration of their training. Taking away the hassle of employing young people required the MAS to undertake a diverse range of tasks. At a minimum, it involved helping employers and the apprentices fill in the required paperwork and ensuring the young person kept up with studies. However, post-placement support also involved a considerable amount of mentoring and assistance from the intermediaries to ensure the maintenance of the employment relationship. When asked about what post-placement support was offered, a MAS broker responded as follows.

> *John* (MAS): You're really a bit of a social worker ... You sort out all sorts of problems. I had one yesterday, this kid rang up and said, 'I've lost my licence. What do I do?' A normal employer doesn't have that problem.

> *Interviewer*: Why not?

> *John*: Because he doesn't care whether the kid's got his licence or not, but I care enough to say to the kid, 'Right we've got to get you to Polytechnic for your evening class and make sure you turn up for work'. I go through the whole rigmarole. I say, 'How has this all been arranged?' 'Well my sister is going to take me to polytechnic and my Mum is going to drop me off at work. It's only for three months'. So I go through the whole system and make sure that his apprenticeship is going to carry on.

> *David* (MAS): There's that intimacy factor that the coordinators have. I've been with coordinators, I'm on the road with them all the time, when a kid's rung up and said that he's got a little drunk and the cops have picked him up. Who's the first person he rings? Not Mum, not Dad, not his employer, but the coordinator. Another one, 'My girlfriend's giving me a hard time'. All of these issues that a traditional employer doesn't get and, on some level, the coordinator does become like a Father to these kids ...

David: Now John was with a young apprentice yesterday. If we were a traditional employer with a traditional manager that kid would have been fired yesterday. He perseveres with them against all the odds, you would argue from a rational perspective. I know this guy pretty well and that young guy will get there because John will be gently kicking his butt the whole way through his apprenticeship. I know that's going to be a success story that wouldn't have been. If it hadn't been for John's perseverance with this young guy he would have been unemployed twelve months ago.

Controlling the Tutors' Work

The data presented above suggests that outsourcing is an effective method of controlling the practices of those working with young people. In the main, the use of employment outcomes as a performance measure has led those who work with young people to deliver the outcomes desired by the state. The literature suggests that outsourcing has introduced forms of Taylorism into youth work and community service organisations. The data shows that there is little recognition for those who work with young people and want to pursue aims broader than simply facilitating employment and enhancing training. Nevertheless, the funding model allows considerable scope for the providers to develop their own approach to securing the outcomes purchased by the state. Intermediaries reported using a wide range of strategies to keep the young people focused on the aims of the course. A strength of the approach is that it did not preclude the adoption of strategies typically associated with youth work, for example, building relationships with young people through one-to-one mentoring. However, the compulsive aspect of the programmes and the formal nature of the learning undertaken means that the programmes evaluated cannot be considered to be youth work (Smith, 2002). In this respect, it is reasonable to argue that outsourcing has introduced forms of Taylorism into youth work that were not present in earlier forms of service delivery. Nevertheless, in the MAS this was not problematic for the intermediaries as they had strong faith in the value of apprenticeship training and had been employed specifically to undertake this task. Similarly, for the interviewees who worked for PTEs this was generally not problematic as they had been employed specifically to achieve positive employment outcomes and few, if any, had backgrounds in social work. As a result, they did not feel their practices violated the values upon which their organisations were founded. Thus, most interviewees did not question the politics that underpinned their practices. They were employed for a particular purpose and their livelihoods depend upon placing young people into employment and further training. Indeed, although there was some discomfort with the overwhelming focus on employment, many supported the basic thrust of active welfare systems and felt that young people had lost sight of the value of being in paid employment.

> *Jan* (YT): There is no work ethic there at all. They have no idea. [One young person said], 'I don't really want to work. I just want to play some music and do this or that'. I said, 'Get real. We're all paying taxes'. He said, 'But I'm not earning any money'. I said, 'Excuse me. You're getting paid every week because we all work to get that for you'. He said, 'Oh, okay'. That's what their belief is and we've seen third and sometimes fourth generation unemployed who have never seen someone in their house get up and go to work. They don't have that work ethic because they've never seen it. There is no education there, which we all learn naturally because we watch it everyday. They have learnt some things but it is not what society would like them to learn.

In contrast, interviewees who worked for community service organisations, which have a broader mission than simply placing young people into work, were less comfortable with the focus on employment outcomes. For example, concern was expressed by intermediaries working for community service organisations who were delivering YT that improvements to the trainees' lives were not properly recognised and that with some young people moving directly into employment was not possible nor desirable.

> *Rebecca* (YT): I think that the outcomes model is a huge pressure. I don't think that it is necessarily a bad pressure because we are here to do a service to the kids in a variety of ways. We are here to help improve their lives and with issues but we also need to help them get into a career pathway. I think the dilemma is that it takes some people a long time to get to that decision point. Especially because we are the first step on the ladder there is pressure to pump them into something that might be inappropriate. It might be inappropriate for them to go away and spend six months or a year doing nothing for them to actually think, 'What I did there was good. Now I am making the right decision'. I do believe in readiness and I think very strongly that the outcomes model does pressure you into saying, 'Where are you going? What are you going to do? Come on we've got to get you something'. People have [also] been saying that … [the trainees] get a job that may only last for three months or six months. Then where are they? They are back on the streets again. The whole psyche is, 'Get a job. Get a job' and not, 'Hey maybe I could get a job in two years. What am I going to do before that?'

For community service organisations participation in YT was more commonly simply an aspect of the broader mission and these workers tended to see YT as a means of obtaining financial support for their broader work with young people. Of course outcomes were critically important for future funding, but their organisation's mission always informed their practice. For example, one PTE, which is based in a youth organisation, tried to take all young people who applied in the belief they could help all-comers.

> *Paula* (YT): We have a community-focused mission. So bottom line, we accept everyone that we can. I'm aware that other providers have entry criteria and will turn people away but we will accept everyone and work with them the best we can. That does affect our outcomes at the end of the course because often we get the low motivation, low social skills, 'low foundation' type people.
>
> *Interviewer*: Do you think there is tension between your mission and the aims of the TEC?
>
> *Paula*: I wouldn't say tension. It's probably a point of difference, which is understandable. One of the TEC's strategies is to get young people into employment or further training, so it is reasonable for them to want to do that. Here we are looking more at the holistic person, the body, mind and soul, rather than just the mind … If we could get funding from another avenue we would still continue to do the programmes. I don't think we have to compromise, just work a lot harder. Rather than allowing students to develop at their own natural pace we have to speed some things up for them. Like encourage them into a job or another course rather than say, 'I know you have an issue at home. We need to find you a flat'. It's is more focus on the TEC outcomes rather than what the student needs for themselves. There is a sacrifice of the youth work approach.

Conclusion

The data presented in this chapter show that the creation of social networks comprises an important aspect of the intermediaries who work in the three main labour market interventions to improve transitions into employment. In the making of networks, an important aspect of the intermediaries' work is the way they work to supply personnel or 'products' which employers can use. However, given the difficulties and the expense of reconfiguring the identities of some young people such that they are productive in the workplace, outcome-based funding always offers financial encouragement to intermediaries to recruit those young people who they perceive present the fewest barriers to employment. Thus, new forms of selection have been introduced.

When selecting trainees and placing them into work, the intermediaries draw upon their industry experience by addressing those skills, qualities, and attitudes necessary to ensure the best possible match. Intermediaries undertake these practices as they have proved to be the most efficient and profitable way to produce the outcomes purchased by the state. However, in the YT programme a lack of supply of young people meant that selecting the most suitable recruits was not always possible and the intermediaries reported feeling under pressure to take a young person even though they knew they would have difficulty producing an employment outcome. Where young people lacked the skills, qualities and attitudes necessary to be successful in the workplace, the intermediaries in YT reported devoting considerable effort to reconfiguring the identities of the trainees to become supportive of the wage-labour relationship. This primarily involves focusing on rectifying 'treating' the attitudes and behaviours held by young people so that they develop pro-work identities and values. Achieving this change required a good deal of one-to-one support over the duration of the full-time training courses, which typically last three months. In the MAS and YT, and to a lesser extent in Gateway, the intermediaries also reported devoting a good deal of attention to post-placement support. This support was needed to ensure the young people were performing in the workplace (in all three programmes) and completing their study (in the case of the MAS).

Finally, although the intermediaries preferred to secure their own trainees' employment and training placements, they worked closely with other providers to improve their own outcomes. Thus, there is evidence of trust developing between competing providers.

Notes

1   The YT Programme is typically offered by providers that also offer the Training Opportunities Programme. The Training Opportunities Programme operates in the same way as the YT Programme but it targets learners aged 18 or older. Until recently, all learners participated in one training programme. However, in order to improve the delivery of services policy-makers decided to separate younger and older learners.

2   This section and some of the arguments presented in the following sections draw upon Strathdee (2004).

3   More recently, the Labour-led Coalition has extended its work-first focus through introducing the 'Job Jolt' range of policies. The Job Jolt is designed to send a clear signal to the unemployed that they have an obligation to be available for work and be actively engaging in activities leading to employment. A range of measures has been introduced, including permitting case managers to 'breach' welfare beneficiaries who move to areas

of the country designated as being of low employment, extending active case management to older workers 55–59 years; and the contracting of employment specialists to work on a one-to-one basis with long term unemployed (eight years or more).

4   Although work-first welfare, outsourcing and contractualism have a neoliberal and conservative heritage, the Labour-led Coalition claims not to support the vision of the previous conservative administration. For example, the current government appears to be more concerned about inequality than the previous administration and aims to create employment that is sustainable and of high quality. An expression of this was the desire to see the YT and Training Opportunities Programmes produce sustainable employment. However, to date little, if any, progress appears to have been made towards realising this goal.

5   The Department of Work and Income offers some in-house training for unemployed people, such as job-search skill development, motivational training, and curriculum vitae writing workshops. However, more substantial training is available for unemployed people who have left school with low levels of qualification, such as attending courses managed by the TEC and provided by Private Training Enterprises.

6   In New Zealand, young people aged 18 years or less are not eligible to receive any unemployment benefit unless they are living with a partner and have children to support.

7   For example, in the United States, the funds authorised by Congress are specifically designed for work-related activities that can move those on welfare into long-term, unsubsidised employment. They cannot be used for stand alone, pre-employment job education or training.

8   All schools are classified on a scale of 1 to 10 depending on the level of disadvantage. A complex formula is used to calculate a school's decile. Decile one schools are the 10 per cent of schools with the highest proportion of students from low socioeconomic communities whilst decile 10 schools are the 10 per cent of schools with the lowest proportion of such students.

Chapter 7

Making Social Networks in England

The previous chapter focused on labour market intervention in New Zealand. The focus in this chapter shifts to England, where New Labour, like the Labour-led Coalition, is keen to facilitate transitions into employment and training. A key element in New Labour's strategy is the introduction of the Connexions Service and the creation of a new youth worker known as a Personal Advisor (PA). These comprise a 'front line' of support for young people. Connexions aims to facilitate learning and employment by giving young people aged between 13 and 19 years the advice and support needed to make transitions into training and employment. For those with disabilities and learning difficulties, the service is available until the age of 25.

Connexions is a unique service – there are no similar programmes in operation worldwide – supported by substantial funding. For instance, in the 2003–2004 financial year approximately £513 million was allocated to support the service. The funding comes from three main sources: the old careers service, which was funded by the DfES through its contracts with careers advice companies; the Local Education Authorities from their youth services budgets; and newly allocated funds. The funds are distributed according to a complex formula that recognises local needs. Areas of high need receive more per young person than areas of low need (Department for Education and Skills, 2002b).

Closely related to Connexions is the introduction of a new training programme for young people who need additional support to guide them into mainstream training and employment, known as Entry to Employment (E2E). Whilst Connexions and E2E are separate programmes, there exists a close relationship between them as PAs enhance personal performance by referring young people to E2E. Essentially, E2E providers work with those young people who require more intensive assistance by offering training and organising work experience.

This chapter contends that the Connexions Service and E2E are attempts to provide a solution to disruption by remaking social networks. This contention is supported by the qualitative data gathered in semistructured telephone interviews with 10 PAs and 10 E2E tutors. The first two sections of the chapter detail the structure and aims of the Connexions Service and the E2E programme. The third briefly reviews New Labour's visions for youth work. The fourth draws on data to identify the practices which PAs and E2E tutors believe aid them in producing the training and employment outcomes needed to meet their performance targets. The final section summarises this chapter.

The Connexions Strategy and Entry to Employment Programme

The origins of the Connexions Service go back to a series of influential reports produced by the Social Exclusion Unit, which was established in 1997 shortly after New Labour came to power. In one of these, 'Bridging the Gap', some young people's attitudes, values, and beliefs were identified as a major cause of social exclusion. New Labour successfully argued that more could be done to prevent these developing and it was decided that greater cooperation and coordination between providers of services to youth would increase the impact of state investment (Social Exclusion Unit, 1999). Connexions was born from this vision and is a so-called 'joined up' strategy. It is designed to provide better coordination of a range of social and educational services which have, to date, individually attempted to address issues facing those socially excluded. Of central importance is the creation of PAs, who work as part of multi-agency teams to coordinate service delivery to young people across numerous agencies, including schools, employers, youth justice services, and drug action teams. Ultimately, the PAs are responsible for the service young people receive and must ensure that they get the support they need to make successful transitions into employment or training.

It is possible to view this strategy as not being new, as it primarily involves the better coordination of existing services. However, creating a web or network of provision to better coordinate existing services prevents young people from slipping through the cracks or being passed from agency to agency and thus not receiving the support they need. The stated purpose is to provide this service to all young people aged between 13 and 19 years and older in specified circumstances. However, clearly politicians will look most closely at the impact of the service on those not in employment, education or training (NEET), with a reduction of the number of such young people being a key indicator of service effectiveness (Twigg, 2002).

Connexions is underpinned by the belief that although VET systems are well-developed and provide routes into employment, some young people will fail to take advantage of the opportunities offered because they are insufficiently embedded in an appropriate social infrastructure. For instance, they may lack quality information about employment and training opportunities and may generally lack access to forms of social capital that are required to make effective transitions into employment. In addition, they may lack 'employability' skills or have personal issues that require treatment prior to commencing mainstream training or obtaining employment. In this latter context, it is the role of the PAs to ensure that young people receive counselling or other services necessary to make effective transitions. Connexions is also designed to provide support to parents who want their children to enter work or training but who may not be able to provide the information necessary to enable them to make good decisions. Thus, a role of Connexions is to '... reinforce and underpin the informal network of support systems which exist in the family, neighbourhoods and the wider community including support in schools and colleges, and through teenagers' own peer groups' (Department for Education and Skills, 2000a, p. 3). Where such support systems do not support the state's goals, Connexions may be seen as an attempt to liberate young people from the forms of social capital that present barriers to participation in training and employment. It is an attempt to replace systems which no longer effectively regulate transitions into work with state-backed intermediaries which create new ladders of opportunity in order to break the cycle of non-participation and low academic achievement.

Due to the recency of Connexions and E2E, few empirical evaluations regarding their ability to create this infrastructure have been completed and it is too soon to assess any longer term impact properly. Nevertheless, by drawing on the research that has been completed – the DfES evaluations and the data gathered from interviews with PAs and E2E tutors – a reasonable picture of practice can be developed. However, prior to exploring this and raising some critical questions about the strategy, it is necessary to briefly describe Connexions' structure and its relationship to E2E.

The Structure of the Connexions Service

Although the basic idea underpinning the Connexions Strategy is straightforward, the sheer scope and the number of different agencies brought together to create the webs of service delivery complicate the structure. The Connexions Strategy has four key themes:

- developing a flexible curriculum that engages different young people and leads to relevant, sought-after qualifications;

- ensuring high quality provision in school sixth forms, further education colleges and work-based training;
- targeting financial support for those in learning;
- providing outreach, information, advice, support and guidance, through a range of programmes including the new Connexions Service (Department for Education and Employment, 2002, p. 4).

In addition, the strategy is designed to achieve the following aims:

- raising aspirations – setting high expectations for every individual;
- meeting individual need – and overcoming barriers to learning;
- taking account of the views of young people – individually and collectively, as the new service is developed and as it is operated locally;
- inclusion – by keeping young people in mainstream education and training and preventing them moving to the margins of their community;
- partnership – agencies collaborating to achieve more for young people, parents and communities than agencies working in isolation;
- community involvement and neighbourhood renewal – through the involvement of community mentors and through personal advisors brokering access to local welfare provision, health, arts, sport and guidance networks;
- extending opportunity and equality of opportunity – raising participation and achievement levels for all young people, influencing the availability, suitability and quality of provision, and raising awareness of opportunities;
- evidence-based practice – ensuring that new interventions are based on rigorous research and evaluation into 'what works' (Department for Education and Skills, 2000b, p. 11).

To achieve these aims the Connexions Partnerships have been formed in distinct geographical areas. These have been structured according to three models: direct delivery, subcontracting or lead body arrangement. In the direct delivery model, Connexion Partnerships have been formed through career companies or the merging of career companies and deliver the services directly to youth. In the subcontracting model, the Connexion Partnerships are newly-formed companies that deliver services directly subcontracting to other providers. In the lead body model, Connexion Partnerships utilise a third party to complete the major operational functions.

In the initial roll out of the service, the delivery of Connexions was not subject to a fully contestable tendering process. However, where services are subcontracted by Connexions Partnerships, a competitive tendering process is mandatory (Department for Education and Employment, 2000). The specification of outcomes makes the move to a fully contestable model possible in the future. Nevertheless, regardless of the funding method, reaching target outcomes is critical and is likely to have an important impact on the practices of those working in the strategy.

The strategy is delivered through three main, inter-related components: the Connexions Service, Connexions Direct, and the Connexions Card. The Connexions Service provides a network of PAs who provide outreach, information, advice, support, and guidance to young people. As noted, the PAs are responsible for ensuring that young people get the 'joined up' support they need and do not get passed from agency to agency. PAs have been recruited from a range of existing youth service agencies, voluntary and community organisations, and, in particular, the established career companies. However, many are newly recruited and it is estimated that approximately 15,000 PAs will be needed to provide a universal service throughout England. Broadly speaking, PAs can be classified according to the type of work they do. The first type provides general career advice to a large number of students, whilst the second type provides intensive assistance to those that need it. Some Partnerships are experimenting with a third type of PA, who works mainly with those hardest to help. The service is also diversely delivered, with the creation of 'one-stop shops' which bring together a range of services in locations and at times convenient to young people.

Connexions Direct is a new call centre and web-based system offering information, guidance and advice to young people. It has a free telephone line service that allows young people to communicate with PAs via telephone, email and a private chat room. Connexions Direct intends to provide guidance to young people at times when they need it and thus augments the work of the PA by extending the hours during which advice can be delivered and expanding the mode of service delivery.

Whilst the PAs provide advice and mentoring to young people to aid smooth transitions, the Connexions Card offers incentives for young people to remain in education and training. In part this is being achieved by allowing young people to collect reward points for engaging in learning, work-based training, and voluntary activities. The Connexions Card contains an electronic chip that records the points accrued by each young person for engaging in behaviour the state endeavours to encourage. For instance, the card can be used to electronically record attendance at school and other activities. Reward points can be exchanged for a range of free goods and services advertised on the Connexions website. In addition, the card can be used for discounts and special offers from registered outlets, businesses, and on public transport.

New Labour has also introduced a new allowance for those aged 16 to 19 years, known as the Educational Maintenance Allowance (EMA). The allowance is intended to encourage young people to stay on in education and training beyond Year 11 and to bind them to their learning agreements with their training provider. The allowance is means tested, but some young people may earn up to £30 a week and receive a bonus of £100 per term for abiding by their training agreements. Although the EMA and the Connexions Card contribute to New Labour's aims by increasing the incentive to learn, the PAs are at the heart of the service.

As noted, the service is promoted as being available to all young people and particularly targeted at those NEET. In practice, three levels of provision are identified. The policy documentation states that the majority of young people at level one, approximately 60 per cent, ought to make useful decisions by accessing advice about career and training options through Connexions Direct. Level two young people, approximately 30 to 40 per cent, or those 'at risk' of underachieving or disengaging from education and training and those with barriers to learning such as learning difficulties or disabilities, are deemed to require more support. This will come in the form of more intensive assistance from PAs to ensure that these young people get the support they need from other agencies. Finally, level three young people, approximately 10 per cent, are thought to face severe and complex barriers to participation. PAs act as brokers to provide the specialist support required, whether from professionals working in education, health, drugs, housing, criminal justice or other social services. PAs undertake a range of tasks in supporting youth to gain employment and engage in training. At a basic level, this involves identifying and overcoming barriers that may prevent young people obtaining employment or embarking in mainstream training. In addition, PAs work with employers to develop strategies aimed at filling vacancies, including brokering employment relationships and organising suitable training for new and existing young employees who do not hold a level two qualification.

The development of Connexions has major implications for existing agencies. This is not only in terms of the balance and focus of their work but also in terms of the interactions and working practices that take place within and between these agencies.

Entry to Employment

As noted, an important source of the PAs' outcomes is the E2E programme. E2E is offered nationally through almost 600 providers contracted to the Learning and Skills Council. The stated aim of E2E is to provide young people who encounter minor barriers to employment with the assistance they need to make transitions into work or mainstream training. The extent of participation is based on the recognition that young people differ in the amount of attention needed to become employable, therefore attendance may be short- or long-term. The majority of young people attend E2E between 16 to 40 hours per week and receive an allowance of £40. Young people in E2E are typically offered training and work experience with the hope of this leading to subsequent employment and training, ideally in employment with training, for example, a foundation modern apprenticeship. Research suggests that more than one-quarter of E2E trainees had experience of employment before joining the programme. Most of this experience had been short-term or casual in nature and few young people had found it to be a fulfilling experience (Spielhofer et al., 2003). A key role of E2E is to facilitate employment and training opportunities, and thus provide an important source of outcomes for PAs. E2E providers are funded according to the number of young people in their courses and given a bonus for successful employment and training outcomes that are measured once an individual leaves the programme. In addition, a bonus is paid to providers if trainees obtain level one equivalent qualifications while they are in the programme.

In total, there exist four main types of post-programme outcomes which are recognised as positive by the Learning and Skills Council and which qualify for the outcomes bonus. These are other level two training, entry to a foundation modern apprenticeship, employment with training and, where it is deemed appropriate by a PA, employment without training. An evaluation of the initial phase of the establishment of E2E on a national basis reported that roughly one-third of young people who participated on E2E went on to positive destinations. Over one-half of these went into employment with or without training. Relatively few went into foundation modern apprenticeships (GHK, 2004).

A New Vision for Youth Work

When releasing New Labour's vision for youth work the then Minister for Education and Employment, Malcolm Wicks, argued that, to date, some of the provision of services to youth had been of poor quality. The Office for Standards in Education reports were utilised to support this claim, showing that the quality of existing youth services were at best variable. Amongst the problems with provision were an 'absence of clear outcomes, scant recording of achievements and poor methodologies for delivering youth work' (Department for Education and Employment, 2001, p. 10). In addition, the provision of resources was uneven and not enough support was reaching those most in need. The training and quality of youth workers was also patchy and the retention and recruitment of staff had proved problematic. Tackling the regrettable increase in intergenerational tensions and conflict in England and other social and economic issues required intervention from the state to improve the quality and volume of services available to young people (Twigg, 2002).

In response, a new tailor-made, diploma level qualification has now been developed and all PAs are required to obtain this. It is hoped this will overcome the perceived inadequacies in the delivery of services to youth. Whilst introducing youth workers to the social context of youth work in modern England, the course also teaches the use of an assessment tool designed to assist in the diagnosis of problem areas affecting youth. These areas include education and training, family and environment, health, social and behavioural development. To improve the impact of the strategy, Connexions has also been developed as an evidence-based service. This means the tangible outcomes are closely monitored to ensure that it provides value for money. PAs are in charge of daily activities, however, the performance of the strategy is carefully measured against clearly specified targets. There are unique targets for the Connexions Service, including reaching 25 per cent of the target group.[1] From this, 60 per cent are to undergo personal and social development that results in an accredited outcome and 70 per cent of those participating in youth services must express satisfaction. Other goals are 'cross cutting' or apply to more than one agency and other goals are agency specific. Establishing clear targets for the service is deemed necessary in order to measure improvements in performance and to help identify best practice.

As discussed in earlier chapters, the effects of neoliberal methods of governance may be significant for community groups and debate exists regarding whether the practice and activities the state sponsors are consistent with the underlying values of these organisations. Similar claims have been advanced in relation to the Connexions Service. For example, in a critique of the Connexions Service, Smith (2002) argues that the strategy promotes a narrow view of youth work as merely delivering predetermined outcomes. In this respect, the introduction of performance measures may have a deleterious impact on youth work by reducing the ability of youth workers to develop meaningful and, arguably, effective relationships with certain groups of young people. It is argued that youth work is a much broader concern than simply achieving predetermined outcomes, as it involves the cultivation of associational life and its central benefits cannot be easily identified (Smith, 2002). Similarly, the introduction of performance outcomes leads to a focus on achieving quantitative rather than qualitative outcomes (McDonald, 2002). For example, PAs and their associated organisations may be able to demonstrate that they have improved the lives of the young people, yet because these outcomes are not recognised in the funding arrangements, they remain unrecognised and unrewarded. Some argue that if agencies continue to deliver welfare-related services to young people they must meet the needs of the target population more or less unconditionally (Smith, 2002). The alternative, where providers limit support and account for expenditure by demonstrating outcomes of service, will see some clients excluded from receiving support (Short and Mutch, 2001). As outlined in the previous chapter, a reason for this is that the most employable in the target population are the most likely to get the greatest access to resources.

As noted, there has been little research into the impact of the Connexions strategy. However, this situation will improve over time as the Department for Employment and Skills looks more closely at the impact of the strategy on the proportion of young people NEET. However, there has been some debate about the ideological assumptions that underpin the strategy and its likely role within youth work generally. Moreover, although policy documents produced by New Labour emphasise the need to create relationships with young people, the strategies employed by PAs to facilitate transitions into work and mainstream training remain open to question.

Method

The method used to explore the practices of the PAs and E2E tutors is similar to that adopted in the previous chapter. The participants were 10 PAs and 10 E2E tutors working in various settings. Two methods were utilised to recruit the participants. Firstly, through a youth workers' mailing board where an advertisement seeking assistance was placed; and secondly, through the Connexions and Learning and Skills Council's websites where the contact details of individual PAs and E2E brokers were provided. Both methods yielded some participants. Additional participants were recruited through the PAs' and E2E tutors' networks. It is important to acknowledge that this study explores the strategies used by PAs and E2E tutors with a small number of participants who live in particular locations. Moreover, it is also important to reiterate that Connexions Services are delivered diversely. For example, some Connexions providers are former careers companies whilst others are newly established. In addition, alternative kinds of partnerships have been developed. In sum, the delivery of the strategy is complex and the practices of the PAs and E2E providers are likely to reflect a combination of factors, including the nature of the local labour market and the particular institutional cultures in which the PAs and E2E tutors work. The aim of this chapter is to highlight some of the practices used by PA and E2E tutors that help them meet their required outcomes. Caution is required when generalising the findings broadly to the Connexions Strategy or E2E.

The PAs and E2E Tutors as 'Market Makers'

As argued, the Connexions Strategy may be seen as an attempt to decommodify knowledge and social contacts that are embedded within social networks and that contribute to patterns of advantage and disadvantage. Expressed another way, Connexions aims to allow everyone access to quality information about the labour market, VET options and contacts with employers. A lack of quality information and contacts need no longer be a source of disadvantage. It is an attempt to bridge gaps in the social infrastructure that have to date limited the ability of some young people to get quality employment information and to develop the direct contacts with employers necessary to make effective transitions into work.

Consistent with the literature, the interview data gathered indicates that much of the PAs work involves bridging gaps by providing general career advice and related information to all students. However, a significant minority of young people are unable to make successful transitions and, although they are 'employable', need additional support. Such young people received varying degrees of more intensive help to get them into training and employment. For some, this help involved providing more specific careers advice and information about current vacancies in the labour market that the PAs had gathered as part of their daily activities. For others, this help involved linking them with employers directly. To maximise their effectiveness in facilitating transitions amongst the target group of young people, the PAs needed to be embedded in the social infrastructure and know just what training and employment opportunities were available. In addition, they had to gain a good knowledge of the young people with whom they worked. This knowledge was needed to maximise the likelihood of achieving a good match between the young people and the available employment and training opportunities. The PAs utilised a number of strategies to become embedded. For example, some PAs reported that they were required to visit employers and to develop relationships with them in order to gather information about demand for new workers and to generate placements for young people. Essentially, the PAs reported that they were 'market makers' and attempted to match employer demand for young workers with particular skills with the supply of suitable workers. An important technique used to gather this information was through interviewing young people and assessing their employment interests, strengths and motivation, and meeting with employers to discuss their labour power needs. Only those young people identified as possessing the relevant qualities required for particular vacancies were provided with contact details of recruiting employers. The PAs undertook this matching exercise because they wanted to achieve their outcomes and to build their reputation as a source of suitable labour power for employers.

> *Toby* (PA): In our system, when they are interviewed about employment, which is quite intensive ... [the young people are asked] what kind of job they are looking for and what they know about it, we grade their choices and they are kept on the [computer] system. Also ... employers will ring us about vacancies ... For instance, a hairdressing job comes up, all the young people that have identified hairdressing as a choice will get notification of the job ... So employers know that all of the people that apply for the job have shown they are interested in the job. Otherwise you get [young] people who think, 'It pays £150, I'll have a go at that' but there is no interest [in the kind of work on offer].

In cases where this kind of 'market making' was insufficient to produce employment outcomes, some PAs reported placing 'employable' young people directly with employers in the hope that it would offer work experience leading to employment. This activity was also underpinned by an assessment of the suitability of a young person for particular kinds of employment, the needs of employers, and the need to build reputation with both employers and young people. For example, one PA who was required to make at least 40 employer visits per year, describes the process as follows:

> *Danny* (PA): We identify people that we think could do with a placement or some kind of work experience. We say to employers, 'We've got this young

person who wants to be a joiner. Any chance of taking him on for one or two days a week or a whole week and see what you think [of them]?' ... I've also got a lad on a farm at the moment and they want to take him on full time when he leaves school because they [the employer] are very impressed with him. His maths and English aren't up to scratch, but he has a farm attitude and understanding ... We try to match the placement with something the young person wants ... If we can match their choices with something they are looking at then, super. If they say they are interested in working with dairy animals and we get them a placement on a farm, in all likelihood it will be a successful placement ... What we try and do is match up what people are looking for in a job and their particular interests so that it becomes a successful placement. If it is not a successful placement it will jeopardise the possibility of placement next time. So we try to make it a successful placement for everybody.

An important aspect of the PAs work is to feed information to young people about suitable vacancies and the qualifications, skills, and the attributes needed to gain these. For example, some PAs reported that some young people had higher employment expectations than was warranted given their qualifications and the conditions of the local labour market. In other instances, a mismatch existed between young people's areas of employment interest and the training available. In both cases, as 'market makers', the PAs reported having to align young people's aspirations and interests to better match the realities of the labour and training markets. The PAs also fed labour market information to employers. In addition to providing specific information about the skills and qualities of young people, the data suggest that the PAs also worked to align the expectations of employers with what could reasonably be expected regarding the young people and to convince them that the young people had as yet unmeasured qualities which made them employable. As a PA put it:

> *Sam* (PA): Employers will always over-aspire and our job is to talk them down in their expectations and their criteria so it fits what we have available. I think it is a general thing throughout the country. Employers will say, 'I want them to have the qualifications I got', or 'I want them to have more qualifications than what I got'. We have to say, 'This is what we've got. Don't be put off that they haven't got x, y, and z. They've really got other qualities which will make them good employees'.

Unlike in New Zealand, where providers selected young people they felt were most likely to produce the outcomes demanded by the TEC (see Chapter 6), PAs are required to work with all young people irrespective of employability. Nevertheless, the role played by PAs as 'market makers' is closely associated with selection processes that impact on the delivery of support. On the one hand, some PAs report being able to give less assistance than in the past to those young people not at risk of becoming NEET. This is due to the critical outcomes involved reducing the proportion of those NEET.

> *Peter* (PA): The kind of work done in 6th forms was historically to do with careers advice and applications for higher education. However, this work has declined considerably in recent times as PAs' [time] under Connexions ... has been rescheduled towards working in harder to help settings. So I'd say that two or three years ago a lot of work might have been done to help a young person apply for university – this work has been significantly reduced ... with the emphasis on doing work with hard to help young people.

On the other hand, amongst those at risk of becoming NEET the more employable young people can more easily access the PAs' employment and networks. For young people with significant barriers to employment and not ready to enter the labour market or engage in further education and mainstream training, direct access to the PAs employment networks is more restricted. This group of young people are typically offered additional support and training through programmes that provided pre-employment activities, particularly E2E. The aim of E2E is to increase the confidence and motivation of young people and help them develop the basic and vocational skills needed to obtain employment. Thus, a key aim of E2E is to reduce barriers to employment. An additional aim of Connexions and E2E is to prevent the formation of poor forms of 'social capital'. As one PA stated, E2E aimed to 'keep young people in circulation' and prevent them from becoming 'isolated or getting involved in subcultures that aren't particularly wholesome'. As with the PAs, creating networks with employers was an important aspect of the E2E providers work and in some instances tutors are employed specifically to maintain and create these. Indeed, producing employment outcomes is a key criterion against which the performance of E2E is measured and PAs reported selecting providers on this basis. Participation in E2E allows targeted young people to access the social networks of a new set of brokers. As one PA stated:

> *Karen* (PA): [Our E2E] provider was picked because they provide apprenticeships for all the local employers and they provide the training for all the local employers. So if you have been on E2E for a while, your confidence is improving and your work is improving then they will take you out for placement with an employer, whom they pay, for a week, four weeks, or six weeks. They might start off at two days, then three days, then four days, and end

up working full time but their wages are still paid by E2E, about £40 a week. Eventually the young person comes to a point where they don't need too much more help and the desire then is for the employer to take them on as a proper apprentice. So ... [we] are weaning them off E2E ... lending them to employers on a short-term basis then a longer term basis, then hopefully move them into the company on a full-time basis while still paying their wages and then try to persuade the company to take them on as an apprentice. So it's amassing the labour market through public funds, through a mixture of supported work outside of employment, supported work in an employment placement, weaning them off, and an employer saying that they will take the person on. That's the model, that's how E2E works when it runs successfully ... Good E2E providers have to be social workers and have compassion for down-and-out kids, and be sharp enough to match employers with kids ... The company that provides ... [E2E] has a lot of people who are ex-industry mechanics, caterers, retailers, childcare and so on, so they know the local industry very well.

The data gathered in the interviews conducted with the E2E providers builds upon that gathered in the interviews with the PAs by showing additional ways that Connexions is contributing to the remaking of social networks. Although the E2E providers have little control over the quality of young people referred by PAs, student access to E2E broker networks is underpinned by selection procedures and workforce development strategies, which are designed to increase the match between employer needs for skilled labour and the human capital produced as a result of participation in E2E. Industry-specific knowledge is very useful and enhances the E2E brokers' matching process. In this respect, knowledge of the needs of industry informs the development of human capital in E2E training and the subsequent placement of young people into workplaces. Creating a match between the skills and attitudes of the trainees with those required by industry was underpinned by a desire on the part of E2E providers to build their reputation with employers such that they would offer placements in the future. Where the existing networks of E2E tutors contain employers with whom they could place a young person, they tend to draw upon this resource; where it did not, they were required to form new networks. To form these, E2E brokers 'cold called' employers either in person or by telephone and asked if they would be willing to take on a young person. When E2E providers were asked about how work placements were generated, the following responses were typical:

Tony (E2E): I come from the commercial world so I have quite a bit of contact within areas of industry ... In some cases, I do some cold calling. I've seen new businesses start up and I've gone in and asked if there was a possibility [of a placements]. I do telephone calling but mainly I ... [make placements] from personal contact ... I know industry. I know where there are possibilities for training within certain industries ... I was asked to join [E2E] because I had a wide commercial background ... Our better placements are those we have repeat business with.

Mandy (E2E): We are quite lucky because we have a work placement person on our team who has a lot of experience in various industries and who has been a key worker for our local city council for many years. As a result he knows a lot of people in a lot of different job areas. So he goes out and discusses with employers the opportunities for young people ... We've got to consider which young person would be right with each employer ...

Interviewer: Are you trying to build reputation with employers?

Mandy (E2E): Yes, very much so because we have always got to be thinking about the next vacancy for the next young person. So if the person who is with them moves on to a different type of placement or opportunity, if it's good placement, we need keep that open so that another young person gets the same opportunity.

For young people, participation in E2E and Connexions more generally, offers an opportunity to obtain the support and the contacts needed to obtain employment. For employers, there is an incentive to take on trainees in that they are provided an opportunity to assess the suitability of young people for existing positions in the workplace without financial cost. For employers with recruitment difficulties, E2E providers reported that this was seen as a way of expanding networks and thus expanding the pool of potential workers whilst gaining additional support for new workers.

However, like the PAs, the E2E providers reported that when completing the matching process, they assess the quality of employment offered and attempt to secure quality places for trainees. However, E2E tutors reported tension between the desire to secure quality placements – for example, those leading to a foundation modern apprenticeship – and the need to meet target employment outcomes. Thus, 'quality placements' need to offer more than just training in the form of work experience; they need to offer the possibility of future employment.

Karl (E2E): Sometimes you can see quite quickly that ... [employers] are just after cheap labour because we actually pay the student and they don't. So you have to be very selective about where you place a young person and what industries you actually go to. For example, in this area it's very rural and we have a lot of big growers and ... foodstocks and we wouldn't want to put a trainee in with one of those companies because it's slave labour basically ... We're actually quite selective. [However], I am actually judged or graded on my ability to get these people employed. My goal is to get them employed, not just trained ... and when I look at a placement I'm always saying to myself, 'is this a job or is this just ... training'. The ultimate goal is to get them employed, of course ... I'm asked to find [young people] training that ends in a job.

At the moment, the performance of the E2E providers in producing positive outcomes is not used by the LCSs to determine who can offer E2E. Nevertheless, some providers were aware that their ability to produce positive outcomes could ultimately prove critical in securing future funding from their LCS. One E2E provider who reported a performance target of 60 per cent positive outcomes expressed it as follows:

Mandy (E2E): [We] ... have targets and in the future, exactly how we perform will inform our next year's contract ... At the moment in our county ... there are nine training providers offering entry to employment. Now the Learning and Skills Council who fund us have said it might be they might cut down to three or four providers next year. So, you know, exactly where we are in our quality and how many positive outcomes we are getting is going to be absolutely crucial in keeping ahead of the game ... We know that we have to stay ahead in terms of quality to keep in the market for a good contract.

For some critics, problem with Connexions is that it subjects youth to new forms of surveillance through, for example, developing a database of all 13–19-year-olds. The associated publicity material touts several benefits to providers of education, including the capacity to develop an electronic registration system to track student attendance, particularly where patterns of attendance are complex, for monitoring the use of accommodation and the effective use of tutor time. A claimed result of the deployment of these new technologies is that Connexions is reaching 'young people that slipped through the net' because now the net is so small. The PAs reported that the databases that they work with are a vital tool in the identification of young people at risk of becoming NEET. Thus, the data speak of the creation of webs through which different agencies monitor, attempt to police and thus better regulate, the behaviour of youth. One PA described how he 'went after' young people who were NEET.

James (PA): I telephone them and if necessary I will get in a car and go and do a home a visit and knock on the door and say hi, my name is James Barr, I've come to see if you're looking for details about looking for work or training. Basically part of the PAs' … [role] is to literally hook them in [to training] by telephoning or knocking on their doors or by referring them to youth agencies, youth offending teams, social workers and youth workers. And to offer them E2E as step back into education …

Interviewer: So how do you manage to convince young people they should go on an E2E programme?

James (PA): … Some of them do get bored and fed up and want to do something. Some of them do genuinely aspire to practical, active careers such as construction … However, there're few, if any, construction jobs in this part of the world … we try and say to them they will gain from the experience and we try and use interpersonal skills and training to basically talk them into training.

However, for those young people on welfare who cannot be talked into Connexions' offerings such as E2E, other measures are available which are designed to encourage them to get a job or to enter training. Thomas, a PA, stated:

Thomas (PA): There are no sanctions [with Connexions]. It is purely a voluntary relationship. But when they do leave school, sanctions come from elsewhere. For instance, if they want to apply for particular benefits, then the Job Centre, which is separate from us, will send them to us and we will do the forms. Then the Job Centre will ring every so often and ask if they have been in. We have to draw up a contract with that young person saying that they will come in weekly, will see a personal advisor fortnightly, and will check the newspapers for jobs. So when the Job Centre rings we will look up the database and say, 'Yes, they've been in looking up jobs in the newspaper' or 'No, we haven't seen them'. Then the Job Centre will do the chasing … The only policing we would do is to say to the Job Centre whether or not a young person has been in. That's the only kind of sanction that we're involved in.

Some Critical Issues with the Connexions Strategy

The literature and the data gathered in the interviews suggests that Connexions and E2E are creating a social infrastructure that facilitates transitions into training and employment. However, there are a number of critical issues that must be addressed if the effectiveness of the service is to be maximised.

Looking broadly at the Connexions Strategy, the web of service provision established is likely to increase participation in education and training. However, in terms of increasing participation in VET, it remains unclear how this will create new ladders of opportunity for all unless it is matched by broader changes in VET. For example, through their knowledge of VET and employment opportunities, embedded PAs are likely to increase the likelihood of young people receiving the training necessary to gain employment. However, although embeddedness is highly desirable, it is not an essential feature of the strategy as participation in any form of VET training is deemed sufficient to meet the key performance outcome of reducing the proportion of young people NEET. In terms of the outcomes, the quality of the training or the value of the qualifications obtained is of relatively little importance in the short term at least. In the longer term, if the training is ineffective, the caseloads of PAs could remain the same, as young people are recycled through ineffective programmes. More broadly, as Fevre et al. (1999) argue, simply increasing the number of people in training will achieve relatively little if the individuals concerned are operating in a 'mimic' or instrumental fashion. Transformative forms of VET need to be developed to help England break out of the low skill equilibrium (Finegold and Soskice, 1988).

At a deeper level, there are grounds for questioning whether or not focusing intervention on individuals, rather than on the social context in which they live, is likely to be effective for all young people. For example, increasing the incentive to stay in education and training through introducing conditionality to unemployment benefits may encourage participation in VET but not affecting other individual attributes or the conditions of schooling that limit motivation to achieve. Thus if young people who are encouraged to return to school by the EMA or their PAs continue to participate in subcultures that resist learning, this may simply increase the proportion of young people who remain in education as discouraged workers.

Early research suggests that significant numbers of young people, particularly ethnic minorities, are missing out on support and that youth workers will find it increasingly difficult to keep track of young people, particularly where professional help is resisted. This research indicates that the Connexions Service is not aware of a high proportion of those NEET. Moreover, it was difficult to keep in touch with the young people to gain a second interview and many 'disappeared' (Britton et al., 2002). This raises questions about how PAs with larger caseloads will help the hardest-to-reach young people, especially where they are reluctant to be involved. As Britton (2002, p. 1) argues, 'many young people who have had lots of 'care professionals in their lives are very reluctant to visit what they see as another one'. In addition, it remains unclear whether or not what PAs can supply is what such young people want. Where young people had been in contact with PAs, it was found that a mismatch existed between the advice young people wanted and the kind of advice they received. Although many young people want jobs, much of the advice offered by the Connexions Service was about training and college courses (Britton et al., 2002).

Related research has also highlighted the importance of the social context in which some young people live, when considering the likely impact of interventions. In a study of homeless youth it was found that some young people have 'fear of the fall'. In other words, there exists a fear held by some that use of the state to improve their lives was not worth the risk as 'they saw any advancement as bringing with it a greater chance of returning to an even worse condition of existence' (Blackman, 1997, p. 116). Thus, the risk of losing existing networks and forms of support did not outweigh the possible benefits of engaging with the state.

The ability of PAs to work effectively with young people who have this fear is also likely to be hampered by the need to steer them into employment and training. In this respect, the claims of critics of youth work in England, who cite a lack of clear outcomes as a reason for introducing performance targets into the Connexions Strategy, resonate with the findings of a recent review of the impact of mentoring on young people. Hall (2003) points out that there is a dearth of quantitative evidence on the impact of mentoring in the UK. In the USA, a recent meta-analysis of 55 studies into mentoring is worth noting in some detail, as it is one of the few large-scale, statistically-based studies conducted to date and has shed light on the impact of mentoring. The authors reported that, while mentoring programmes have a small to modest benefit for the average youth, programme effects are significantly enhanced 'when greater numbers of both theory-based and empirically based "best practices" are utilized and when strong relationships are formed between mentors and youth' (DeBois et al., 2002, p. 1). The authors also state 'that multiple features of relationships, such as frequency of contact, emotional closeness, and longevity, each may make important and distinctive contributions to youth outcomes' (DeBois et al., 2002, p. 188). The authors are careful to document that they are unable to demonstrate that mentoring is the cause of the effects they observe. However, their analysis strongly suggests that young people from backgrounds of environmental risk and disadvantage, such as low socioeconomic family backgrounds, benefit most.

Barriers to success in mentoring schemes identified in Hall's (2003) review, include a lack of shared values or beliefs that lead to 'social distance' or a 'mismatch' between mentors and mentorees; a lack of mentor training and/ or expertise; a mismatch between the aims of the mentor and the mentoree; and conflicting roles such that it becomes unclear upon whose behalf the mentor is acting. For example, as the focus on rewarding practices which lead young people to engage in employment or training indicates, New Labour is attempting to change the behaviour of young people in ways supportive of the wage-labour relationship through the Connexions Service. Hall's (2003) review of the literature suggests that this focus is unlikely to be conducive to the development of relationships between young people and PAs that characterise effective mentoring, particularly with those hardest to help. For example, it may create ersatz relationships that are underpinned by the need of the PAs to impose the state's wishes upon young people within predetermined periods of time. This process is buttressed by other measures, particularly the New Deal for Young People in which young people can be financially penalised for failing to work with PAs. Such measures help cement power relationships between mentors and mentorees that may actually restrict the production of social capital. For example, PAs may be able to encourage young people to return to education or employment. However, if young people are not ready for work or training they are unlikely to be successful in either environment. As a result, the reputations of the PAs with employers, training providers and, critically with the young people themselves, will be damaged. Thus, all groups are likely to be reluctant to build the kind of relationships with PAs that are necessary to achieve the outcomes policy-makers desire.

Finally, there is a group of young people who do not display typical signs of risk. Such young people are likely to have work-poor backgrounds, low educational attainment, low expectations, and live at home supported by their parents (Britton, 2002). In the longer term, their low level of educational achievement and general disengagement from the workforce suggests that such young people are likely to face difficult transitions.

Conclusion

The central argument of this chapter is that the introduction of the Connexions Strategy and the related E2E programme are intended to provide a solution to disruption by making social networks. According to the new sociology of economics, these programmes represent good social policy as they recognise the embeddedness of decision-making processes and attempts to create institutions that complete functions no longer effectively completed in the sociocultural subsystem (Carnoy, 2000; Coleman, 1993). It is recognised that not all have access to the social or cultural resources needed to make transitions into work and so the strategy is designed to provide all young people with access to forms of social and cultural capital needed to make effective transitions into work.

To ensure that all have access to these forms of capital, it is intended that the strategy will create a net so tight that no young person can slip through and burden society. The creation of this net is buttressed by the development of information technologies designed to monitor the actions of young people and the introduction of schemes designed to motivate young people to participate. Once identified, the aim is to ensure that all young people receive the treatment needed to rectify pathologies that currently create barriers to employment. As such, Connexions and E2E represent the latest development of the tutelage society (Donzelot, 1977). By creating social networks, the strategy is trying to repair functional deficits in the social infrastructure as identified by New Labour.

The role of PAs and E2E tutors in creating webs of service provision indicates that the location of social networks has shifted from the now-eroded familial and community networks into an apparatus of the state. Their role in this process highlights the positional nature of social capital. Those young people who are most employable represent a more valuable resource to employers, to the PAs and to the E2E tutors. This is because these young people are best placed to be effective in the workplace and in VET, and to produce the required employment and training outcomes.

Note

1   Local target populations will 'include a locally agreed target for those assessed as ... NEET or who are at risk of or who already fall into the following categories: teenage pregnancy, drugs, alcohol or substance abuse or offending' (Department for Education and Skills, 2002b, p. 18).

Chapter 8

The Commodification of Social Capital

The revolutionary nature of capitalism leads to constant shifts in labour power needs as entrepreneurs seek out new ways of making profits and new markets in which to sell products. A consequence of these shifts is that employment relationships and the individual identities developed as a result are disrupted. The introduction of new labour-saving technology and new social technology – for example, in weaving, cropping, and numerous other industries in eighteenth-century England – caused widespread disruption to existing work practices and led to the erosion of particular work-based identities and cultures (Thompson, 1968). In addition, the introduction of the factory model of production caused workers to coordinate their activities around the 'working day' in which time became commodified through the development of the clock. In the 1850s, further development and expansion of the factory system necessitated the spread of time-consciousness amongst the masses. Due to the expense of purchasing a personal clock at the time, a 'knocker-up' was employed to wake workers at an appointed time (Mumford, 1934). The creation of time-consciousness was buttressed by developments in morality and the associated emergence of the sin of 'time-wasting' within schooling, church, and the workplace.

The rise of industrialisation and the emergence of the factory model of production divided workers from their products and provided the basis for the industrial (or Fordist) era institutions, including the industrial family, trade unions and the corporation (Brown and Lauder, 2001). These institutions aided the formation of new worker and new gender identities, for example male workers had to dispense with identities as craftworkers and adjust to the discipline of the production line. In addition, the new rules of production gave rise to the development of new social groupings, new sources of identity, and solidarity. Essentially, the industrial working class was the product of the industrial society (Scott, 1996).

In the contemporary era, changes in production brought about by continuing globalisation and technological innovation have intensified economic competition as entrepreneurs seek new ways to maximise profits. For example, the development of new computer and production technologies allows information to be transmitted and goods transported around the globe rapidly.

In addition, these developments have allowed producers to keep inventories to a minimum and have made it easier to get goods into markets.

An important economic and political response to increasing competition has been to increase labour market flexibility. Essentially, firms have responded to competition by dismantling the Fordist structures built during industrial capitalism and by creating post-Fordist structures. For many workers this has meant the demise of internal career structures in which progression through levels of remuneration was automatic. Now we see the emergence of flexible labour markets in which employment is based on individual performance-based contacts. Political reform, including the gradual removal of protectionist policies designed to insulate domestic producers from global competition, and changes to employment law, including the reduction of trade union power, have aided this process. Thus, a new set of rules has come to govern how production is undertaken. Of particular significance are the new rules of production that favour those with the flexibility to shift production to different locations around the globe, for example, those who are able to shift production from high labour cost to low labour cost environments. In addition, flexible production has been associated with a decline in the influence of local communities on production. For example, where workplaces are merely links in a global production network, decisions made by global elites to eliminate individual producers from their network can have deleterious local effects.

In essence, continual revolution of the means of production has altered social relationships between individuals. Capitalist development continues to separate some young people from traditions, identities and the networks created during the post-war boom which facilitated transitions into employment. Until recently, institutions such as the family and the social networks surrounding them ensured the continuing viability of the economic system by helping to reproduce the social relations of production, fostering skill transmission between generations, and providing direct and indirect links with the labour market. Thus, they provided an effective internal guidance system that facilitated transitions into work. The precise configuration of these networks was contextually and historically specific and their functioning was buttressed by developments in the schooling system, which was designed to limit participation and achievement to the elite. During the post-war economic boom this approach was effective as it reflected the demands of production. The state could reduce participation and limit achievement and young people could reject schooling, adopt identities as workers, and find employment by utilising resources made available through their social networks. Thus, young people could be brought into labour market relationships with limited assistance from the state. However, continual economic and social change have disrupted this relationship and, in declining sectors of the labour market, young people must distance themselves from identities and the employment networks that were built during an earlier era. A central argument in this book is that state intervention in education and the welfare state are designed provide a solution to disruption. Through introducing active welfare policies, implementing new forms of VET, and by creating educational markets, the state is attempting to remake identities conducive to the new labour market realities and provide individuals with a means to embed themselves within the emerging social infrastructure.

Clearly, continued globalisation and technological innovation, and the political response to these developments, have altered the nature of the competition for advancement. Those likely to benefit from this new economic environment will not only have the skills needed by employers but will also have the social and cultural skills needed to access valuable networks and to create new networks. In this context it is important to recognise that the privileged are likely to have access to resources that enable them to compete effectively in the new environment. Young people who are better educated, who have access to wider social networks and who have the cultural skills necessary to both utilise existing networks and grow new ones, will be best placed to succeed. Alternatively, the continuation of problems, such as the discouraged worker effect, the proportion of young people NEET, and welfare dependency indicate that not all have access to the social, cultural and economic resources necessary to become embedded in networks that lead to the formation of sustainable employment relationships. Moreover, to date, VET reform and new qualifications systems have failed to replace functions formerly completed by social networks. As a result, new institutions are needed to embed individuals into employment rich social networks. Where are these new institutions going to come from? Although Coleman (1993) did not provide an answer to this question, he emphasised that the opportunities for the 'rational' reconstruction of society, following the decline in primordial organisations, lay in the construction of institutions, organisations, and social environments where positive incentives and rewards for performance are emphasised.

A problem with the perspective adopted by Third Way governments and some social capital theorists, for example, Szreter (1998), is that simply increasing access to networks will not in itself address fundamental questions of social exclusion. Moreover, the concept of social capital has tended to be utilised by Third Way administrations as a way to maintain their left-wing credentials while advancing neoliberal strategies to enhance the efficiency of the economic system. Indeed, an achievement of the reforms introduced by previous neoliberal administrations and built upon by Third Way administrations by for instance, increasing the cost of higher education, has been to give the positional nature of social capital added emphasis. Nevertheless, the concept of social capital has provided useful grounds for advancing claims about the apparent destruction of social solidarity and social cohesion that has been exacerbated by the uncritical adoption of neoliberalism.

This chapter aims to draw the themes of this book together and note some of the ways the social infrastructure may be strengthened. It begins by summarising the major themes of the book and by briefly comparing the remaking of social networks in New Zealand to the English experience. The commodification of social networks is explored in light of Habermas' theory of the emergence of legitimation crises, as introduced in Chapter 1. Finally, the limits and possibilities of social capital are considered.

The Commodification of Social Capital

Compared to the level of intervention apparent today, the state has historically played a relatively minor role in facilitating transitions into employment. However, the emergence of disruption suggests that families, the communities in which they live, and the welfare or education systems are all unable to regulate youth labour effectively. The current inability of these institutions to regulate transitions into employment has been recognised by Third Way governments and has led to the adoption of three main strategies by the state to better regulate the supply of youth labour.

The first strategy is the development of improved educational technologies in the form of CBET. This represents an attempt to replace standards of achievement, gather labour market information, and create worker identities that were formerly established and transmitted as part of a cultural inheritance. Standards of achievement, labour market information, and worker identities are established and mandated by the state. However, the continuation of social problems, for instance, the discouraged worker effect and youth unemployment, has raised questions regarding the effectiveness of VET systems in achieving these aims. Although the development of new educational technologies in VET and elsewhere continues to capture the imagination of policy-makers, this influence is waning as the state recognises its ineffectiveness.

The second broad strategy identified is the introduction of outcomes-based funding in VET and welfare programmes. Operating within an environment of labour market growth, this strategy has proved highly effective in facilitating transitions into work in New Zealand. In Chapter 7 it was shown that the key strategies utilised by the tutors in the three programmes devised to produce the employment outcomes purchased by the state included drawing upon their existing networks and creating new employment networks. These networks provided information about the skills and qualities required in the labour market, and provided direct links with recruiting employers. However, the making of networks requires the supply of a suitable 'product'. The tutors in these programmes employed two main strategies to ensure this. Firstly, they recruited young people who they thought already had the skills and the worker identity necessary to be effective in the workplace. Secondly, where the new recruits lacked suitable skills and identity, they worked to produce them. An important aspect of intermediaries' work is the development of relationships between themselves and young people and between themselves and employers.

The third strategy identified is in the area of career guidance where New Labour has introduced the Connexions Strategy. In England the Connexions Strategy is designed to create a social infrastructure that will provide the internal guidance system necessary to facilitate transitions into employment. Although the reform is at an early stage and it is too soon to properly assess its impact, the limited data reported in this book and the secondary sources of evidence suggest that creating and maintaining social networks is an important aspect of the Personal Advisor's (PAs) work. For example, using new information technology, PAs are able to track young people's transitions beyond school and identify those who are at risk of failing to attach to the labour market. Once identified, the PAs can draw upon a range of resources to increase the likelihood of a young person making a successful transition into work or training. Some young people will receive intensive career advice and assistance with applying for employment – others will be placed directly into employment either by a PA or through E2E. To gather useful career advice and create the placement, the PAs had become conduits through which labour and training market information flowed. As one PA put it, they had become 'market makers'.

However, whilst the strategy is clearly an attempt to embed young people in productive networks, there are grounds to question its effectiveness in helping all young people. The Connexions service aims to be both a general service for all and a service targeting those NEET. Thus, PAs are required to work with a large number of young people and it is likely to be very difficult for them to develop the quality relationships needed to embed the hardest to help in education and work. In this respect, the data show that, like the situation with the MAS, YT and Gateway, new forms of selection are being introduced through Connexions. Secondly, in terms of education, it remains unclear just how measures such as the Educational Maintenance Allowance, which is designed to increase participation in conventional education and training, will enhance transitions into employment for those the measure is designed to help. For example, little evidence exists to support the claim that young people find low-level qualifications useful in the attainment of employment. Moreover, it is important to note that those NEET have already rejected the attitudes and values of mainstream society and many will have developed 'damaged' learner identities. Alternative approaches, such as those offered through E2E, are available: however, in the main, schools remain conservative organisations which do not readily adjust to the needs of a minority of young people who require intensive assistance.

Despite some important differences between the programmes assessed in this book, a common practice is the creation of networks. In New Zealand, this practice plays a pivotal role in achieving the outcomes purchased by the state and in ensuring the intermediaries' continued employment. In this context, social networks have become commodified and part of the way in which production is organised. The commodification of social capital is accompanied by the identification and ultimate remuneration of intermediaries who possess the technical, cultural, and social skills necessary to cultivate the networks which lead to the employment and training outcomes purchased by the state. In this way, the state is reconfiguring networks and allowing their value to be established by market forces as well as better regulating the practices of those working with young people. Those young people who are disembedded from the social infrastructure due to the natural functioning of markets can be re-embedded by intermediaries. For those who participate in such programmes, the commodification of social capital increases their ability to find work. As a result, a new form of social closure is introduced.

It is worth remembering that an advantage of this approach is that it primarily occurs in the context of local labour markets. Purchasing employment outcomes ensures that local providers employ intermediaries who understand the needs of employers in their particular labour market. It is possible that employers will discount the use of their own networks because these programmes complete labour exchange functions. By financing network creation and work-related training, the state can provide employers with a more reliable source of suitably skilled employees than that provided through other means. However, the occurrence of this could increase employers' dependency upon intermediaries and ultimately upon the state as a source of labour. In turn this may contribute to the further erosion of the value of familial and community-based networks. Conversely, it is possible that over time the networks commodified by the state may become self-sustaining if those who find satisfying jobs through these programmes feed labour market information into their 'network poor' communities.

The insights of Durkheim, Weber, and Habermas can improve our understanding of the remaking of social networks. Durkheim (1933) believed that the state, or an agency representing the general interests of all, was needed to regulate economic life. In addition, he believed that the division of labour and the associated institutions of industrial society, such as the industrial guilds, would promote social cohesion. Similarly, Weber (1968) believed that the rationalisation of society and increased state intervention was inevitable, as the state provides the most efficient method of organising social life. Although each of these perspectives may be drawn upon to better understand the role of the state in remaking social networks, the perspective explored in detail here is mostly in debt to the insights of Habermas (1976).

According to Habermas, advanced capitalist society comprises three inter-related subsystems: the economic, the political-administrative, and the sociocultural. This model, represented in Figure 8.1, is taken from Habermas (1976, p. 5). Each subsystem has tendencies towards crises that undermine the ability of society to maintain and reproduce itself. Different kinds of crises elicit different types of responses. For example, a crisis in the economic subsystem might elicit a response from the political-administrative subsystem. However, state interventions in the economic and the political-administrative subsystems are problematic, as historically their maintenance has destroyed aspects of the sociocultural subsystem. This is significant because state intervention has eroded many cultural practices and other resources upon which capitalist

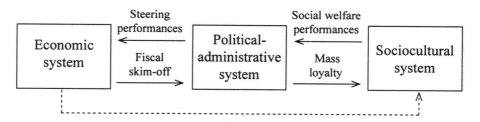

Figure 8.1   Habermas' model of advanced capitalist society

production depends but neither capitalism nor the state can efficiently replace these. In modern society, the imperatives of crisis management and the forces of technocratic rationality have undermined these cultural practices and related resources and this has led to the colonisation of the sociocultural subsystem, or the life-world. Essentially, state intervention and economic development have reduced the cultural supports and the ability of the everyday interactions that exist between people to give meaning and motivation to life. This robs the life-world of its ability to organise human interaction. As Young (1990) notes, the economic and political-administrative subsystems have been borrowing significance from the life-world for some time.

Replacing functions formerly completed in the life-world presents further problems. In order for intervention to be perceived as legitimate, the state must create a rational consensus among the public. According to Habermas, the state attempts to create this by drawing on scientific-technological knowledge and by developing technocratic interventions. Scientific-technological knowledge and technocratic interventions normally provide the strongest sources of legitimation because they mystify power relations and present the interests of the few as 'generalisable interests'. The development of technocratic interventions to political problems is an attempt to limit doubt regarding the integrity of the political-administrative subsystem. However, the inability of state intervention to resolve the contradictions in capitalist production means that there is always a tendency towards crises of rationality.

Social networks that exist within families and the communities in which they live are aspects of the life-world because they reflect the everyday interactions that exist between people. In the past, young people were able to organise transitions into work by drawing upon resources made available through their social networks. For example, young people could learn about the world of work by inheriting a cultural tradition similar to that described by Cohen (1983). This practice and these understandings were significant because they helped establish standards that governed labour market behaviour, enabled the formation of individual worker's identity, and guided individuals in finding employment. Moreover, this process occurred with minimal levels of state intervention. However, disruption has reduced the ability of social networks to fulfil this process. In order to maintain the social relations of production, the state has been compelled to fulfil functions formerly completed by social networks. In effect, these measures are attempts from within the political-administrative subsystem to ease problems created by functional weaknesses within the sociocultural subsystem, which are the result of continued economic change. More specifically, these measures are technocratic solutions designed to compensate for the erosion in the value of social networks and the emergence of related social and economic problems.

Although Habermas' theory presents a compelling explanation for state intervention and the likely form of this intervention, it has less to say about the limits and possibilities of network creation. Indeed, as the programmes evaluated indicate, the way in which networks are remade has important implications regarding the kind of contribution networks make to broader social and economic goals. Moreover, Habermas' theory offers little to policy-makers and practitioners regarding the alleviation of disruption.

The Limits and Possibilities of Network Creation

Third Way administrations perceive the creation of social capital as providing the possibility for increasing social cohesion and empowering individuals to take greater control of their lives. However, it may be expected that the Third Way's commitment to the creation of social capital, broadly conceived, is limited. An explanation for this can be found in the concepts of exit and voice. As noted in Chapter 4, in market societies the ability to facilitate change through exit is emphasised (Hirschman, 1970). An important reason for this is that it enhances the legitimation of inequality, which is seen to be the result of individual choices rather than the result of structural barriers to advancement. An alternative means of facilitating change is through voice, which depends upon loyalty and social cohesion. In other words, it depends on social capital. Attempts to create broader forms of social capital may ultimately be resisted by the state as they may reduce the legitimacy of the functioning of the economic system through increasing voice. Thus, attempts to increase voice, for instance, through increasing participatory democracy, may be resisted on the grounds that it challenges the position of existing elite groups.

Although for an administration committed to creating and maintaining free markets the incentive to create broader forms of social capital is likely to be limited, it is important to consider the contribution the creation of network capital has made to broader Third Way goals. In short, the programmes reviewed have increased their chances of obtaining employment through developing bridging social networks. However, the way networks are remade impacts on the young people's longer-term employment outcomes. Contrasting YT with the MAS is illustrative.

In the YT case, the remaking of social networks has increased the supply of labour at the bottom of the labour market without increasing wage pressure.

However, this does little to increase demand for skilled labour. Indeed, an emphasis upon increasing the supply of labour may secure low-wage/low-skill employment strategies in some sectors of the labour market. In turn, this may have a depressing effect on the incentives for individuals to be self-regulating and make networks that themselves lead to employment. The kinds of networks made and the resources these networks provide access to do not appear to encourage the creation of sustained employment. Although human capital development is an aspect of the programme, it appears that both the young people in YT and their employers need greater encouragement to adopt strategies that increase the likelihood for sustained employment.

Unlike YT, in the MAS case, the making of social networks is linked to the development of skilled labour. The intermediaries provide support throughout the period of apprenticeship to ensure that young people complete the training and that employers provide skills necessary to sustain employment. Although apprentices typically sacrifice higher wages for training, the completion of an apprenticeship offers reasonable security that future employment will be sustained.

Three factors suggest that the importance of networks in the recruitment process is likely to continue. Firstly, growth in service sector employment. Essentially, where the skills necessary for success in the workplace are poorly measured by school qualifications, employers will seek out and draw upon other sources to assess the suitability of new recruits. Networks are ideally placed to transmit the required information. Secondly, the saturation of the labour market with credentialed job seekers means that employers require additional sources of information about the quality of potential recruits. Young people will need to find ways of securing valuable qualifications. Again networks are ideally placed to provide this information. Thirdly, case study evidence such as that provided by Bowles and Gintis (2002) demonstrates that communities have the capacity to solve contemporary social and economic problems by improving social coordination, although a cost of this is social closure. They point out that community-based solutions may be more important in the future as production becomes increasingly based on quality rather than quantity, as information-intensive team production and the associated multilateral monitoring and risk sharing replaces Fordist 'low-trust' methods of production.

Given the tendency for economic development to constantly disrupt existing relationships in the search for more profitable methods of production, an unanswered question concerns the ways policies can improve social coordination. It is possible to identify three broad areas that are important to the improvement of social coordination. Before describing these it is worthwhile noting that elite groups continue to prosper under current arrangements and there is little reason for the beneficiaries of neoliberal policies to support change. Although New Labour and the Labour-led Coalition have maintained a rhetoric of general improvement for all, for example, through pursuing a high-wage/ high-skill training and labour market strategy, in practice their commitment to such a strategy is limited and it is difficult to judge where the required political will is going to stem from. Nevertheless, the broader issue concerning the impact of disruption on marginalised groups and the longer-term sustainability of neoliberal strategies suggests that new ways of facilitating employment relationships are desirable (Brown and Lauder, 2001). Indeed, whilst Third Way policies continue to effectively maintain company profits, policy-makers need to look beyond the immediate needs of the labour market and move beyond narrow perceptions of citizenship. An imperative step in developing a new policy foundation designed to improve social and social outcomes is to move beyond the limiting Third Way view of citizenship. Accordingly, New Labour and the Labour-led Coalition have adopted a Durkheimian position in which integration into the division of labour is the central key to the maintenance of social cohesion and solidarity (Fergusson, 2002). Durkheim believed that social cohesion could be maintained if individuals perceived their place in the division of labour as rational and saw personal benefits in the resulting membership of society (Parkin, 1992). However, if integration into the division of labour lacked rationality – for example, if recruitment into prestigious positions in the labour market was not meritorious or if individuals saw their work in isolation rather than as contributing to a collective project – the social cohesion would be undermined. In this respect, the approach of New Labour and the Labour-led Coalition differs from that advocated by Durkheim, as they have yet to consider the broader context in which work is undertaken and the relations of trust that emerge from this. Moreover, the approach adopted by New Labour and the Labour-led Coalition is further limited as it does not consider other forms of exclusion (Fergusson, 2002). In this respect, Third Way administrations in New Zealand and United Kingdom have tended to emphasise paid employment as the primary means to overcome social exclusion. Full participation in the labour market is perceived to be reducing social exclusion and promoting social cohesion. Whilst work is clearly an important aspect of social inclusion, research suggests that all employment is not equal in this respect and the extent to which social inclusion is promoted may vary accordingly (Pavis et al., 2001). Simply placing young people into work tends to privilege the initial transition into employment under an assumption that this will help people achieve the first rung on the ladder of opportunity (Peck and Theodore, 2000). To help overcome these weaknesses, policy-makers ought to direct their attention to the following areas.

The first area owes much to Szreter's (1998) and Brown and Lauder's (2001) analyses of New Labour's policies in which the tradition of increasing the communicative competence of individuals, given impetus by Dewey (1916), is followed. One way to create social capital is to redistribute resources by investing in an education system that improves the communicative competence of individuals. This requires a shift away from the current emphasis on the integrative function of education and an increased focus on the educative and democratic functions (Dewey, 1916). Although the introduction of competency-based assessment has yet to replace functions formerly completed by social networks in the recruitment process, its development is nevertheless a positive move. It embodies a positive view of human potential, promotes diversity of provision, and allows for assessment to be undertaken in a variety of contexts. In the VET area, increasing communicative competence is likely to involve the development of communities of practice that facilitate learning. The current obsession with human capital approaches to learning, in which learning is primarily viewed as an individualised process which ends when a credential is obtained, is limited because of its failure to recognise the importance of social and group learning processes. VET systems may continue to flounder due to the failure of human capital theory to recognise the importance of embeddedness in training decisions. For example, whilst the measures employed by the Labour-led Coalition have encouraged YT intermediaries to develop good networking strategies, it is unclear whether they impart this skill to trainees. Arguably, the making of networks and creation of sustainable employment outcomes requires that young people adopt a complex mix of abilities that stretch beyond a simple link with employers. Whilst providing young people with the skills enabling participation, it is important to recognise that networks can change rapidly and the cultural and aesthetic skills needed to make use of them are not universally available.

Other measures that limit participation in employment-rich networks should also be discouraged. A society in which individuals are divided from one another reduces social capital and arguably reduces economic competitiveness. This is why the commodification of higher education may limit the access of students from particular social groups to particular social networks. In this respect, the commodification of higher education also entails of the commodification of social networks, albeit through a different method.

By increasing the cost of higher education, New Labour and the Labour-led Coalition are heightening social division, fuelling domestic positional competition, and heralding a new era based on market, rather than meritocratic, rules of competition (Brown, 2000).

Although the changes suggested above may improve the provision of VET, it is unlikely that it will replace the role of social networks in the recruitment process. It is clear that other strategies need to be adopted. One way forward for policy-makers is to support the creation of high quality intermediaries. If the state is to do more than simply compel young people to acquire work in the contingent labour market, then how the intermediaries funded by the state are to act needs to be reconsidered. The analysis presented above suggests two ways the state could purchase access to social networks. Firstly, the MAS could be described as the 'high skills' route into employment. There, intermediaries work for the duration of the apprenticeship to ensure that employers provide the training young people need to obtain useful qualifications. Intermediaries also generally support apprentices in the workplace. YT may be thought of as a 'low skills' route, as relatively little consideration is devoted to the quality of the employment offered, and little or no post-placement support is provided beyond the date outcome measures are recorded. The broadening of outcomes to include aspects of work beyond simply placing young people in any kind of employment is necessary if sustainable forms of work are desired. Simply being in work is unlikely to contribute to future employment if it is in a declining sector of the labour market and if the employee does not develop personal human and network capital. For example, one aspect of high quality intermediary work may be to focus on the ongoing career development of young people, including their human and social capital development. In an era when many entry level positions are 'dead end' jobs, there is a need to look beyond initial employment to subsequent employment. For example, an intermediary can help by providing young people with quality advice regarding training and employment options beyond their first job.

In a similar vein, placing some young people directly into work is not always the best option either for them or for employers. The data from YT tutors show that some young people need support and training over extended periods and that going directly into work after a short course is not the best option for them. The poor longer-term outcomes of Training Opportunities attest to this. One way forward would be to broaden the outcomes measures beyond work-first to include non-work yet socially valuable outcomes. For example, young people can contribute to broader social goals by undergoing self-development that may not result in employment.

However, the potential of these measures to improve the social infrastructure is likely to be limited if they are not matched by measures to improve the quality of work. Although conservative commentators may dispute the point, improvements in the quality of work are an important aspect of improving the social infrastructure. Without the creation of quality jobs, the incentives for young people to become self-regulating and to build employment-rich social networks is likely to be reduced. Policies that can improve the quality of work are critical.

A Concluding Note

The argument within this book is that economic and social change has failed to erode the importance of networks in facilitating transitions into employment. In the past, families and the communities in which they lived brought young people into labour market relationships by linking them with employers and transmitting to them skills necessary to be successful in the workplace. Whilst the transitions differed according to class, gender and location, whatever the context, families and the communities in which they lived provided resources to facilitate transitions. However, economic and social change has disrupted this relationship, and in particular segments of the community, the connection between family- and community-based resources and transitions into employment have been severed. For those on the Right, this severing has been closely followed by a rise in social pathologies, including welfare dependency and teen pregnancy. From this perspective, the solution is to heighten the incentive to work by increasing the punishing consequences of remaining on welfare. The Right envisions and hopes that weakening the welfare state will strengthen the family. For those on the Left, numerous problems, including the discouraged worker effect and youth unemployment, reflect structural changes in the economy that have reduced the demand for young workers. As a result, older workers can no longer 'speak for' young people and their own positions in the labour market are under threat. In contemporary society, the state is attempting to reconnect young people with the labour market. An important strategy designed to achieve this is the creation of labour market and training intermediaries. It is their role to replicate functions formerly completed in what Habermas (1976) has termed the sociocultural subsystem. In contrast to many authors, including Castells (1996) and Kelly and Kenway (2001), who refer to transformations in social relations and the creation of porous, open networks, the argument in this book maintains that access to social networks remains closed and has become commodified. As a result, new forms of social exclusion have been introduced into the VET and welfare systems.

This book is an attempt to describe and explain how the state is facilitating transitions into employment in the search for a solution to disruption. If it has improved our understanding of broader changes in the social infrastructure that affect young people's transitions into work and the state's response to these, it will have achieved its purpose.

References

Adler, P. and Kwon, S.W. (2000), 'Social Capital: The Good, the Bad, and the Ugly', in C. Lane and R. Bachmann (eds), *Trust Within and Between Organizations: conceptual Issues and Empirical Applications*, New York: Oxford University Press, pp. 89–115.

Ahier, J. and Moore, D. (1999), 'Post-16 Education, Semi-dependent Youth and the Privatisation of Inter-age Transfers: Re-theorising Youth Transition', *British Journal of Sociology of Education*, 20 (4), pp. 515–30.

Aldridge, S. (2001), *Social Mobility*, discussion paper, London: Performance and Innovation Unit.

Apple, M. (1993), 'The Politics of Official Knowledge: Does a National Curriculum Make Sense?', *Teachers College Record*, 95 (2), pp. 222–41.

Aronowitz, S. and De Fazio, W. (1994), *The Jobless Future: Sci-tech and the Dogma of Work*, Minneapolis: University of Minnesota Press.

Audretsch, D. and Fritsch, M. (2003), 'Linking Entrepreneurship to Growth: The Case of West Germany', *Industry and Innovation*, 10 (1), pp. 65–73.

Auhion, P. and Howitt, P. (2000), 'Wage Inequality and the New Economy', *Oxford Review of Economic Policy*, 18 (3), pp. 306–23.

Australian Industry Commission (1996), *Competitive Tendering and Contracting by Public Sector Agencies*, Report No. 48, Melbourne: Australian Government Publishing Service.

Ball, S., Bowe, R. and Gewirtz, S. (1995), 'Circuits of Schooling: A Sociological Exploration of Parental Choice in Social Class Contexts', *The Sociological Review*, 43, pp. 52–78.

Ball, S. and Vincent, C. (1998), '"I Heard it on the Grapevine": "Hot" Knowledge and School Choice', *British Educational of Sociology of Education*, 19 (3), pp. 77–400.

Banfield, P., Jennings, P. and Beaver, G. (1996), 'Competency-based Training for Small Firms – An Expensive Failure', *Long Range Planning*, 29 (1), pp. 94–102.

Barnett, P. and Newberry, S. (2002), 'Reshaping Community Health Services in a Restructured State: New Zealand 1984–97', *Public Management Review*, 4 (2), pp. 187–208.

Baron, S., Field, J. and Schuller, T. (2000), *Social Capital: Critical Perspectives*, Oxford: Oxford University Press.

Barrell, R. and Genre, V. (1999), *Labour Market Reform in the UK, Denmark, New Zealand and the Netherlands*, London: National Institute of Economic and Social Research.

Bebbington, A. (1997), 'Social Capital and rural Intensification: Local Organisations and Islands of Sustainability in the Rural Andes', *The Geographical Journal*, 163 (2), pp. 189–97.

Beck, U. (1992), *Risk Society: Towards a New Modernity*, London: Sage.

Beck, U. (1999), *World Risk Society*, Cambridge: Polity Press.

Bell, D. (1973), *The Coming of the Post-industrial Society: A Venture in Social Forecasting*, New York: Basic Books.

Benner, C. (2003), 'Labour Flexibility and Regional Development: The Role of Labour Market Intermediaries', *Regional Studies*, 37 (6/7), pp. 621–33.

Bertrand, M., Luttmer, E. and Mullainathan, S. (2000), 'Network Effects and Welfare Cultures', *The Quarterly Journal of Economics*, 115 (3), pp. 1019–55.

Biggart, A. and Furlong, A. (1996), 'Educating "Discouraged Workers": Cultural Diversity in the Upper Secondary School', *British Journal of Educational Sociology*, 17 (3), pp. 253–66.

Blackburn, M., Bloom, D. and Freeman, R. (1990), 'The Declining Economic Position of Less Skilled American Men', in G. Burtless (ed.), *A Future of Lousy Jobs*, Washington DC: Brookings Institute, pp. 31–67.

Blackman, S. (1997) '"Destructing a Giro": A Critical and Ethnographic Study of the Youth "Underclass"', in R. MacDonald (ed.), *Youth, the 'Underclass' and Social Exclusion*, London: Routledge, pp. 113–29.

Blaiklock, A., Kiro, C., Balgrave, M., Low, W., Davenport, E. and Hassall, I. (2002), *When the Invisible Hand Rocks the cradle: new zealand children in a Time of Change*, Innocenti Working Paper, Report No. 93, Florence: UNICEF Innocenti Research Centre.

Blair, T. (1996), Speech given at Ruskin College, Oxford, 16 December.

Blunkett, D. (1999), 'Pessimistic Pundits Put on Notice', *The Guardian*, 11 August, p. 25.

Blunkett, D. (2001), *Education into Employability: The Role of the DFEE in the Economy*, London: Department for Education and Employment.

Bonjour, D., Knight, G. and Lissenburgh, S. (2002), *Evaluation of New Deal for Young People in Scotland*, Edinburgh: Scottish Executive Central Research Unit.

Borland, J., Gregory, R.G. and Sheehan, P. (2002), *Work Rich, Work Poor: Inequality and Economic Change in Australia*, Melbourne: Centre for Strategic Economic Studies.

Bowles, S. and Gintis, H. (1976), *Schooling in Capitalist America: Educational Reform and the Contradictions of Economic Life*, London: Routledge and Kegan-Paul.

Bowles, S. and Gintis, H. (2002), 'Social Capital and Community Governance', *The Economic Journal*, 112, November, F419–F436.

Bradley, H. (1996), *Fractured Identities: Changing Patterns of Inequality*, Cambridge: Polity Press.

Breen, R. and Goldthorpe, J. (2001), 'Class, Mobility and Merit: The Experience of Two British Birth Cohorts', *European Sociological Review*, 17 (2), pp. 81–101.

Brennan, G. and Buchanan, J. (1985), *The Reason of Rules: Constitutional Political Economy*, Cambridge: Cambridge University Press.

Britton, L. (2002), *Can Connexions Bridge the Gap?*, Working Paper, Report No. 131, London: Centre for Economic and Social Inclusion.

Britton, L., Chatrik, B., Coles, B., Craig, G., Hylton, C. and Mumtaz, S. (2002), *Missing Connexions: The Career Dynamics and Welfare Needs of Black and Minority Ethnic Young People at the Margins*, Bristol: The Policy Press.

Brown, G. (2003), 'A Modern Agenda for Prosperity and Social Reform', accessed 15 May, <http://www.hm-treasury.gov.uk/newsroom_and_speeches/press/2003/press_12_03.cfm>.

Brown, P. (2000), 'The Globalisation of Positional Competition', *Sociology*, 34 (4), pp. 633–53.

Brown, P. and Lauder, H. (2001), *Capitalism and Social Progress: The Future of Society in a Global Economy*, New York: Palgrave.

Brown, P. and Lauder, H. (2002), 'Human Capital, Social Capital, and Collective Intelligence', in T. Schuller, S. Baron and J. Field (eds), *Social Capital: Critical Perspectives*, Oxford: Oxford University Press, pp. 226–42.

Brown, P. and Scase, R. (1997), 'Universities and Employers: Rhetoric and Realities', in A. Smith and F. Webster (eds), *The Postmodern University? Contested Visions of Higher Education in Society*, Buckingham: Open University Press, pp. 85–98.

Buckingham, A. (2000), 'Welfare Reform in Britian, Australia and the United States', in P. Saunders (ed.), *Reforming the Australian Welfare State*, Melbourne: Australian Institute of Family Studies, pp. 72–90.

Bull, I. (2002), 'Merchant Households and Their Networks in Eighteenth-century Trondheim', *Continuity and Change*, 17 (2), pp. 213–31.

Burchell, B., Day, D., Hudson, M., Ladipo, D., Mankelow, R., Nolan, J., Reed, H., Wichert, I. and Wilksinson, F. (1999), *Job Insecurity and Work Intensification: Flexibility and the Changing Boundarie of Work*, York: Joseph Rowntree Foundation.

Burnett, J., Jentsch, B. and Schucksmith, M. (2001), *Paypird Final Report*, Aberdeen: Arkleton Centre.

Burt, R. (1997), 'The Contingent Value of Social Capital', *Administrative Science Quarterly*, 42, pp. 339–65.

Burt, R. (2001), 'Structural Holes Versus Network Closure', in L. Nan, K. Cook and R. Burt (eds), *Social Capital: Theory and Research*, New York: Aldine de Gruyter, pp. 31–56.

Callister, P. (2001), *A Polarisation into Work-rich and Work-poor Households in New Zealand? Trends from 1986 to 2000*, Occasional Paper 2001/2003, Wellington: Department of Labour.

Carnoy, M. (2000), *Sustaining the New Economy: Work, Family, and Community in the Information Age*, Cambridge, MA and London: Harvard University Press and Russell Sage Foundation.

Castells, M. (1996), *The Rise of the Network Society*, London: Blackwell.

CBI Scotland (2000), *Competitive Scotland*, CBI Scotland working paper, Glasgow: CBI Scotland.

Charles, N. and James, E. (2003), 'The Gender Dimension of Job Insecurity in a Local Labour Market', *Work, Employment and Society*, 17 (3), pp. 531–52.

Chisholm, L. and Du Bois-Reymond, M. (1993), 'Youth Transitions, Gender and Social Change', *Sociology*, 27, pp. 259–80.

Clark, A. (2003), 'Unemployment as a Social Norm: Psychological Evidence from Panel Data', *Journal of Labor Economics*, 21 (2), pp. 323–51.

Clark, H. (2002), 'Prime Minister's Address to the London School of Economics', Wellington, 21 February, New Zealand Parliamentary Speech Archive.

Codd, J. (1995), 'NZQA and the Politics of Centralism', paper presented at the Annual Conference of the New Zealand Association for Research in Education, Massey University, New Zealand, 3–5 December.

Codd, J. (1998), 'Educational Reform, Accountability and the Culture of Distrust', *New Zealand Journal of Educational Studies*, 38 (1), pp. 45–53.

Cohen, P. (1983), 'Losing the Generation Game', *New Socialist*, 14, pp. 28–36.

Cohen, S. and Fields, G. (1999), 'Social Capital and Capital Gains in Silicon Valley', *California Management Review*, 41 (2), pp. 108–30.

Coleman, J. (1988), 'Social Capital in the Creation of Human Capital', *American Journal of Sociology*, 94, S95–S120.

Coleman, J. (1993), 'The rational Reconstruction of Society', *American Sociological Review*, 58 (1), pp. 1–15.

Collins, R. (1979), *The Credential Society: An Historical Sociology of Education and Stratification*, New York: Academic Press.

Colmar Brunton Research (1994), *What Are Employers Looking For?*, Wellington: New Zealand Employment Service.

Cox, E. and Caldwell, P. (2000), 'Making Social Policy', in I. Winter (ed.), *Social Capital and Public Policy*, Melbourne: Australian Institute of Family Studies, pp. 43–73.

Creech, W. (1998), 'Launch of the Achievement 2001 School Qualifications for 16 to 19 year olds', paper presented to the New Zealand Parliament, 5 November.

Crompton, R. (1993), *Class and Stratification: An Introduction to Current Debates*, Cambridge: Polity Press.

Curriculum, Evaluation and Management Centre (no date), 'Underaspirers – How Can We Help Them?', unpublished paper, Durham: Curriculum, Evaluation, and Management Centre.

Deacon, A. (2000), 'Learning from the US? The Influence of American Ideas upon "New Labour" Thinking on Welfare Reform', *Policy and Politics*, 28 (1), pp. 5–18.

Dean, M. (1995), 'Governing the Unemployed Self in an Active Society', *Economy and Society*, 24 (4), pp. 559–83.

DeBois, D., Holloway, B., Valentine, J. and Cooper, H. (2002), 'Effectiveness of Mentoring Programmes for Youth: A Meta-analytic Review', *American Journal of Community Psychology*, 30 (2), pp. 157–97.

Department for Education and Employment (2000), *The Connexions Service: Prospectus and Specification*, Nottinghamshire: Department for Education and Employment.

Department for Education and Employment (2001), *Transforming Youth Work: Developing Youth Work for Young People*, Nottinghamshire: Department for Education and Employment.

Department for Education and Skills (2000a), *Connexions: The Best Start in Life for Every Young Person*, Nottinghamshire: Department for Education and Employment.

Department for Education and Skills (2000b), *The Connexions Service: Prospectus and Specification*, Nottinghamshire: Department for Education and Employment.

Department for Education and Employment (2002), *Connexions Annual Report 2001–02*, Nottinghamshire: Department for Education and Employment.

Department for Education and Skills (2002a), *14–19: Extending Opportunities, Raising Standards (Summary)*, Nottinghamshire: Department for Education and Skills.

Department for Education and Skills (2002b), *Transforming Youth Work: Resourcing Excellent Youth Services*, Nottinghamshire: Department for Education and Skills.

Department for Education and Skills (2003), *21st Century Skills: Realising our Potential, Individuals, Employers, Nation*, London: Department for Education and Skills.

Department of Education (1943), *The Post-primary Curriculum: Report of the Committee Appointed by the Minister of Education in November*, Wellington: Government Printer.

Department of Labour (2000), *Objectives, Key Features and Issues for Industry Training in New Zealand*, Wellington: Department of Labour.

Department of Labour (2003), *Work Trends: How Work is Changing in New Zealand*, Wellington: Department of Labour.

Department of Social Security (1998), *New Ambitions for Our Country: A New Contract for Welfare*, Cm 3805, London: Her Majesty's Stationery Office.

Department of Statistics (1972), *New Zealand Official Yearbook*, Wellington: Department of Statistics.

Department of Statistics (1993), *New Zealand Social Trends*, Wellington: Department of Statistics.

Dewey, J. (1916), *Democracy and Education: An Introduction to the Philosophy of Education*, New York: The Free Press.

Dex, S. and Taylor, M. (1994), 'Household Employment in 1991', *Employment Gazette*, 102 (10), pp. 353–7.

Dickens, R., Gregg, P. and Wadsworth, J. (2000), 'New Labour and the Labour Market', *Oxford Review of Economic Policy*, 16 (1), pp. 95–113.

Dockery, A.M. and Stromback, T. (2001), 'Devolving Public Employment Services: Preliminary Assessment of the Australian Experiment', *International Labour Review*, 140 (4), pp. 429–51.

Doeringer, P., Christensen, K., Flynn, P., Hall, D., Katz, H., Keefe, J., Ruhm, C., Sum, A. and Useem, M. (1991), *Turbulence in the American Workplace*, Oxford: Oxford University Press.

Donzelot, J. (1977), *The Policing of families: Welfare Versus the State*, London: Hutchinson.

Doogan, K. (2001), 'Insecurity and Long-term Employment', *Work, Employment and Society*, 15 (3), pp. 419–41.

Dorsett, R. (2001), *The New Deal for Young People: Relative Effectiveness of the Options in Reducing Male Unemployment*, London: Policy Studies Institute.

Drucker, P. (1993), *Post-capitalist Society*, London: Butterworth and Heinemann.

Durkheim E. (1933), *The Division of Labor in Society*, London: The Free Press.

Eardley, T. (1997), *New Relations of Welfare in the Contracting State: The Marketisation of Services for the Unemployed in Australia*, Report No. 79, Sydney: University of New South Wales, Social Policy Research Centre.

Elliott, L. and Atkinson, D. (1998), *The Age of Insecurity*, New York: Verso.

Ellison, N. (1997), 'Towards a New Social Politics: Citizen and Reflexivity in Late Modernity', *Sociology*, 31 (4), pp. 697–719.

Ewert, G. (1991), 'Habermas and Education: A Comprehensive Overview of the Influence of Habermas in the Education Literature', *Review of Educational Research*, 61 (3), pp. 345–78.

Fattore, T., Turnbull, N. and Wilson, S. (2003), '"More Community!" Does the Social Capital Hypothesis Offer Hope for Untrusting Societies?', *The Drawing Board: An Australian Review of Public Affairs*, 3 (3), pp. 165–79.

Felstead, A., Gallie, D. and Green, F. (2002), *Work Skills in Britain 1986–2001*, Leicester: Center for Labour Market Studies.

Fergusson, R. (2002), 'Rethinking Youth Transitions: Policy Transfer and New Exclusions in New Labour's New Deal', *Policy Studies*, 23 (3/4), pp. 173–90.

Fernandez, R., Castilla, E. and Moore, P. (2000), 'Social Capital at Work: Networks and Employment at a Phone Center', *American Journal of Sociology*, 105 (5), pp. 1288–356.

Fevre, R. (2000), 'Socializing Social Capital: Identity, the Transition to Work, and Economic Development', in S. Barton, J. Field and T. Schuller (eds), *Social Capital: Critical Perspectives*, Oxford: Oxford University Press, pp. 94–110.

Fevre, R., Rees, G. and Gorard, S. (1999), 'Some Sociological Alternatives to Human Capital Theory and Their Implications for Research on Post-compulsory Education and Training', *Journal of Education and Work*, 12 (2), pp. 117–40.

Fine, B. and Green, F. (2000), 'Colonizing the Social Science', in S. Barton, J. Field and T. Schuller (eds), *Social Capital: Critical Perspectives*, Oxford: Oxford University Press, pp. 94–110.

Finegold, D. (1999), 'Creating Self-sustaining, High Skill Ecosystems', *Oxford Review of Economic Policy*, 15 (1), pp. 60–81.

Finegold, D. and Soskice, D. (1988), 'The Failure of Training in Britian: Analysis and Prescription', *Oxford Review of Economic Policy*, 4 (3), pp. 21–53.

Fitsimmons, P. (1997), *What Difference does the NQF Make for Young People: A Longitudinal Study Tracking Ninety-eight Students (The First Report of the First Cohort to NZQA)*, Wellington: New Zealand Council for Educational Research.

Foley, M. and Edwards, B. (1999), 'Is it Time to Disinvest in Social Capital?', *Journal of Public Policy*, 19 (2), pp. 141–73.

Fremstad, S. (2004), *Recent Welfare Reform Research Findings: Implications for TANF Reauthorization and State TANF Policies*, Washington: Centre on Budget and Policy Priorities.

Fukuyama, F. (1995), *Trust: The Social Virtues and the Creation of Prosperity*, New York: The Free Press.

Galindo-Rueda, F. and Vignoles, A. (2003), *Class Ridden or Meritocratic? An Economic Analysis of Recent Changes in Britain*, London: Centre for the Economics of Education.

Gallie, D., White, M., Cheng, Y. and Tomlinson, M. (1998), *Restructuring the Employment Relationship*, Oxford: Clarendon Press.

GHK (2004) *LSDA and LSC National Office Evaluation of the Initial Phase of the National Establishment of Entry to Employment (E2E)*, Final Report, Coventry: Learning Skills Council.

Giddens, A. (1998), *The Third Way*, Cambridge: Polity Press.

Goodwin, J. and O'Connor, H. (2003), *Exploring Complex Transitions: Looking Back at the 'Golden Age' of School to Work*, Centre for Labour Market Studies Working Paper No. 42, Leicester: Centre for Labour Market Studies.

Gosling, A. and Machin, S. (1993), 'Trade Unions and the Dispersion of Earnings in UK Establishments', Discussion Paper No. 140, London: London School of Economics.

Government of New Zealand (1995), *Education Act 1989*, in reprinted Act, Education (with amendments incorporated) Sections 246–248, Wellington: Government of New Zealand.

Granovetter, M. (1995), *Getting a Job: A Study of Careers and Contacts*, Chicago: Chicago University Press.

Gray, A. (1997), 'Contract Culture and Target Fetishism: The Distortive Effects of Output Measures in Local Regeneration Programmes', *Local Economy*, 11 (4), pp. 343–57.

Green, A. and Sakamoto, A. (2001), 'Models of High Skills', in P. Brown, A. Green and H. Lauder (eds), *High Skills: Globalisation, Competitiveness, and Skill Formation*, Oxford: Oxford University Press, pp. 56–160.

Green, D. (1996), *From Welfare State to Civil Society: Towards Welfare that Works in New Zealand*, Wellington: New Zealand Business Round Table.

Green, F., McIntosh, S. and Vignoles, A. (1999), *'Overeducation' and Skills – Clarifying the Concepts*, London: London School of Economics, Centre for Economic Performance.

Gregg, P. and Wadsworth, J. (1996), *It Takes Two: Employment Polarisation in the OECD*, Discussion Paper No. 304, London: London School of Economics, Centre for Economic Performance.

Gregg, P. and Wadsworth, J. (2000), 'Mind the Gap, Please: The Changing Nature of Entry Jobs in Britian', *Economica*, 67, pp. 499–524.

Grieco, M. (1987a), 'Family Networks and the Closure of Employment', in G. Lee and R. Loveridge (eds), *The Manufacture of Disadvantage: Stigma and Social Closure*, Milton Keynes: Open University Press, pp. 33–44.

Grieco, M. (1987b), *Keeping it in the Family: Social Networks and Employment*, London: Tavistock.

Grieco, M. (1996), *Workers' Dilemmas: Recruitment, Reliability and Repeated Exchange: An Analysis of Urban Social Networks and Labour Circulation*, London and New York: Routledge.

Grover, C. (2003), ''New Labour', Welfare Reform and the Reserve Army of Labour', *Capital and Class*, 79, Spring, pp. 17–23.

Guerin, D. (1997), 'Public Subsidies for Students in Private Training Providers', *New Zealand Annual Review of Education*, 7, pp. 59–77.

Habermas, J. (1976), *Legitimation Crisis*, London: Heinemann.

Hall, J. (2003), *Mentoring and Young People: A Literature Review*, Glasgow: The Scottish Council for Research in Education.

Hall, R., Bretherton, T. and Buchanan, J. (2000), *"It's Not My Problem": The Growth of Non-standard Work and its Impact on Vocational Education and Training in Australia*, Leabrook: Australian National Training Authority.

Halsey, A. (1993), 'Trends in Access and Equity in Higher Education: Britain in International Perspective', *Oxford Review of Education*, 19 (2), pp. 124–40.

Hargreaves, A. (1989), *Curriculum and Assessment Reform*, Milton Keynes: Open University Press.

Harkness, S. and Machin, S. (1999), *Graduate Earnings in Britian, 1974–1995*, London: Department for Education and Employment.

Hazeldine, T. (1998), *Taking New Zealand Seriously: The Economics of Decency*, Wellington: HarperCollins.

Heath, A. (1999), 'Job-search Methods, Neighbourhood Effects and the Youth Labour Market', discussion paper, Sydney and London: Reserve Bank of Australia and London School of Economics, Centre for Economic Performance.

Hendel, M. (2000), *Is There a Skills Crisis? Trends in Job Skills Requirements, Technology and Wage Inequality in the United States*, New York: The Jerome Levy Economics Institute of Bard College.

Hewlett, S. (1993), *Child Neglect in Rich Nations*, New York: United Nations Children's Fund.

Hirschman, A. (1970), *Exit, Voice and Loyalty: Responses to Decline in Firms, Organisations and States*, Cambridge, MA: Harvard University Press.

HM Treasury (1999), *Top Experts Draw Up Five Point Action Plan to Tackle Variations in Performance across the Public Sector 1998/1999*, London: HM Treasury.

HM Treasury (2000), *The Goal of Full Employment: Employment Opportunity for All throughout Britain. Trends in Regional and Local Vacancies and Unemployment*, London: HM Treasury.

Hodgson, A. and Spours, K. (2002), 'Curriculum, Learning and Qualifications 14–19', in The Nuffield Foundation (ed.), *14–19 Education: Papers Arising from a Seminar Series held at the Nuffield Foundation*, London: The Nuffield Foundation.

Hollands, R. (1990), *The Long Transition: Class, Culture and Youth Training*, London: MacMillan Education.

Holzer, H. (2000), 'Mismatch in the Low-wage Labour Market: Job Hiring Perspective', in K. Kaye and D. Nightingale (eds), *The Low-wage Labor Market: Challenges and Opportunities for Economic Self Sufficiency*, Washington: US Department of Health and Human Services Office of the Assistant Secretary for Planning and Evaluation, pp. 127–15.

Hughes, D.C. and Lauder, H.C. (1990), 'Public Examinations and the Structuring of Inequality: A Case Study', in H.C. Lauder and C. Wylie (eds), *Towards Successful Schooling*, Lewes: Falmer Press, pp. 151–73.

Hyland, T. (2002), 'Third Way Values and Post-school Education Policy', *Journal of Education Policy*, 17 (2), pp. 245–58.

Jackson, M. (1984), *The Formation of Craft Labor Markets*, Orlando, FL: Academic Press.

Jacob, M. (2003), 'Rethinking Science and Commodifying Knowledge', *Policy Futures in Education*, 1 (1), pp. 125–42.

James, R. (2002), *Socioeconomic Background and Higher Education Participation: An Analysis of School Students' Aspirations and Expectations*, Canberra: Department of Education, Science and Training.

Jeffs, T. and Smith, M.K. (2004), 'The Problem of "Youth" for Youth Workers', accessed 8 April, <http://www.infed.org/archives/youth.htm>.

Jenkins, R., Bryman, A., Ford, J., Keil, T. and Beardsworth, A. (1983), 'Information in the Labour Market: The Impact of Recession', *Sociology*, 17, pp. 260–67.

Johnson, P. and Reed, R. (1996), 'Intergenerational Mobility among Rich and Poor: Results from the National Child Development Survey', *Oxford Review of Economic Policy*, 12 (1), pp. 127–42.

Jones, C. and Novak, T. (1980), 'The State as Social Policy', in P. Corrigan, H. Ramsay and D. Sayer (eds), *Capitalism, State Formation and Marxist Theory*, London: Quartet Books, pp. 143–70.

Kanter, R. (1995), *World Class: Thriving Locally in the Global Economy*, New York: Simon and Schuster.

Katz, M. (1989), *The Undeserving Poor: From the War on Poverty to the War on Welfare*, New York: Pantheon.

Kazis, R. (1999), *Improving Low Income Job Seekers' Employment Prospects: The Role of Labour Market Intermediaries*, Boston: Jobs for the Future.

Keep, E. and Mayhew, K. (1999), 'The Assessment: Knowledge, Skills, and Competitiveness', *Oxford Review of Economic Policy*, 15 (1), pp. 1–15.

Kelly, P. and Kenway, J. (2001), 'Managing Youth Transitions in the Network Society', *British Journal of Sociology of Education*, 22 (1), pp. 19–33.

Kelly, R. and Lewis, P. (1999), *The Impact of Intergenerational Effects and Geography on Youth Employment Outcomes: A Study of the Perth Metropolitan Region*, Perth: Murdoch University, Centre for Labour Market Research.

Kenworthy, L. (1997), 'Civic Engagement, Social Capital, and Economic Co-operation', *American Behavioral Scientist*, 40 (5), pp. 645–56.

Kerr, C., Dunlop, J., Harbison, F. and Myers, C. (1973), *Industrialism and Industrial Man: The Problems of Labour and Management in Economic Growth*, Harmondsworth: Penguin.

Kerr, M. (2002), 'Why Does Workplace Learning Work', paper presented to the New Directions in Workplace Learning Conference, Wellington, 22 May.

King, S. (1994), 'Competitive Tendering and Contracting Out: An Introduction', *The Australian Economic Review*, 171 (3rd Quarter), pp. 75–8.

Lachnit, C. (2001), 'Employee Referral Saves Time, Saves Money, Delivers Quality', *Workforce*, 80 (6), June, pp. 67–72.

Latham, M. and Botsman, P. (2001), *The Enabling State: People Before Bureaucracy*, Sydney: Pluto Press.

Learning Skills Council (2003), *Key Messages from Skills in England*, Coventry: Learning Skills Council.

Lee, G. and Lee, H. (1992), *Examinations and the New Zealand School Curriculum: Past and Present*, Delta Research Monograph No. 12, Palmerston North: Massey University, Department of Education.

Levine, D. (1999), *Choosing the Right Parents: Changes in the Intergenerational Transmission of Inequality between the 1970s and Early 1990s*, Working Paper No. 72, Berkeley: University of California.

Lewis, I. (2003), 'Offenders Learning and Skills Unit 2003', paper presented to the Offenders' Learning and Skills Unit, Wakefield, 8–9 May.

Lin, N. (1999), 'Social Networks and Status Attainment', *Annual Review of Sociology*, 25, pp. 467–87.

Livingstone, D. (1999), 'Lifelong Learning and Underemployment in the Knowledge Society: A North American Perspective', *Comparative Education*, 35 (2), pp. 163–86.

Long, M., Ryan, R., Burke, G. and Hopkins, S. (2000), 'Enterprise-based Education and Training', report prepared for the New Zealand Ministry of Education, Wellington.

Loprest, P. (1999), *Families who Left Welfare: Who Are They and How Are They Doing?*, Washington: Urban Institute.

Maguire, S. (2002), 'Employers' Demand for Youth Labour and their Recruitment Strategies', *Career Research and Development*, 6, Summer, pp. 3–8.

Maharey, S. (2000), 'Partnership, Politics and the Social Democratic Project', paper presented to the New Zealand Parliament, Wellington, 25 March, New Zealand Parliamentary Speech Archive.

Maharey, S. (2001), 'Building Social Capital', paper presented to the New Zealand Parliament, Wellington, 7 September, New Zealand Parliamentary Speech Archive.

Maharey, S. (2002a), 'Education and Work Partnerships for the Knowledge Economy', paper presented to the New Zealand Parliament, Wellington, 21 March, Parliamentary Speech Archive.

Maharey, S. (2002b), *Maharey Notes*, Issue No. 79, Wellington: Government of New Zealand.

Mallard, T. (2000), Speech delivered to the NCEA Forum, presented to the New Zealand Parliament, Wellington, accessed 10 August, Parliamentary Speech Archive, <http://www.executive.govt.nz/speech.cfm?speechralph=31951&SR=1>.

Mallard, T. (2001), Speech to secondary principals conference, presented to the New Zealand Parliament, Wellington, acessed 29 March, Parliamentary Speech Archive, <http://www.executive.govt.nz/speech.cfm?speechralph=34193&SR=1>.

Manwaring, T. (1982), *The Extended Internal Labour Market*, Berlin: IIM.

Marginson, S. (1997), *Markets in Education*, New South Wales: Allen and Unwin.

Marquand, D. (1997), *The New Reckoning: Capitalism, States and Citizens*, Cambridge: Polity Press.

Matlay, H. (2000), 'S/NVQs in Britian: Employer-led or Ignored?', *Journal of Vocational Education and Training*, 52 (1), pp. 135–48.

McDonald, J. (2002), 'Contestability and Social Justice: The Limits of Competitive Tendering of Welfare Services', *Australian Social Work*, 55 (2), pp. 99–108.

McIntosh, S. (2004), *Further Analysis of the Returns to Academic and Vocational Qualifications*, London: Centre for the Economics of Education.

McKenzie, D., Lee, G. and Lee, H. (1990), *The Transformation of the New Zealand Technical High School*, Delta Research Monograph No. 10, Palmerston North: Massey University, Department of Education.

McIlroy, R. (2000), *How is the New Deal for Young People Working?*, Warwick: Warwick Business School.

McMurrer, D., Condon, M. and Sawhill, I. (1997), *Intergenerational Mobility in the United States*, Washington: Urban Institute.

Mead, L. (1986), *Beyond Entitlement: The Social Obligations of Citizenship*, New York: The Free Press.

Mead, L. (2003), 'The Primacy of Institutions', *Journal of Policy Analysis and Management*, 22 (4), pp. 577–80.

Millar, L., Acutt, B. and Kellie, D. (2002), 'Minimum and Preferred Entry Qualifications and Training Provision for British Workers', *International Journal of Training and Development*, 6 (3), pp. 163–82.

Miller, P. (1998), 'Youth Unemployment: Does the Family Matter', *Journal of Industrial Relations*, 40 (2), 247–76.

Miller, P. and Volker, P. (1987), 'The Youth Labour Market in Australia', *Economic Record*, 63 (182), 203–19.

Miller, S. and Rosenbaum, J. (1997), 'Hiring in a Hobbesian World: Social Infrastructure and Employers' Use of Information', *Work and Occupation*, 24 (4), pp. 498–523.

Mizen, P. (1999), 'Ethics in an Age of Austerity: "Work-welfare" and the Regulation of Youth', in S. Banks (ed.), *Ethical Issues in Youth Work*, London: Routledge, pp. 21–36.

Mizen, P., Bolton, A. and Pole, C. (1999), 'School Age Workers: The Paid Employment of Children in Britain', *Work, Employment and Society*, 13 (3), pp. 423–38.

Montgomery, J. (1992), 'Job Search and Network Composition: Implications of the Strength-of-weak-ties Hypothesis', *American Sociological Review*, 57, pp. 586–96.

Mumford, L. (1934), *Technics and Civilisation*, New York: Harcourt.

Muntaner, C., Lynch, J. and Smith, G. (2000), 'Social Capital and the Third Way in Health', *Critical Public Health*, 10 (2), pp. 107–24.

Murnane, R. and Levy, F. (1993), 'Why Today's High-school-educated Males Earn Less than their Fathers Did: The Problem and Assessment of Responses', *Harvard Educational Review*, 63 (1), pp. 1–19.

Murphy, R. (1988), *Social Closure: The Theory of Monopolization and Exclusion*, Oxford: Clarendon Press.

Muschamp, Y., Jamieson, I. and Lauder, H. (1999), 'Education, Education, Education', in M. Powell (ed.), *New Labour, New Welfare State: The Third Way in British Social Policy*, Bristol: Polity Press, pp. 101–22.

Nahapiet, J. and Ghoshal, S. (2000), 'Social Capital, Intellectual Capital, and the Organization of Advantage', in E. Lesser (ed.), *Knowledge and Social Capital*, Boston: Butterworth Heinemann, pp. 119–57.

Neven, M. (2002), 'The Influence of the Wider Kin Group on Individual Life-course Transitions: Results from the Pays de Herve (Belgium), 1846–1900', *Continuity and Change*, 17 (3), pp. 405–35.

New Zealand Labour Party (1999), *Labour's Training Strategy: 21st Century Skills, Building Skills for Jobs and Growth*, Wellington: New Zealand Labour Party.

New Zealand Ministry of Social Development (2002), *Briefing to the Incoming Government*, Wellington: New Zealand Ministry of Social Development.

New Zealand Qualifications Authority (1991), *Developing the National Qualifications Framework: A Report to the Board*, Wellington: New Zealand Qualifications Authority.

New Zealand Qualifications Authority (1996a), 'Many Roads to Excellence', *Learn*, 7, pp. 7–13.

New Zealand Qualifications Authority (1996b), *The National Qualifications Framework – Issues*, Wellington: New Zealand Qualifications Authority.

New Zealand Qualifications Authority (1997), *Company Use: The National Qualifications Framework and the Workplace*, Wellington: New Zealand Qualifications Authority.

New Zealand Treasury (1987), *Government Management*, brief to the incoming government, vol. II, Wellington: New Zealand Treasury.

Newman, J. (1999), 'The Future of Welfare in the 21st Century', *National Press Club*, Canberra, 29 September.

Newman, K. (1999), *No Shame in My Game: The Working Poor in the Inner City*, New York: Vintage.

Nickson, D., Warhurst, C. and Cullen, A. (2003), 'Bringing in the Excluded: Aesthetic Labour, Skills and Training in the "New" Economy', *Journal of Education and Work*, 16 (2), pp. 185–203.

Nolan, P. (2001), 'Shaping Things to Come', *People Management*, 7 (25), pp. 30–32.

O'Regan, K. and Quigley, J. (1991), 'Labor Market Access and Labor Market Outcomes for Urban Youth', *Regional Science and Urban Economics*, 21, pp. 277–93.

Office for Standards in Education (2002), *Connexions Partnerships: The First Year 2001–2002*, London: Office for Standards in Education.

Office of the Associate Minister of Education – Tertiary Education (2001), *Skills for a Knowledge Economy: A Review of Industry Training in New Zealand*, Wellington: Office of the Associate Minister of Education – Tertiary Education.

Office of the Prime Minister (2002), *Growing an Innovative New Zealand*, Wellington: The Office of the Prime Minister.

Okano, K. (1995), 'Habitus and Intraclass Differentiation: Nonuniversity-bound Students in Japan', *Qualitative Studies in Education*, 8 (4), pp. 357–69.

Organisation for Economic Cooperation and Development (2000), *Making Transitions Work: From Initial Education to Working Life*, Paris: Organisation for Economic Cooperation and Development.

Osterman, P. (1999), *Securing Prosperity*, Princeton, NJ: Princeton University Press.

Parkin, F. (1992), *Durkheim*, Oxford: Oxford University Press.

Parsons, D., Barry, J., Bysshe, S. and Foster, P. (2003), *Evaluation of the Connexions Direct Pilot, Research Report*, Nottinghamshire: Department for Education and Skills.

Parsons, T. (1951), *The Social System*, New York: The Free Press.

Patterson, L. (2003), 'The Three Educational Ideologies of the British Labour Party, 1997–2001', *Oxford Review of Education*, 29 (2), pp. 165–85.

Pavis, S., Hubbard, G. and Platt, S. (2001), 'Young People in Rural Areas: Socially Excluded or Not?', *Work, Employment and Society*, 15 (2), pp. 219–309.

Payne, J. (2000), 'The Unbearable Lightness of Skill: The Changing Meaning of Skill in UK Policy Discourses and Some Implications for Education and Training', *Journal of Education Policy*, 15 (3), pp. 353–69.

Peck, J. (1997), 'From Federal Welfare to Local Workfare? Remaking Canada's Work-Welfare Regime', in A. Herod, G.O. Tuathail and S. Roberts (eds), *An Unruly World?: Globalization, Governance, and Geography*, London: Routledge, pp. 95–115.

Peck, J. (2000), 'Local Discipline: Making Space for the "Workfare State"', in P. Edwards and T. Elger (eds), *The Global Economy, National States and the Regulation of Labour*, London: Mansell, pp. 64–86.

Peck, J. (2001), *Workfare States*, New York: Guilford Press.

Peck, J. and Theodore, N. (2000), '"Work First": Workfare and the Regulation of Contingent Labour Markets', *Cambridge Journal of Economics*, 24, pp. 119–38.

Performance and Innovation Unit (2002a), *Adult Skills in the 21st Century: Part One*, London: Cabinet Office.

Performance and Innovation Unit (2002b), *Adult Skills in the 21st Century: Part Two*, London: Cabinet Office.

Performance and Innovation Unit (2002c), *Social Capital: A Discussion Paper*, London: Cabinet Office.

Piven, F.F. and Cloward, R.A. (1972), *Regulating the Poor: The Functions of Public Welfare*, New York: Vintage Books.

Platt, T. (2003), 'The State of Welfare: United Stated 2003', *Monthly Review*, 55 (5), pp. 13–27.

Podder, N. and Chatterjee, S. (1998), 'Sharing the National Cake in Post Reform New Zealand: Income Inequality Trends in Terms of Income Sources', paper presented to the Annual Conference of the New Zealand Association of Economists, Wellington, 2–4 September.

Popham, I. (2003), *Tackling NEETs, Connexions Research Report*, Nottinghamshire: Department for Education and Skills.

Portes, A. and Landolt, P. (1996), 'The Downside of Social Capital', *The American Prospect*, (26), May/June, pp. 18–21.

Prime Ministerial Task Force on Employment (1994), *Employment: The Issues*, Wellington: The Government of New Zealand.

Priven, F. (1998), 'Welfare and Work', *Social Justice*, 25 (1), pp. 67–81.

Propper, C. and Wilson, D. (2003), 'The Use and Usefulness of Performance Measures in the Public Sector', *Oxford Review of Economic Policy*, 19 (2), pp. 250–67.

Pusey, M., Wilson, D., Turnbull, N. and Fattore, T. (2003), *The Experience of Middle Australia: The Dark Side of Economic Rationalism*, Cambridge: Cambridge University Press.

Putnam, R. (2000), *Bowling Alone: The Collapse and Revival of American Community*, New York: Simon and Schuster.

Putnam, R., Leonardi, R. and Nanetti, R. (1993), *Making Democracy Work: Civic Traditions in Modern Italy*, Princeton, NJ: Princeton University Press.

Pye, D., Haywood, C. and Mac an Ghail, M. (1996), 'The Training State, De-industrialisation and the Production of White Working-class Trainee Identities', *International Studies in Sociology of Education*, 6 (2), pp. 133–46.

Questions Answered Limited (2000), *A Survey of Employers' Awareness of NTOs*, Research Report No. 209, Norwich: Department for Education and Employment.

Quiggin, J. (1994), 'The Fiscal Gains from Contracting Out: Transfers or Efficiency Improvements', *The Australian Economic Review*, 107 (3rd Quarter), pp. 97–102.

Reay, D. and Lucey, H. (2003), 'The Limits of "Choice": Children and Inner City Schooling', *Sociology*, 37 (1), pp. 121–42.

Reenen, V.J. (2001), *No More Skivvy Schemes? Active Labour Market Policies and the British New Deal for Young People in Context*, London: Institute for Fiscal Studies.

Rees, G. (1997), 'Making a Learning Society: Education and Work in Industrial South Wales', *Welsh Journal of Education*, 6 (2), pp. 4–16.

Reich, R. (1991), *The Work of Nations: Preparing Ourselves for 21st Century Capitalism*, London: Simon and Schuster.

Reingold, D. (1999), 'Social Networks and the Unemployment Problem of the Urban Poor', *Urban Studies*, 36 (11), pp. 1907–32.

Rhodes, M. (2000), 'Desperately Seeking a Solution: Social Democracy, Thatcherism and the "Third Way" in British Welfare', *West European Politics*, 23 (2), pp. 161–86.

Robinson, P. (1997), 'The Myth of Parity Esteem', Discussion Paper No. 354, London: London School of Economics, Centre for Economic Performance.

Robison, L., Schmid, A. and Siles, M. (2002), 'Is Social Capital Really Capital?', *Review of Social Economy*, LX (1), March, pp. 1–21.

Rosenbaum, J. (2002), *Beyond College for All: Career Paths for the Forgotten Half*, New York: Sage.

Rosenbaum, J. and Binder, A. (1997), 'Do Employers Really Need More Educated Youth?', *Sociology of Education*, 70, pp. 68–85.

Rosenbaum, J., Kariya, T., Settersten, R. and Maier, T. (1990), 'Market and network Theories of the Transition from High School-to-work: Their Application to Industrialised Societies', *Annual Review of Sociology*, 16, pp. 263–99.

Rowthorn, R. (1999), *The Political Economy of Full Employment in Modern Britain*, Oxford: University of Oxford, Department of Economics.

Saxenian, A. (2002), 'Transnational Communities and the Evolution of Global Production Networks: The Cases of Taiwan, China and India', *Industry and Innovation*, 9 (3), pp. 183–202.

Schneider, M., Teske, P., Roch, C. and Marschall, M. (1997), 'Networks to Nowhere: Segregation and Stratification in Networks of Information about Schools', *American Journal of Political Science*, 41 (4), pp. 1201–23.

Schuller, T. (2001), 'The Complementary Roles of Human and Social Capital', *ISUMA*, 2 (2), pp. 18–24.

Scott, A. and Freeman-Moir, J. (1990), 'Work and Education', in H. Lauder and C. Wylie (eds), *Towards Successful Schooling*, London: Falmer Press, pp. 151–74.

Scott, J. (1996), *Stratification and Power: Structure of Class, Status and Command*, Cambridge: Polity Press.

Sennett, R. (1998), *The Corrosion of Character: The Personal Consequences of Work in the New Capitalism*, New York: W.W. Norton.

Shah, S., Rayner, E., White, R., Dawes, L. and Tinsley, K. (2000), *Evaluating the Jobseeker's Allowance: A Summary of the Research Findings*, Norwich: Department of Social Security.

Shavit, Y. and Muller, W. (2000), 'Vocational Secondary Education: Where Diversion and Where Safety Net?', *European Societies*, 2 (1), pp. 29–50.

Short, P. and Mutch, A. (2001), 'Exchange, Reciprocity, and Citizenship – Principles of Access and the Challenge to Human Rights in the Third Sector: An Australian Perspective', *Social Justice*, 28 (4), pp. 114–27.

Simmie, J. (2003), 'Innovations for Urban Regions as National and International Nodes for the Transfer and Sharing of Knowledge', *Regional Studies*, 37 (6/7), pp. 607–20.

Siora, G. and Chiles, M. (2000), *A Study of the NTO Network*, Research Report No. 210, Norwich: Department for Education and Employment.

Skill New Zealand (1999a), *Investing in Skills for Competitive Advantage*, Wellington: Skill New Zealand.

Skill New Zealand (1999b), *Training Opportunities: Research into Longer Term Outcomes*, Wellington: Skill New Zealand.

Skill New Zealand (2001a), *Formative Evaluation of the Modern Apprenticeships Pilots*, Wellington: Skill New Zealand.

Skill New Zealand (2001b), *Update: Youth Training – 2001*, Wellington: Skill New Zealand.

Skill New Zealand (2002), *Interim Process Evaluation of the Gateway Pilots*, Wellington: Skill New Zealand.

Smith, M.K. (2002), 'Transforming Youth Work – Resourcing Excellent Youth Services. A Critique', accessed 8 January 2003, Informal Education homepage, <http://www.infed.org/youthwork/transforming_youth_work_2.htm>.

Smithers, A. (1993), 'All our Futures: Britain's Education Revolution', Channel 4 Television Dispatches Report on Education, London.

Smithers, R. (2002), 'Parents Get 12 Week Deadline on Truancy', *The Guardian*, accessed 15 May 2004, <http://education.guardian.co.uk/schools/story/0,5500,808860,00.html>.

Social Exclusion Unit (1999), *Bridging the Gap: New Opportunities for 16–18 Year Olds Not in Education, Employment or Training*, London: Her Majesty's Stationery Office.

Solon, G. (1992), 'Intergenerational Income Mobility in the United States', *American Economic Review*, 82 (3), pp. 393–408.

Spielhofer, T., Mann, P. and Sims, D. (2003), *Entry to Employment (E2E) Participant Study*, Learning and Skills Council: Coventry.

Spours, K. and Young, M.F.D. (1990), 'Beyond Vocationalism: A New Perspective on the Relationship between Work and Education', in D. Gleeson (ed.), *Training and its Alternatives*, Milton Keynes: Open University Press, pp. 213–24.

Stack, C. (1974), *All Our Kin: Survival Strategies for Survival in a Black Community*, New York: Harper and Row.

Statistics New Zealand (1998), *New Zealand Now: Young New Zealanders*, Wellington: Statistics New Zealand.

Statistics New Zealand (2003), *Human Capital Statistics*, Wellington: Statistics New Zealand.

Steedman, H. (2002), 'Employers, Employment and the Labour Market', in *14–19 Education: Papers arising from a seminar series held at the Nuffield Foundation*, London: The Nuffield Foundation, pp. 24–37.

Stone, W., Grey, M. and Hughes, J. (2003), *Social Capital at Work: How Family, Friends and Civic Ties Relate to Labour Market Outcomes*, Research Paper No. 31, Melbourne: Australian Institute of Family Studies.

Stone, W. and Hughes, J. (2002), *Social Capital: Empirical Meaning and Measurement Validity*, Research Paper No. 27, Melbourne: Australian Institute of Family Studies.

Strathdee, R. (2003), 'The Qualifications Framework in New Zealand: Reproducing Existing Inequalities or Disrupting the Positional Conflict for Credentials', *Journal of Education and Work*, 16 (2), pp. 147–64.

Strathdee, R. (2004), 'Outsourcing and the Provision of Welfare-related Services to Unemployed Youth in New Zealand', *Cambridge Journal of Economics*, 28 (1), pp. 59–72.

Strathdee, R. and Hughes, D. (2000), 'Social Networks and the "Training Gospel"', *New Zealand Journal of Educational Studies*, 35 (2), pp. 131–43.

Strathdee, R. and Hughes, D. (2001), 'The National Qualifications Framework and the Discouraged Worker Effect', *New Zealand Journal of Educational Studies*, 36 (2), pp. 155–69.

Streeck, W. (1989), 'Skills and the Limits of Neo-liberalism: The Enterprise of the Future as a Place of Learning', *Work, Employment and Society*, 3 (1), pp. 89–104.

Stuart, S. (1995), 'Future of the Family', *Dominion Sunday Star – Times*, 9 October, Wellington, C1.

Sullivan, M. (1989), *Getting Paid: Youth Crime and Work in the Inner City*, Ithaca: Cornell University Press.

Swift, J. (1995), *Wheel of Fortune: Work and Life in the Age of Falling Expectations*, Toronto: Between the Lines Press.

Szreter, S. (1998), *A New Political Economy for New Labour: The Importance of Social Capital*, PERC Policy Paper No. 15, Sheffield: Political Economy Research Centre.

The Australian Bulletin (1887), 'Australia for Australians', *The Australian Bulletin*, 2 July, Sydney, p. 4.

Thompson, E.P. (1968), *The Making of the English Working-class*, Harmondsworth: Pelican Books.

Thrupp, M. (2001), 'Education Policy and Social Class in England and New Zealand: An Instructive Comparison', *Journal of Education Policy*, 16 (4), pp. 297–314.

Thurow, L.C. (1992), *Head to Head: The Coming Economic Battle among Japan, Europe, and America*, New York: Morrow.

Tilly, C. (1998), *Durable Inequality*, Berkeley: University of California Press.

Trades Union Congress (2001), *Permanent Rights for Temporary Workers: Findings from a TUC Survey on Temporary Working*, London: Trade Union Congress Organisation and Services Department.

Trow, M. (1977), 'The Second Transformation of American Secondary Education', in J. Karabel and A. Halsey (eds), *Power and Ideology in Education*, New York: Oxford University Press, pp. 105–18.

Tucker, D. (2002), *'Precarious' Non-Standard Employment – A Review of the Literature*, Wellington: Department of Labour.

Twigg, S. (2002), 'Speech to the Connexions Partnership's National Forum', accessed 1 September 2003, <http://www.connexions.gov.uk/partnerships/documents/CNXspeechSTwigg.doc>.

Unwin, L., Fuller, A., Turbin, J. and Young, M. (2004), *What Determines the Impact of Vocational Qualifications? A Literature Review*, Nottinghamshire: Department for Education and Skills.

Vanstone, A. (2001), 'The Third Way', paper presented in the Australian Parliament, Canberra, 13 July, Australian Parliamentary Speech Archive.

Walby, S. (1991), *Theorizing Patriarchy*, Oxford: Basil Blackwell.

Waldinger, R. (1986*), Through the Eye of the Needle: Immigrants and Enterprise in New York's Garment Trades*, New York: New York University Press.

Wallace, C., Boyle, F., Cheal, B. and Dunkerley, D. (1993), 'The Employment and Training of Young People in Rural South West England', *British Journal of Education and Work*, 6 (3), pp. 25–44.

Weber, M. (1968), *Economy and Society*, New York: Bedminister Press.

Webster, D. (2000), 'The Geographical Concentration of Labour Market Disadvantage', *Oxford Review of Economic Policy*, 16 (1), pp. 114–28.

West, A. (2001), 'A Vital Element in the Knowledge Society', *QA News*, 38, June, Wellington, 1–2.

White, M. (1999), 'Evaluating the Effectiveness of Welfare-to-work: Learning from Cross-national Evidence', in C. Chitty and G. Elam (eds), *Evaluating Welfare to Work*, London: Department of Social Security and National Centre for Social Research, pp. 57–70.

White, M. and Riley, R. (2002), *Findings from the Macro Evaluation of the New Deal for Young People*, Department for Work and Pensions Research Report No. 166, Leeds: Department for Work and Pensions.

Willis, P. (1977), *Learning to Labour: How Working-class Kids get Working-Class Jobs*, Farnsborough: Saxon House.

Wilson, J. W. (1987), *Truly Disadvantaged: The Inner City, the Underclass and Public Policy*, Chicago: University of Chicago Press.

Wilson, J. W. (1996), *When Work Disappears: The World of the New Urban Poor*, New York: Knopf.

Winch, C. (2003), 'Education and the Knowledge Economy: A Response to David and Foray', *Policy Futures in Education*, 1 (1), pp. 50–70.

Winter, I. (2000), *Social Capital and Public Policy in Australia*, Melbourne: Australian Institute of Family Studies.

Wintour, P. and Smithers, R. (2001), 'Blair Pledges to Cut Class Sizes in Problem Schools', *The Guardian*, 14 February, p. 6.

Wolf, A. (2002), *Does Education Matter: Myths about Education and Economic Growth*, London: Penguin.

Wolfe, A. (1989), 'Market, State and Society as Codes of Moral Obligation', *Acta Sociologica*, 32 (3), pp. 221–36.

Wong, S. and Salaff, J. (1998), 'Network Capital: Emigration from Hong Kong', *British Journal of Sociology*, 49 (3), pp. 358–74.

Woolcock, M. and Narayan, D. (2000), 'Social Capital: Implications for Development Theory, Research and Policy', *The World Bank Research Observer*, 15 (2), pp. 225–49.

Young, M. and Willott (1957), *Family and Kinship in East London*, London: Routledge and Kegan Paul.

Young, R. (1990), *A Critical Theory of Education: Habermas and our Children's Future*, New York: Teachers College Press.

Zemsky, R. (1998), 'Labor, Markets and Educational Restructuring', *Annals of the American Academy of Political and Social Science*, 559, pp. 77–90.

Zucker, L. (1986), 'Production of Trust: Institutional Sources of Economic Structure, 1840–1920', *Research in Organisational Behaviour*, 8, pp. 53–111.

Index